DCU LIBRARY

971079536

D1756428

SUBJUGATED KNOWLEL

MAIN LENDING   **3 WEEK LOAN**   DCU LIBRARY

Fines are charged **PER DAY** if this item is overdue.
Check at www.dcu.ie/~library or telephone (01) 700 5183 for fine rates and
renewal regulations for this item typ
Item is subject to recall.
Remember to use the Book I... ... libr... ...d.
... for return o... ...b

i

Also by Laurel Brake

INVESTIGATING VICTORIAN JOURNALISM
(*co-editor with Aled Jones and L. Madden*)

PATER IN THE 1990s (*co-editor with Ian Small*)

THE YEAR'S WORK IN ENGLISH STUDIES, Vols 62–8
(*editor*)

Subjugated Knowledges

Journalism, Gender and Literature in the Nineteenth Century

Laurel Brake

WITHDRAWN

MACMILLAN

© Laurel Brake 1994

All rights reserved. No reproduction, copy or transmission of
this publication may be made without written permission.

No paragraph of this publication may be reproduced, copied or
transmitted save with written permission or in accordance with
the provisions of the Copyright, Designs and Patents Act 1988,
or under the terms of any licence permitting limited copying
issued by the Copyright Licensing Agency, 90 Tottenham Court
Road, London W1P 9HE.

Any person who does any unauthorised act in relation to this
publication may be liable to criminal prosecution and civil
claims for damages.

First published 1994 by
THE MACMILLAN PRESS LTD
Houndmills, Basingstoke, Hampshire RG21 2XS
and London
Companies and representatives
throughout the world

ISBN 0–333–47590–9 hardcover
ISBN 0–333–60672–8 paperback

A catalogue record for this book is available
from the British Library.

Printed in Great Britain by
Antony Rowe Ltd
Chippenham, Wiltshire

820.9008 BRA

971079536

For Simon

Contents

List of Illustrations

Acknowledgements

Working with periodicals is a time-consuming business, and this book has been many years in gestation. I am grateful to the British Academy and the Leverhulme Trust for large and small grants on more than one occasion to support this research; without their encouragement and the time and travel they funded, it would not have accreted and come to fruition. The Department of English at UCW, Aberystwyth, offered me ample opportunity to pursue these interests at undergraduate and postgraduate levels and through regular study leave, and the supportive interest of busy colleagues from a range of departments and institutions at Aberystwyth, particularly Desmond Slay, Lyn Pykett, Moira Vincintelli, Aled Jones, Ned Thomas and Lionel Madden, was particularly formative, and is gratefully acknowledged. The other community to which this book is indebted is the Research Society for Victorian Periodicals under whose auspices much of the book has been conceived. The partnership of Stephen Brake made the whole project imaginable and possible. To Simon Brake, whose ebullient life developed alongside that of the book, and informed it, the book is dedicated.

Most of the periodical research has been carried out in four libraries, the National Library of Wales, the British Library, the Bodleian, and the Periodicals Room at Senate House, University of London, whose patient and expert staff have located lost or arcane material. I am particularly grateful to have been able to work in the dedicated space and open stacks of Senate House which offers rare facilities to readers of Victorian periodicals. I want to thank too the staff of the Library of Congress for the special help they provided in connection with the Harper and *McClure's* material, and the Sydney Jones Library, University of Liverpool, for access to their copies of *The Savoy*. Quotation from the Diary of A.C. Benson is by kind permission of the Masters and Fellows, Magdalene College, Cambridge; from the MS letter from Alfred Douglas to Kains-Jackson by kind permission of M. Holland for the Estate of Oscar Wilde; and from the Diary of Mark Pattison by kind permission of the Bodleian Library, the University of Oxford.

Versions of a number of the chapters have appeared in print before. They are published with the generous permission of the editors and publishers as follows. A version of Chapter 1 appeared in the 'Literary Periodicals' issue of *Yearbook of English Studies*, 16 (1986) 92–116. Chapter 3 on the *Nineteenth Century* appeared in *Victorian Periodicals Review* (Spring 1992) 16–21. Chapter 7 on the *Woman's World* appeared in *Women: A Cultural Review* 2 (Summer 1991) 149–62, and I am grateful to OUP for permission to reprint it. Early versions of Chapter 9 on the DNB appeared in the *Modern Language Review*, (October 1975) 731–42, and Chapter 10, 'Judas and the Widow' in *Prose Studies*, 4 (May 1981) 39–54. Chapter 4 appeared in *Pater and the 1990s*, eds. L. Brake and I. Small. (ELT Press, Greensboro, NC: 1991) pp. 43–61, and Chapter 5 in *Papers for the Millions*, ed. Joel Wiener (Greenwood Press, Westport, Conn.: 1988) pp. 1–24.

Introduction

This book pertains to print in culture, the relations of certain forms of nineteenth-century printed texts – articles, periodicals, and part-issues in the main – to their modes of production and to each other, in their own period and in ours. These materials are 'subjugated' interestingly, not only in their own period where they were prime and highly visible quiddities in a struggle between literature and journalism, but also in the twentieth-century construct of 'literature' which is predicated on their defeat, devaluation and invisibility as subjects.

My work is historical, but not exclusively 'literary' history, as it is not characteristically author (or genre or theme) centred; and although it is also textual, it largely treats non-book texts and forms. Where it does engage with books, it is volumes of criticism and biography, discourses which sit uneasily with the academic definition of Literature – at times and in specific instances included within it and at times disowned. Historical, textual, *and* (but not only) literary, and drawing on contemporary theory, this work lies within that enhanced area of historical bibliography mapped by D.F. McKenzie in the Panizzi lectures of 1985 and called 'the sociology of texts'.

Noting that 'print is only a phase in the history of textual transmission' (52), McKenzie never pauses, as he goes on to topography and film, to look at other *print* forms of 'non-book' texts. That is the remit of *Subjugated Knowledges*.[1] My choice of Victorian periodicals as subject stems from two facets of the construction of Victorian literature by modernism: the first is the assumption that modes of production and circulation have little to do with textuality, and that texts were circulated then in the forms we read them today, as books, with a nod to part-issue; the second is that fiction is the overwhelmingly dominant genre of the time. The third element of modernist criticism to which this book is addressed is the formalist insistence, in various guises, on the isolation of texts of all periods from history, culture, gender, production and ideology, and the relegation of textuality to the high ground of aesthetics. It was my increasing impatience with this defensive pursuit of denials that as a young student of Pater I

traversed a path from formalist aestheticism to cultural material-
ism, feminism, and post-structuralism.

This book begins with a section on literature and journalism
which probes in a number of ways the long gestation and volcanic
birth, in the latter part of the nineteenth century, of a specialist
notion of 'Literature', to which English Literature and the academy
attached themselves, and an alternative kind of writing for the
common reader. This latter was now theorised as a down-market
'consumer' rather than 'reader' of the periodical press and
contemporary fiction. Derisively called 'journalism', writing so
designated was associated by its critics (such as Matthew Arnold)
with the forces of democracy and the 'new journalism'. Yet the
attempt to create a clear-cut dichotomy between literature and
journalism belied the involvement of almost all Victorian writers
with the periodical press, as contributors, editors and/or proprietors. The nature of 'authorship' in the period almost inevitably
included periodical publication as one source of readers and
income, and a determining format. George Saintsbury, a Victorian
looking back in 1896, insists that the development of 'periodical
literature' is the most 'distinctive and characteristic' feature of
nineteenth-century literary history (Saintsbury 166).

At the same time, in the 1880s and 90s, the formal study of
English literature to degree level was under scrutiny and in the
offing. This required the vernacular literature to present itself as
sufficiently demanding and recondite, or *inaccessible*, to justify
study at Oxbridge. Implicated in this model was that of the only
literature taught at university, classical literature, which required
'mastery' of ancient languages, with all the expensive education
and time that such acquisition involved. The idea that literature in
English was accessible to all those who could read their native
language carried the twin taints of opening higher education to
those men outside the gateways of public school or private tuition,
and to women whose access to higher education was increasing
through the extension system and the new residential halls and
tuition for women in place in Oxford and Cambridge by 1880.

Another important factor in the equation that came to formulate
English literature at this time was the demonstrable weakness of
the standard of attainment and teaching of classics at the
universities. The fragility of classics made the strength and fortunes
of English appear very threatening. A second contender for degree
status was modern languages which met the criterion of

prerequisite linguistic attainment. While it held out the notion of systematic study of valued works in German, it also would provide access for the new breed of students to politically revolutionary work in French and Italian, and to French literature; its modernity, like that of English, might also attract students away from the classics. Two results of these combined pressures on English were the predominance of language over literature in the early appointments to Chairs in English and in the constitution of the subject, and the reinforcement of the role of English literature in an ongoing nationalist agenda, which has only recently again been invoked by government in the debate on the place of English in the new National Curriculum.

The access of higher education to women was one element of what Victorians knew, familiarly, as the 'woman question' but it is clear in contemporary responses to this question that the gender issues of the period were not confined to women. Definitions of manliness were at issue, and gay men moved into visibility and discourse in public arenas such as the stage, the novel, and the periodicals. While the 'causes' of gay men and the new women were not necessarily perceived as allied internally, in the perception of outsiders they were often yoked as a twin threat to the extant cultural order.

Nervousness about gender questions is indicated in the first number of the *Albemarle*, dated January 1892, where it is announced that 'An Original Story by Mr. Rudyard Kipling's Sister (Mrs. Fleming)' (iii) will be published in February. In the event it describes her on the contents page as 'Mrs. Fleming (née Kipling)'. The first number also publishes *two* articles, by a woman and a man, for and against 'The Primrose League', a Conservative club which was open to both sexes. Aiming at male and female readers, the *Albemarle* uneasily tackles what it constructs as a divided readership, and shows its own confusions: *which* man is [Alice] Fleming defined by, her brother or her husband?

Notions of authorship were significantly affected by issues of gender throughout the period: George Eliot worried about 'silly' lady novelists; Thomas Hardy and George Moore felt that the censorship of fiction in the name of 'family' readers was intolerable; a perception of a feminisation of fiction from mid-century was addressed at its end by a series of aggressively masculine novels. But notions of authorship were also assailed by a series of biographies in the latter half of the century which undermined romantic ideas of the author as 'hero', or 'genius'. Just as material conditions such as growing literacy, disposable income, and population helped create more accessible kinds and formats of writing, so a 'new biography' which relied on letters, research and documentation was fostered by the growth of methods of social research into problems of the 'condition of England' as seen in blue books, investigative reporting in the press, and the introduction of the personal, including the interview, into the 'new journalism'. Biographies of Thomas Carlyle and Robert Burns, and a bio-graphical account of R.L. Stevenson for example, all presented accounts of writers whose lives were shown to violate and to call into question religious, sexual or ethical norms of this period, rooting the origins of literary achievement firmly in the ordinary and culpable. The politics of biography thickened throughout the century, and by the 1880s writers, their potential subjects, publishers, reviewers and readers were alike alert to the issues, the profits and the losses.

In the desire to establish English as an academic subject, it was attempted to sever the links between literature and journalism, and to obscure their intimate material involvement and intertextuality in the period. This subjugation has prevailed: if periodicals appear at all in the university syllabus at present, it is usually under the rubric of 'popular culture' or media studies, and it is normally the twentieth-century press which is studied. The professionalisation of English was paralleled by that of journalism which is itself anxious, as a field, to date its existence from the period of *mass media*; it too is characterised by an exclusion of pre-twentieth century journalism history from its syllabuses, and a wish to separate itself from literary and all academic forms of writing.

This book begins and ends in our own century, and moves from a general mapping of the relations between literature and journal-ism and their respective formations to studies of individual periodical texts and of relations between (the construction of) authorship and publishing history. While most of the publishing space discussed here is male – written by men for men – the discourses are explicitly gendered and fissured, articulating eloquently a full spectrum of gender, and a cacophony of presence and absence, of subjugating and subjugated.

Notes

1.   The concept and phrase are Foucault's (81–2)

Works Cited

Foucault, M. (1980) *Power/Knowledge*, ed. Colin Gordon. Brighton, Sussex.
McKenzie, D.F. (1986). 'Bibliography and the Sociology of Texts'. The
    Panizzi Lectures. London.
Saintsbury, G. (1895). *History of Nineteenth-Century Literature*. London.

I

Literature and Journalism

1

Criticism and the Victorian Periodical Press[1]

Perhaps there is no single feature of the English literary history of the nineteenth century, not even the enormous popularisation and multiplication of the novel, which is so distinctive and characteristic as the development in it of periodical literature. For this did not, as the extension of novel-writing did, concern a single department only. The periodical – it may almost for short-ness' sake be said the newspaper – not only became infinitely multiplied, but it gradually absorbed almost every department, or a share of almost every department, into itself. Very large numbers of the best as well as of the worst novels themselves have originally appeared in periodicals; not a very small pro-portion of the most noteworthy nineteenth-century poetry has had the same origin; it may almost be said that all the best work in essay, whether critical, meditative or miscellaneous, has thus been ushered into the world. Even the severer and more academic divisions of history, philosophy, theology and their sisters, have condescended to avail themselves of this means of obtaining a public audience; and though there is still a certain conventional decency in apologising for reprints from periodicals, it is quite certain that, had such reprints not taken place, more than half the most valuable books of the age in some departments, and a considerable minority of the most valuable in others, would never have appeared as books at all. (Saintsbury: 166)

It is still not as clear to most scholars, lecturers, and especially students of literature, as it was to George Saintsbury in 1896, that a corpus of Victorian criticism of quality and range exists; neither are its authors known. Still, numerous books and articles from different angles and disciplines attest to the criticism and avail themselves of it; the author-centred Critical Heritage volumes or works-centred

Casebooks, for example, present it referentially, as a satellite of illustrious planets. Biographies of individual critics, research on non-fictional prose as a genre, and even belle-lettrist essays[2] serve more self-consciously to bring it to notice, but the most appropriate and revelatory approach has been through the Victorian periodicals where almost all the criticism first appeared.[3] The periodicals themselves, and work associated with them such as Walter Graham's outline of *English Literary Periodicals* (1930), bibliographies such as *The Wellesley Index* (1966–89), Alvin Sullivan's *British Literary Magazines* (1983–6), and the MLAA two-volume *Victorian Periodicals: A Guide to Research* (1978, 1989); and criticism such as Armstrong's *Victorian Scrutinies* (1972), Shattock and Wolff's *The Victorian Periodical Press* (1982), and Wiener's *Innovators and Preachers* (1985) have been instrumental in the identification and understanding of Victorian criticism and critics. I shall try to show here some of the ways that Victorian critical discourse is connected with periodicals as a form of production and with the particular periodical in which the criticism appears.

From their critical cradles to their graves, writers were accommodated by the periodicals which operated an informal system of apprenticeship for the would-be writer, initially through anonymous contributions over a range of subject areas. Common among Victorian critics and criticism between 1840 and 1870, this breadth of interest, which served as protective colouring, may also have hidden them from later critics. In particular, the lack of specialisation in English literature was part of a period in which English was not firmly established as a subject for study in British schools and universities, or as a separate subject more generally. The terms 'critic' and 'criticism' functioned as our terms 'reviewer' and 'review', with no special association with what we have since defined as 'literature'. Even late in the century, Clement Shorter classifies a motley lot as 'critics' – philosophers, scientists, theologians and economists, as well as critics of literature; neither critics who wrote about literature nor individual periodicals *confined* themselves to literature, and in 1876 Leslie Stephen was forced to use the term 'aesthetic criticism' (Stephen 1876: 559) to distinguish criticism where 'aesthetic questions' were at issue, from 'criticism' concerning history or science.[4] Most of the 'higher journalism' periodicals resembled their descendants – our *Spectator* and *New Statesman* – in their general coverage, rather that the specialist *Review of English Studies*. With the exception of Matthew Arnold,

Walter Bagehot and Walter Pater, who held other jobs, and Ruskin who was independently wealthy, many Victorian critics such as G.H. Lewes, R.H. Hutton and Leslie Stephen were journalists and the bulk of their work remains buried in the journals. Matthew Arnold presents an unusual case because, as a poet, his criticism is only a part of his literary activity, and as an educator and moralist, it consists of an even smaller proportion of his total work. Arnold's fame and survival as a critic are due to the totality of his achievement, and the same might be said of Walter Pater who has a secure alternative existence in the world of letters as an Oxford don and as an initiator of English aestheticism. Lewes, Bagehot, Hutton and Stephen edited periodicals at one time or another, while contributing to them regularly, and of these only Bagehot made his main income from a source outside journalism, as a banker; but then he edited *The Economist* as well as the *National Review*. Lewes and Hutton were bread and butter journalists, professionals. Leslie Stephen, while both a contributor and an editor in the early part of his working life, was for a short time Professor of English at Cambridge; and in the latter part of his life, from 1882, he edited the *Dictionary of National Biography*, which appeared in serial form from 1886 quarterly; this was an editorial endeavour so historic, sustained and exacting that it bordered on the scholarly. But it is certain from many of Stephen's articles, some autobiographical, some on other writers, and some specifically on editing and writing for the periodicals, that he considered himself a journalist.

VICTORIAN CRITICS ON THEIR CRITICAL PRACTICE

This medley of activity, by authors who in retrospect are regarded primarily as literary critics, attests to a chaotic time in the transition and fragmentation of the critics into journalists, literary and other scholars, and literary critics who publish in periodicals. That this growth of the profession of the critic and the genre of criticism is recognised by the Victorian critics is shown by the many articles in which they grope their way through problems of identity, method and language. Their self-conscious questions and answers provide considerable insight into the nature of Victorian criticism as an activity and discourse. As late as the 1870s Swinburne, for example, addresses himself to the morality of puffing and defends his right to review – but openly and honestly – the work of his friends, and in *Under the Microscope* (1872) he scornfully acknowledges, referring to his enemy Robert Buchanan, the relation between young critics and certain periodicals which he dub 'nursing journals', in that they 'nurse' talent. Beside defending and attacking puffing, Swinburne resists the increasing specialisation of criticism and argues for the competence of the literary critic who wants to comment on art or music (Swinburne 1875: ix). John Morley is another critic who emphasises professionalism in writing rather than in subject, and he similarly defends general rather than specialist knowledge (Morley 1882).

In a keynote essay in the first volume of the *National Review* in 1855 Walter Bagehot, co-editor with Hutton, wryly if frankly attempts to define the genre and limitations of the periodical review:

In this transition from ancient writing to modern, the review-like essay and the essay-like review fill a large space. Their small bulk, their slight pretension to systematic completeness, their avowal, it might be said, of necessary incompleteness, the facility of changing the subject, of selecting points to attack, of exposing only the best corner for defence, are great temptations. Still greater is the advantage of "our limits". A real reviewer always spends his first and best pages on the parts of a subject on which he wishes to write, the easy comfortable parts which he knows. The formidable difficulties which he owns, you foresee by a strange fatality he will only reach two pages before the end; to his great grief there is no opportunity for discussing them. As a young gentleman, at the India House examination, wrote "Time up" on nine unfinished papers in succession, so you may occasionally read a whole review, in every article of which, the principal difficulty of each successive question is about to be reached at the conclusion. Nor can any one deny that this is the suitable skill, the judicious custom, of the craft. (Bagehot 1855: 256–7)

Elsewhere he aggrandises the method of this type of essay and dubs it 'allusive criticism':

In Shelley's case, it may be said that we allowed a certain defined intensity to have a higher imaginative value than a more diffused fertility and a less concentrated art; why is not Wordsworth entitled to share the benefit of this doctrine also? The plea is very specious, but we are not inclined to think that it is sound. Shelley has shown in a single direction, or in a few directions, an immense general power of imagination and mind. We may not pause to prove this: it is in the nature of allusive criticism to be dogmatic; we must appeal to the memory of our readers. (Bagehot 1859: 392)

This double perspective (and occasional conflict) characterises an allusive criticism which assumes its audience well-read enough to provide its own proof, and criticism which caters to the more general reader and popular audience who have no interest in proof. 'Allusive criticism' reflects an increasing sense of professionalism both as journalist and critic, whereas the cynicism of the *National Review* essay tends to regard journalism and criticism as debased and lax forms.

Even after Matthew Arnold's sustained defence of the function and dignity of criticism in the essays of the late 1850s and 1860s Swinburne, in *Under the Microscope*, has cause to be defensive about self-conscious analysis, and sceptical of it as was Bagehot:

Will it again be objected that such dissection as this of a poem is but a paltry and injurious form of criticism? Doubtless it is; but the test of true and great poetry is just this; that it will endure, if need be, such a process of analysis or anatomy; that thus tried…it comes out after all renewed and reattested in perfection of all its parts, in solid and flawless unity, whole and indissoluble. (Swinburne 1872: 34)

For criticism, Swinburne defends rational method, and in his criticism he provides some good analysis, as in his judgement of Tennyson's conception of the *Idylls*:

Thus it is that by the very excision of what may have seemed in his eyes a moral blemish Mr Tennyson has blemished the whole story; by the very exaltation of his hero as something more than man he has left him in the end something less. The keystone of the whole building is removed, and in place of a tragic house of song where even sin had all the dignity and beauty that sin can retain, and without which it can afford no fit material for tragedy, we find an incongruous edifice of tradition and invention where even virtue is made to seem either imbecile or vile. (Swinburne 1872: 39)

But ten pages later, in commentary on the work of Walt Whitman, he regrets the formalist or didactic element in poetry, and registers a preference for the passages which result from a compulsion to speak, the hallmark for Swinburne of sincerity. In his view the adoption of scientific method, favoured for the critic, is not admissible in the poet. However, if Swinburne upholds the dignity of the professional critic in his outline of method, he ends *Under the Microscope* with a diatribe against them, aimed at Robert Buchanan whose 'self-criticism' consisted of anonymously reviewing his own poems. Critics, Swinburne muses, are beneath the notice of science, and of no historical interest. In a conflation of Darwin and Genesis he finally situates them in a lower species than the toad, among the snakes.

Among the many pronouncements on criticism by Leslie Stephen, certitude and singlemindedness are discernible, as though for him criticism is no longer under siege or a matter of personal dignity. Commenting below on a fulsome criticism of praise, Swinburne's more common practice, Stephen may be supposed to reflect Arnold's campaign for 'disinterestedness' in his defence of reason in criticism:

> though criticism cannot boast of being a science, it ought to aim at something like a scientific basis, or at least to proceed in a scientific spirit. The critic, therefore, before abandoning himself to the oratorical impulse, should endeavour to classify the phenomena with which he is dealing as calmly as if he were ticketing a fossil in a museum. The most glowing eulogy, the most bitter denunciation have their proper place; but they belong to the art of persuasion, and form no part of scientific method. Our literary, if not our religious, creed should rest upon a purely rational ground, and be exposed to logical tests. Our faith in an author must in the first instance be the product of instinctive sympathy, instead of deliberate reason. It may be propagated by the contagion of enthusiasm, and preached with all the fervour of proselytism. But when we are seeking to justify our emotions, we must endeavour to get for the time into the position of an independent spectator, applying with rigid impartiality such methods as are best calculated to free us from the influence of personal bias....To be an adequate critic is almost to be a contradiction in terms: to be susceptible to a force, and yet free from its influence; to be moving with the stream, and yet to be standing on the bank. (Stephen 1877: 723)

Where Swinburne sneers 'We live in an age when not to be scientific is to be nothing' (Swinburne 1872: 1), Leslie Stephen genuinely embraces science as a principal element in his method. Notably, Stephen's middle-of-the-road poise between passion and coldness, and his temperate mode of arguing accords with the family-oriented character of the *Cornhill*, the periodical in which his remarks appeared. R.H. Hutton too, editor of the rigorously judicious *Spectator*, seldom betrayed any uncertainty about the status of literary criticism. But by the end of the century the avowedly élitist *Academy* has to dismiss, with some despair, the claim of criticism to adequacy, disinterestedness, or the last word: the judgement of literature has become ultimately a subjective one, and criticism, while a profession, is limited to technical authority. The effectiveness of puffing earlier in the century was largely dependent on the absolute authority accorded the periodical of one's choice, without intervening signatures. The relativism implicit in the *Academy's* observation in the extract below made effective puffing on a large scale impossible, and hastened the reliance of publishers on more open advertising. As professionalism in the practice of criticism and the conduct of the higher periodicals prevailed, the authority of the journal and of criticism waned under the concommitant and more general triumph of scientific relativism and increasing literacy, and the inevitable pluralism and fragmentation in their wake:

The day has gone by when persons bought a critical organ under the impression that what it said was law....Upon every book, particularly of poetry, may be passed as many just and differing opinions as it has readers. It is not in any one man's power to say how another will receive it. Expert criticism can deal only with the technique of a work; its individuality is to be summed by every reader for himself, however humble and illiterate he may be. The wise know this, and choose accordingly the organs which they will read. (Anon. 1897a: 182)

The self-consciousness of the Victorian critics and their preoccupation with their own critical practices and discourse indicate the perceived importance at the time of this mode of literary production. Contemporary theorising on periodical cirticism occurs in the periodicals with a frequency comparable to that on realism and the novel, another important focus of criticism in the nineteenth century.[5]

THE PERIODICALS AND THE FORM OF CRITICISM

Many of these authors collected their articles into volumes during their lifetime, such as Arnold's *Essays in Criticism*, Pater's *Studies in the History of the Renaissance*, and Stephen's *Hours in a Library*, and posthumous collected editions followed; the bound volume is the form in which the essays, extracted from their periodical context, are known today, if they are known at all. Though the prose of Arnold and Bagehot has recently been reordered and edited in scholarly, expensive, multi-volume (largely library) editions, tiny selections from Lewes, Pater, Stephen and Hutton appear and disappear. The texts required to study Victorian criticism are in short supply, and the relation between criticism and the periodicals is yet to be foregrounded and theorised. How did particular periodicals, and the whole Victorian phenomenon of the startling growth of the periodicals from quarterlies to monthlies and weeklies influence the kinds and forms of Victorian criticism? This is a matter of what Foucault calls the episteme.

Other questions that invite consideration pertain to the ways in which criticism is shaped to a greater or lesser extent by the specific periodical in which it appeared, and is informed by the critical debates in other periodicals of the day. The subject and length of an article, its style and tone, the audience to which it is addressed, whether it is anonymous or signed, and its political and theological assumptions are aspects open to control by the character of the journal and its editor. A significant factor is the extent to which the piece was influenced and even revised by the editor or other influential personages. One of the critics of *The Times*, E.S. Dallas, was not above puffing for John Blackwood, his patron and friend. Finally the financial circumstances should be probed: whether authors were paid, and how much.

Frequency of pay is important; Walter Graham has suggested that the advent of the weekly journal professionalised periodical criticism (Graham: 340). No payment suggests a commitment to the periodical's fortunes and politics which is likely to be reflected in the article; or the amount of payment may affect the quality of the piece, in that low-paid professional critics, for quarterlies for example, who were dependent on the periodicals for their income, may have used the same material for more than one article, in more than one periodical (Shattock 1976: 84–7). High pay is significant too; we find Arnold and others choosing to publish in the *Cornhill*, within the editorial constraints of that journal, only because the *Cornhill* paid best (Cook: 22). The appearance of an author in a periodical did not necessarily mean adherence to its collective ethos.

These financial underpinnings reveal another, perhaps unexpected, phenomenon: the links rather than the differences among periodicals, with the links resulting from authors contributing simultaneously to sundry periodicals, for a variety of reasons. These range from an author using the same material more than once to a critic who genuinely honours distinctions between periodicals, as Leslie Stephen did when he published in the *Pall Mall Gazette* and *Fraser's*, certain articles which violated the policies of the *Saturday Review* and the *Cornhill*, periodicals to which in certain periods of his life he contributed most frequently (Stephen 1903: 620). Moreover, in 1871, Stephen was offered the editorship of each of a pair of his alternates, of *Fraser's* and the *Cornhill*. Though he accepted the offer of the latter, he frequently resented the limitations of the *Cornhill*: F.W. Maitland reports him as writing 'What can one make of a magazine which excludes the only subjects in which reasonable men take any interest: politics and religion' (Maitland: 257–8). Stephen's letters to Hardy, for example, show that he distinguished his personal beliefs and taste from those of his professional persona as editor of the *Cornhill*, and that he subordinated himself to his understanding of the 'family' character of the *Cornhill* as established by George Smith, its founder, Thackeray and G.H. Lewes, its previous editors, and, allegedly, its readers.

Neither in his multiple contributions to periodicals, nor in his practice of using certain journals as alternates to the more restricted partisan journals or popular magazines is Stephen untypical. *Fraser's*, the *Westminster Review*, the *Nineteenth Century*, and the *Fortnightly Review* at various times in their history functioned as alternatives for many authors, and it may be instructive in future to look at the new and irregular contributors to these periodicals in this light.[6] Nor is Stephen's disinterestedness as editor unparalleled, although it is less common in this period. The *Cornhill* in particular attracted a succession of editors, in Thackeray, Lewes and Stephen, who agreed to observe intellectual and moral tenets professionally which contradicted their personal beliefs. By contrast the periodicals which Hutton and Bagehot edited (the *Spectator*, and the *National Review* and *The Economist*) might be said to reflect their personal convictions. Clearly the gendering of the space in this set of examples is significant, with the *Cornhill* targeting women readers as well as men, and the *Spectator*, the *National Review* and *The Economist* – including politics and economics and carrying no fiction – largely aiming at male readers. Lewes's personal and professional commitment to the *Leader*, a radical weekly which he edited and founded, is clear from the frequency of his contributions as 'Vivian' in the 1850s, just as his estrangement from the *Cornhill* is reflected in the comparative sparsity of his work there in the 1860s. But the variety of other periodicals to which he contributed in his life as a journalist and critic is prodigious, as is his variation of tone and seriousness. His work appeared in a great range of Victorian journals including, among others, the *Athenaeum*, *Blackwood's*, the *British Quarterly Review*, *Cornhill*, *Edinburgh Review*, the *Fortnightly*, *Fraser's*, the *Leader*, *Nature*, *Once a Week*, the *Saturday Review*, and the *Westminster* – weeklies, monthlies, quarterlies; Tory, Radical, Whig.[7] J.G. Lockhart, a former contributor to *Blackwood's*, while editing the *Quarterly* was heavily involved in the founding of *Fraser's*, a rival to both, and may even have helped edit it in the beginning.

The Table of Contents from W.M. Rossetti's *Fine Art, Chiefly Contemporary: Notices Re-printed, with revisions* (1867) indicates the fairly typical variety of periodicals to which a young critic, not yet established, might contribute. For ten articles, Rossetti lists eleven different sources which include *Fraser's*, *Edinburgh Weekly Review*, *Spectator*, *Reader*, *Saturday Review*, *London Review*, *Fine Arts Quarterly Review*, *Pall Mall Gazette*, *Critic*, *Liverpool Post*, and *Waldon Register*, some of which occur more than once. The differences of tone, style, politics and audience in the *Edinburgh Weekly Review*, *Fraser's*, the *Spectator*, and the *Saturday Review* are great, and evidently Rossetti who regarded himself as a professional critic (as he explains in the review of Palgrave's *Essays on Art* in the volume) varied his style and level of article accordingly. Many writers, like Ruskin,[8] self-consciously availed themselves of the occasional and serial nature of publication in periodical and serial, and chose their form of publication, including whether to publish in or outside (the constraints or conditions of) the periodicals, according to the nature of the work in hand. It is clear that some mid-century critics, particularly those who regarded themselves as professionals, had many authorial personae, even some of those who had decided, publicly articulated and acknowledged 'views' such as Lewes and

Leslie Stephen. Few associated themselves with a single periodical or a single point of view at any one time.

The policy of anonymity of most of these journals obscured the heterodoxy and overlapping of staff, allowing the professional journalist to contribute freely and to develop, while the corporate identity of the individual periodicals appeared to survive unharmed. But at the same time, studies of specific periodicals repeatedly show that reversals of policy and full-scale alterations of staff often resulted from a change of editor, as in the *North British Review*, and *Fraser's* which became demonstrably more radical concerning religion after 1863; they suggest that the politics, format and contributors of individual journals varied significantly as regimes changed and that the uniformity characteristic of a specific journal is dependent on continuity of its editor. A principal cause for the triumph of uniformity of tone in the *Spectator* is R.H. Hutton's 35-year reign as editor. I say 'triumph' because the illusion of a characteristic 'identity' (whether eclectic or singular) is one of the constitutive conditions of newspapers and periodicals, as commodities competing in the market-place and as forms of cultural production. Both readers and writers are implicated in creating and endorsing these identities.

I want to return to the above outline of the characteristics of a critical essay influenced by the periodicals, and look at each item more closely. It would seem, from various explanations by periodical journalists, that the process of assigning reviews and articles varied considerably. T.H. Escott reports that Douglas Cook of the *Saturday Review* 'personally instructed' his contributors in his chambers at the Albany, and held 'weekly *levées*' of his writers ...every Tuesday' (Escott: 533), but when he contributed to the *Daily Telegraph*, Escott submitted several subjects to James Macdonell who chose one which was topical (Escott: 535). Yet another procedure is outlined by G.H. Lewes who, after reading *Jane Eyre*, went to *Fraser's* to request to review it, but found that it was considered so obscure, that he could only include it in a review with several other books. E.S. Dallas, as a regular reviewer at *The Times*, was free to choose whatever books he wished from the room in which the review copies were displayed, but as John Blackwood put 'kindly but persistent' pressure on Dallas, and as John T. Delane, editor of *The Times*, was similarly predisposed to Blackwood books, 'personal considerations' often dictated Dallas's choice of books (Carruthers: 57–61).

It is difficult to assess, even where an element of choice on the reviewer's part is evident, how much a specific review reflects the critic's initial interest. In most cases the process is not clear at all; for example, it is impossible to say whether Johann Winckelmann, the subject of the second published review by Walter Pater, reflects Pater's choice (from his rooms at Oxford or from a 'table' of available books at the *Westminster*) or that of the editor(s) of the *Westminster Review*,[9] and since Winckelmann's ideas can be seen, retrospectively, to have figured importantly in Pater's developing thought, the process of choice is of considerable interest. Was the *Westminster* responsible for introducing Walter Pater to an important source for his later thought, or did Pater submit 'Winckelmann' to the *Westminster* because he thought that the profile of the journal and its readers coincided with his own in the essay? To put it another way, did Pater gravitate to the *Westminster* because of its reputation for 'wickedness',[10] or was the assignment of a review on Winckelmann an expression of the way the *Westminster* saw itself, in a vanguard particularly receptive to German criticism and inimical to orthodox Christianity? Another characteristic of Pater's review, its tolerance and foregrounding of homosexual love between men, similarly identifies the *Westminster* and its (anonymous) reviewer with a discourse of sexual tolerance and, in nineteenth-century terms, subversion and license. The origin of the subject of reviews is an important factor in assessing the nature of the apprenticeship that the Victorian periodicals as a cultural formation offered young critics.

The relation of length of article to the nature of the criticism is perhaps closer than might be envisaged, and length is a factor on which most periodicals have a norm. Many of Swinburne's rambling essays appeared in the *Fortnightly Review* which, for some reason, published his effusive reviews, apparently unedited, of Hugo, Arnold, Rossetti and Shelley of 24, 31, 28 and 22 pages respectively, as well as his shorter and tighter pieces. Both Bagehot and Hutton produced literary essays of about thirty pages for the *National Review*.[11] The lengthier review allows for the effusions, surveys, moral, philosophical and theological speculations, and long quotations which some of them include. Long articles such as those in monthlies are inherited from the great quarterlies earlier in the century, when length was equated with seriousness. In more popular monthly magazines such as *Blackwood's*, *Macmillan's*

Magazine, and the *Cornhill,* reviews were shorter, with Leslie Stephen's literary articles in *Cornhill* being between 15 and 20 pages long, about half the length of Hutton's and Bagehot's in the *National Review.* That of the three, Stephen's essays are most focused seems related in part to the strictures on length in the *Cornhill.* Few literary journals of our own time publish articles of more than 12–15 pages and, to some extent, our experience of some Victorian criticism as diffuse is a function of the disparities between their periodicals and ours.

The question of the more positive relation between the styles of any single critic and the periodicals in which she or he published is more complex. It is necessarily involved with a journal's house style and the effort the author makes to meet it, the audience of the periodical (particularly its gender(s) and class), and the extent of revision by the editor, as well as the subject and the author's preferred style. As editors, Bagehot, Hutton and Leslie Stephen had working maxims, with Bagehot describing an allusive style, Hutton calling for 'vivacity and crispness' (Anon. 1897b: 221), and Stephen (1903b: 756) demanding succinctness. Interest in prose style was not confined to the editors however, and almost every critic in the period considers the subject of style, either separately or as a recurring interest in their essays. The most influential essays of the century on style were probably those by De Quincey (1840), Herbert Spencer (October 1852 and 1857), and Pater (1888), but Lewes (in *Principles of Success in Literature* (1865), Saintsbury (1876), R.L. Stevenson (1885), William Archer (1885) and J.A. Symonds (1890) also theorised in the periodicals. In 1859 David Masson published a work treating *British Novelists and their Styles,* and Matthew Arnold's *Essays in Criticism* and *Culture and Anarchy* in the 1860s included many observations on style as well as more formal rules.

In 1840, in his plea for a more poetic and idiomatic prose style, De Quincey feared that the bookish formality of newspaper English might take over, but what we are forced to conclude upon consideration of the Victorian periodicals is that variety, not uniformity, of style reigns, for the most part between periodicals, but sometimes, as in the *Fortnightly Review,* within a single journal. Two extremes can be represented by the *Athenaeum,* where reviewing by specialists resulted in a lack of homogeneity (Marchand: 167), and *Blackwood's* of which John Skelton ('Shirley') writes:

Except his contributors (with whom he maintained closely confidential relations) not many know how much of unity and distinct personality the Magazine owed to its Editor – to his fine mother wit and native shrewdness. His marginal notes on the *proofs* of articles – suggestive, anecdotical, brightly conversational – were altogether admirable. He did not, like Jeffrey, rewrite articles, so that their authors did not know them again; but every article was so assimilated by him that anything out of keeping or character, anything inconsistent with the traditions of the Magazine, was at once detected by the practised eye and the fine sense of what was fit. For though neither bigot in politics nor zealot in religion, he stuck to his convictions as a limpet sticks to its rock. He was the great Tory editor....Blackwood's Toryism was indelible – bred in the bone (Skelton 1895: 291–2).

But if one is prone to imagine too readily the disadvantages of such close editorial supervision, the following enlightened editor's pressure on a *Fraser's* reviewer in connection with Swinburne reveals some advantages.

> Aug. 19 [1866]. Since I [J.A. Froude] wrote you [J. Skelton] I have seen Swinburne's volume, and also the "Saturday" and the "Athenaeum" reviews of it. There is much, of course, which is highly objectionable in it, but much also of real beauty. He convinces me in fact for the first time that he has real *stuff* in him, and I think, considering the fatuous stupidity with which the critics have hitherto flattered him, considering that he is still very young, and that the London intellectual life is perhaps the very worst soil which has ever existed in the world for a young poet to be planted in, – considering all this, I am very unwilling to follow the crew of Philistines, and bite his heels like the rest of them. The "Saturday Review" temperament is ten thousand thousand times more damnable than the worst of Swinburne's skits. *Modern respectability is so utterly without God, faith, heart; it shows so singular ingenuity in assailing and injuring everything that is noble and good, and so systematic a preference for what is mean and paltry, that I am not surprised at a young fellow dashing his heels into the face of it.* If he is to be cut up for what he has done, I would lay the blame far more heavily on others than on him, and I would select and especially praise the many things which highly deserve praise. When *there is any kind of true genius, we have no right to drive it mad. We must deal with it, wisely, justly, fairly.* (Skelton 1894: 763)

However, Skelton's review, 'Mr Swinburne and his critics', which appeared in the November issue (Skelton 1866), not only adopted the editor's general approach and tone, but pursued all the specific points included in Froude's letter – such as Swinburne's youthfulness, the attack on the *Saturday Review*, the critics' flattery, the objectionable and the praiseworthy in Swinburne's poems, and the real 'stuff' of the poet. Skelton even quotes Froude verbatim.[12] This interleaving of editor and reviewer provides a fascinating insight into how editors influenced reviewers, how readily reviewers complied with this imposition by the editor, and how periodicals maintained their house style and ethos. Hutton's *Spectator* also occasioned notice of its homogeneity of tone:

> One of the best things one may say of it is, that it is a paper that has known its way. As for its summary of the week's events, more than one man of note describes it, both as regards its meritorious omissions and its concise presentment of the great events that transpire week by week, as quite the best bit of journalism in the English press. The whole journal, indeed, with its fine wholesomeness, its unusual fairness, its suppressed power, its anything but supercilious corrective tone, has about it a quieting effect compared with the hot hurried developments of a press whose note is mere cleverness, and what is known as up-to-dateness…. The *Spectator* has always seemed, to one of its readers at least, as nearly as possible an ideal paper for a cultured, discriminating, leisurely life, which is, however, not too self-indulgent to overlook the more vital movements of the world, although ready, delightedly enough, to "avert its ken" from more than half of the human fate on which, as represented in print, multitudes voraciously feed. To say that the periodical is noted for its earnestness, is certainly not, even in frivolous days like these, to say anything against it (Hogben: 41–2).

Revision, even extensive revision by the editor, for many Victorian critics, must have been a common experience which they accepted as one of their conditions of work. Certainly, G.H. Lewes did not seem to bear Jeffrey any special malice for tampering with his originals; he explained to Elizabeth Gaskell in response to her account of his review of *Shirley* in the *Edinburgh Review* that Jeffrey 'tampered with the article, as usual, and inserted some to me offensive sentences, but the main argument – as far as I recollect it – is complimentary to women, not disrespectful' (Haight 1954–6: II . 316). To some extent then, and probably particularly in the early contributions of a young critic, the published piece was the result of a collaboration between contributor and editor, sometimes with the cooperation of the author and sometimes without it. But before the piece ever reached the editor's desk, the author had pitched it to the style, tone and taste of the periodical for which it was intended. In connection with certain nineteenth-century novels which appeared in periodicals, we are accustomed to think in terms of at least two texts, the original manuscript and the edited or bowdlerised text which appeared serially. In the case of critical essays we are, for the most part, unable to recover the manuscript text except on the odd occasion when the author, like some novelists, has reverted to the original in book publication.

During the worst instances of editorial revision, by J.G. Lockhart and J.W. Croker in the *Quarterly*, the publisher of the periodical was 'now and then compelled to republish as they originally stood articles which had become interpolated…with libels and malicious jokes' (Strahan: 519). However, the phenomenon of the author's republication of periodical essays in book form is more common and of considerable interest. It began in earnest in the early part of the century with Francis Jeffrey (Hatch: 56–62), and the degree of revision, the attempt – or lack of it – to forge a unity initially lacking by reordering, revising, or writing new filler material, is useful in assessing the degree of editorial revision objectionable to the contributor, the process of transition from journalist to critic, and the status of the periodical essay. Authors' attitudes to their periodical writing are implied by the tenor and technique of the editions of collected essays. Leslie Stephen, for example, distinguished periodical from book publication wittingly and quite willingly, reserving his more frank expression for the latter form (Maurer: 85).[13] Other critics of the period, such as Benjamin Jowett and Walter Pater, having experienced adverse reaction to bold periodical essays, used later book publication to modify or to withdraw totally the offending material.

William Rossetti affords an example of an author who stresses the ephemeral nature of periodicals essays by claiming to have revised them substantially for his book, *Fine Art, Chiefly Contemporary: Notices Re-printed, with Revisions*, but upon comparison of the book and periodical texts of one of the earlier essays, the review of Palgrave's *Essays on Art*, the revisions are seen to be perfunctory and minimal. He is only bowing to the alleged inferiority of the periodical essay to the finished piece, while in practice he denies it. By contrast, Swinburne, who seems to have suffered little from the editor's pen in his prose for the *Fortnightly*, praises and defends the periodical form in his Preface to *Essay and Studies*:

> These Essays, written at intervals during a space of seven years, are now reissued with no change beyond the correction of an occasional error, the addition of an occasional note, and the excision or modification of an occasional phrase or passage. To omit or to rewrite any part would be to forfeit the one claim which I should care to put up on their behalf; that they give frank and full expression to what were, at the time of writing, my sincere and deliberate opinions. Only where I have detected a positive error or suspected a possible injustice have I changed or cancelled a syllable. As I see no reason to suppress what I have no desire to recant, I have not allowed myself to strike out the rare allusions, which might otherwise have been erased, to such obscure and ephemeral names or matters as may be thought unworthy even of so slight a record as the notice here conferred on them. (Swinburne 1875: vii)

Some years before, in a piece on periodical literature in the *Dublin Review*, Frederick Oakeley similarly invokes the frankness, fullness, and sincerity of the best of the periodical essays as a source of their strength, rather than weakness, dubbing the book as a form of publication – with some hint of distaste – refined:

> We speak of such specimens of it only as have produced the greatest effect on public opinion, and these will be found, as we believe, to be characterized far beyond other literature, by the easy, natural, and therefore affecting and impressive character of earnest *conversation*. One proof of this is, that no kind of writing is more apt to betray its author, by internal evidence than the periodical essay. One *book* is far more like another than article is like article. The reason, we suspect, is that when a man writes an "article" he does it *currente calamo*, often as a relief rather than a task, as he might converse after dinner with his literary friends, and the consequence is, that just as natural and earnest conversation is "thinking aloud", this easy off-hand writing is a kind of talking on paper....A "book" is a serious undertaking, and is generally kept by its author and revised, till much of its simplicity is

refined away, its sentiment over-qualified, its style over-wrought. An article is written off at the flow of the intellectual tide, goes to the printer in fragments as it is produced, and is "struck off" before the writer has time to recal [sic] the temerarious word, or polish the uncouth sentence. (Oakeley: 544–5)

Both Swinburne and Oakeley seem to be registering a preference for the journalist critic who, by virtue of the profession, retains a liveliness and spontaneity which elude the more staid author of a book whom, it is implied, tends to pedantry. Genuine debate and topicality spice Victorian criticism in the periodicals; this positive journalistic quality contributes to what is deemed the 'new' or 'neutral' unadorned style by twentieth-century critics such as Travis R. Merritt and John Woolford. Kenneth Allott describes it more negatively than Oakeley, as 'looser' than the academic style, and characterised by 'shapelessness' and 'indiscipline', but its qualities are identical:

The new style reflected the mixture of speech-habits in the big towns and cities; it had a richer or more mongrel vocabulary and a more complicated structure; and it was sustained – or, one may prefer to say, preyed on – by half-understood literary influences (including those of journalism). (Allott: xxxi–ii).

So, if the text of a critical essay which first appears in a periodical is bound to inscribe the style and tone of the specific periodical in which it appears (how voluntarily or imposed is something scholars should assess), the text also inscribes what Allott calls 'an expansive energy' (Allott: xviii), a positive and shared element of language found in the critical prose of the period, which derives in part from the conditions of writing for the periodicals of the day.

The audience of the periodical in which criticism appears is another constituent factor. Although little from external evidence is known about Victorian readers of periodicals,[14] editors and contributors do indicate how they perceive their audiences. Leslie Stephen's 'Hours in a Library' in the *Cornhill*, for example, had to be *conceived* within the limits of their notion of a family audience, no politics and no theology. Intellectually cramping overall, these prohibitions must have been particularly significant in their influence on Stephen's articles for the *Cornhill* on 'Art and Morality', 'Cowper and Rousseau', and 'Wordsworth's Ethics'; 'Carlyle's

Ethics' and 'Thomas Carlyle' both appeared in 1881 when Carlyle's politics were as controversial as ever.

ANONYMITY, SIGNATURE AND THE STATUS OF CRITICISM

Whether an article is anonymous or signed is also a governing characteristic of Victorian criticism. Signature eventually became a principal factor in the growth of the respectability of journalism, and in the apprenticeship system on offer to neophytes, but initially anonymity was the principal guarantor.[15] The stridency of tone of some Victorian critics (such as Matthew Arnold) about their peers and their calling, their virulence about the system of reviewing, and the uncomplicated faith in professionalism expressed by some is striking to a twentieth-century reader: high feeling and dissatisfaction suggest imminent change and transition. W.M. Rossetti shows particular concern about the dignity of his profession: in the Preface to *Fine Art, Chiefly Contemporary* (1867) he adumbrates the squalidness of anonymity, and he entitles one of the essays 'Mr Palgrave and Unprofessional Criticisms on Art'. Although he is relatively and condescendingly kind to F.T. Palgrave, he pronounces stentoriously:

> the only criticism of much use in the long run is that by professional men; not only on the ground that they alone are qualified to pronounce upon technicalities, but that this knowledge of technicalities is a powerful sedative to the whole range of opinion upon art, and enables a man to say clearly and almost *ex cathedra* what attempts in art are desirable to be made, compatibly with the limits of technical attainment, as well as how far these limits have been reached in any particular attempt. (Rossetti 1867: 326)

'The whole range of opinion upon art' is Rossetti's reference to a perennial problem, the relation between informed opinion and professional criticism, but it also signals a more specific problem of the authority of criticism in the nineteenth century,[16] which was beset during its first half by a system of anonymity which permitted both editors and publishers a heyday of puffing. J.W. Croker's and Francis Jeffrey's respective vituperative reviews, and interpolations of editorial opinion and slurs in contributors' articles are noted above, but perhaps more common and insidious were the

various forms of puffing afforded to *publishers* by the periodical
system. That the publishers of some periodicals such as *Blackwood's*
and the *New Monthly Magazine* were principally publishers of books
meant that the Houses had a secure source of favourble reviews,
most of which were written by the firm's rather than the
periodical's reviewers. The plight of the editor of such a periodical
is described in Thomas Hood's letter to a prospective reviewer for
Henry Colburn's *New Monthly Magazine* in 1843:

> I write in haste a few lines to put you on yr. guard, by telling you
> of the arrangements for reviewing in the Magazine. I undertook
> to review all books except Colburn's own with the puffing of
> which I of course desired to have no concern. They are *done* by
> the persons of the establishment – Patmore, Williams or Shoberl.
> If you see the Mag. you will know what wretched things these
> reviews are....I am ashamed of them at present or should be
> were it not pretty well known that I have no hand in them.
> (Jerrold: 369–70)

Because in the 1830s most daily papers had no literary staff, they
welcomed 'paid paragraphs' from the publishers as a source of
both income and criticism, and these were sent in turn to the pro-
vincial papers by the publishers, sometimes on puff sheets. The
more familiar pressure of publishers' advertising on the content of
criticism is illustrated by Henry Stebbing's confession later, in the
1870s, that he wrote reviews of books he had never read because
advertising depended on their appearance (Stebbing: 88). Even
William Hepworth Dixon, editor of the *Athenaeum* between 1855
and 1869, abused the anonymity policy of that periodical and
reviewed his own books. Quite apart from publishers, editors and
advertisers, it seems evident that reviewers availed themselves of
the opportunity to praise the work of friends and damn that of
enemies; thus campaigns against authors by individual critics who
refused to consider successive works on merit were tolerated and
even endorsed.

It would seem that objections to puffing date from the earlier
days of that practice in the nineteenth century; Macaulay attacked it
in the *Edinburgh* in April 1830, and C.W. Dilke had to make
strenuous efforts to eradicate it between 1830 and 1846; during his
period as editor of the *Athenaeum*, he avoided society and thus
pressure from friends and associates; he never solicited review

copies from the publishers but bought in a shop copies of books for review that publishers had not sent free and unsolicited. For Marchand, Dilke held 'an almost tyrannical stick over his staff, and even over contributors and foreign correspondents, to see that they remained independent of authors and publishers' (Marchand: 34). *Fraser's* was the other periodical of this period that campaigned against puffery but where Dilke tried to ensure fair reviewing, William Maginn and his staff, although independent of party and publishers, too often vented their spleen and personal prejudices for the resulting criticism to approach judiciousness.

The phenomenon of *Fraser's*, against puffery but often vindictive and irresponsible, reveals that the attempt to establish the respectability of periodical journalism was in two stages; neither the *Edinburgh*, the *Athenaeum*, nor *Fraser's* advocated signature, but rather more responsible and honest anonymity. Although instances of signed articles, and even short-lived periodicals whose editorial policy embraced signature, occurred before 1859, it was with the founding of *Macmillan's Magazine* that a general march toward signature in the Victorian periodicals began, and long after the trumpeted advocacy of signature in the prospectus of the new *Fortnightly Review* in 1865, the majority of periodicals resisted wholesale signature. It should be remembered that anonymity often extended even to the editor's name.

Once the debate over anonymity was launched in 1859, it continued until the end of the century. It is well described by Oscar Maurer, but it is instructive to read some contemporary critics' presentation to Victorian readers of the arguments for and against. Frederick Oakeley, writing anonymously on a collection of periodical essays by Cardinal Wiseman, chooses to devote a large part of his essay to an assessment of periodical essays as a genre. He feelingly outlines the advantage of anonymity to the naturally modest but independent author, and the welcome weight collective authority gives to new or young contributors.

Among the advantages of the literature under consideration, which in turn have no doubt proved its attractions to those who have taken part in it, must be mentioned the shield of reserve and protection which it throws over personal modesty, and by which it modifies personal responsibility. It furnishes a graceful disguise, intermediate between the boldness of profession and the cowardice of concealment; opaque enough to shelter diffidence, transparent enough to verify conjecture....an article, from the very fact of its being for the most part an off-hand expression of the mind, is more apt than any other composition to betray its writer to such as think its authorship worth investigating....

In fact, the benefit of editorial protection did not consist in the opportunity it might afford of shrinking from responsibility, but in the sanction which it gave to individual opinion. The regular contributors to a Review, constitute a kind of corporation, each member of which derives an immense accession of weight from the fact of his forming an integral part of its whole. Men of note, especially in the outset of their career, have ever felt it a gain to be launched upon the great ocean of literary competition under convoy of some established name; nor can any patronage be so complimentary, because none is so hazardous to the patron himself, as that which is implied in the fact of taking an author into this kind of literary partnership. It is no wonder, then, that rising men should covet such a distinction, nor again that even in the heyday of their reputation they should continue to feel the value of an arrangement which stamps such effort of their genius with so powerful an "imprimatur". (Oakeley: 549–50)

Less predictable than these rather orthodox claims is his analysis of the limited influence of periodicals, which reflect public preoccupations and opinions rather than create them. By stressing the effect of the periodical as a whole, he seems, by some sleight of hand, to obviate the individuality of its contributors and to accede to the illusion of unaninmity and monolithic identity.

A journal can hardly be said to *direct* public opinion, which makes that opinion in any material degree the rule of its sentiments, which cautiously sounds the depths of the national mind before it makes up its own, and launches forth tentative articles as aeronauts send up pilot-balloons, to try the direction of currents, before they commit themselves to the bosom of the aerial deep....Do we mean to assert, then, that these journals are merely the victims, and in no sense the arbiters, of public opinion? Not so; they perform a very essential office in supplying the nation with arguments, in giving shape, expression, effect, and currency; to the crude mass of thought which goes to form, on the whole, what is called the mind of England. Nay, they may at times even modify it where it is extravagant, and give it conclusions where it recognizes but the premisses. What they cannot do, is to work any essential change in its views and principles. (Oakeley: 542)

But nowhere does Oakeley acknowledge the undeniable abuse of the system, and the many and travelled paths to the devil of puffing.

Three articles defending signature, by Thomas Hughes in 1861, and by Anthony Trollope (1865) and John Morley (1867) appear in *Macmillan's Magazine* and the *Fortnightly*, the Victorian pioneers of the policy. Morley and Trollope agree with Oakeley that the names of many of the major reviewers are known, with Trollope arguing:

What has he to gain by such [anonymous] efforts that he should give to them the best of his mind and the best of his conscience? I may be told, with truth, that many have gained much...but such men have done so because their work has not in truth been anonymous. They have been known by other marks than those of a signed name, and have received their reward in the recognition given to them. (Trollope: 495)

John Morley, writing in the *Fortnightly* two years later, similarly insists that lack of anonymity is the principal guarantee of respectable work.

The more obscure the journalist, the more reason why he should be known. In the case of the chief writers on the *Saturday Review*, for example, or the *Pall Mall Gazette*, or the *Spectator*, or the *Economist*, there is practically no anonymity. The general public may not know who are their instructors, but each of these writers has a circle of friends who know perfectly well what he writes, and to whose opinion therefore he is virtually responsible. It is, for one thing, because they are thus in fact not anonymous that their general tone is so respectable. (Morley 1867: 290)

But Leslie Stephen, writing in 1876 in the *Cornhill*, which still retained its policy of anonymity, disagrees, arguing that critics who are known, whether by 'publicity' or signature, are more 'slashing' than their anonymous counterparts: 'The most ferocious denunciation, and the most arrogant dogmatism, have, I think, been shown by men whose names were known to everybody, if not actually published' (Stephen 1876: 561). Desiring from critics trust-worthiness and insight without heat, Stephen calls for the critic who is 'a prophet without inspiration' (Stephen 1876: 560).

Even the general public had access to authorship in periodicals and the names of editors, for in a series of knowledgeable articles in *The Critic* in 1851/2 on some of the major titles, 'Herodotus Smith' (the pseudonym of Francis Espinasse, 1823?–1912) identifies past and present editors, staff members, and reviewers of the *Edinburgh*, *Quarterly*, *Fraser's*, *Westminster*, *Blackwood's*, and in less detail, of the *North British Review*, the *British Quarterly*, and the *Prospective Review*. Moreover, each number of *The Critic: London Literary Journal* contains a section, 'The Literary World', or its equivalent, in which authors of anonymous or pseudonymous articles are named, rather casually, in the course of what is essentially literary gossip.

Where Oakeley in the *Dublin Review* argues for anonymity to bastion the dignity of the members of the Catholic establishment who commit themselves to print there, Thomas Hughes in *Macmillan's* opts for impact rather than discretion; he illustrates his argument by using religious criticism within Anglicanism, claiming that published singly the pieces in *Essays and Reviews* would 'have passed unnoticed in one or another of the Quarterlies had they been published anonymously'. This is presumably the 'protection' that Oakeley values. But Hughes goes on to prefer debate embodied in the flesh of personalities and position, and to reject the notion of disembodied pure Ideas which proponents of ideal anonymous journalism invoke.

> Their effectiveness lay, somewhat perhaps in the grouping, but chiefly in the names which were affixed to them. Has it been for the good of the nation, the Church, the writers themselves, that their names were published? I can have no hesitation in answering, yes. (Hughes: 159)

This conflict between belief in discretion, with its underlying assumption that writing in periodicals is beneath the dignity of those in public life, and those who welcome the more brash cut and thrust of ideas and personalities, was one of the basic issues in the anonymity–signature debate.

But, outside the dignity of the great, Oakeley values the collective identity of the journal, and signature would undoubtedly break this illusion, not perhaps so much in regard to the loyalties of the great from other professions who used the organs of their party to further their cause, but with respect to the professional author who contributed to the whole range of periodicals. In his revelatory pieces on the periodicals in *The Critic* in 1852, Francis Espinasse registers self-consciousness of this disillusioning process in his nervous reference to G.H. Lewes whom he is forced to identify as a contributor to successive periodicals. Here he is writing about *Blackwood's:*

> There, too, sometimes are to be seen the sparkles of an unmistakeable and a unique vivacity. The reader has already guessed the name, and with a cordial smile of welcome on his lip already murmurs fondly: "Once more the omnipresent LEWES!" (Espinasse 1852: 114)

But John Morley, writing in 1882 after the initial breakthrough of signature in the 1860s, looks back fondly at the professional writer who, in comparison with the 'expert', possesses some of the charm of the amateur.

> There is a something to be said for the writer by profession, who without being an expert, will take trouble to work up his subject, to learn what is said and thought about it, to penetrate to the real points, to get the same mastery over it as an advocate or a judge does over a patent case or a suit about rubrics and vestments. (Morley 1882: 514)

This curve between uneasy consciousness about professional writers and nostalgia at their passing into experts describes the growth, flourishing and decline of this figure between 1850 and the present. With the anonymity–signature debate, the subterranean practices of the journalist's trade which were relatively unexamined publicly until mid-century emerged to become one of the important issues within it. That certain authors, who wrote anonymously, accepted assignments cavalierly in the confidence that they could work them up as Morley suggests, could expect less work from a policy of signature and therefore opposed it is understandable. But they might write better. Trollope and Thomas Hughes are agreed that

> the writer who is made to give his name will be more careful, when using it, than he is when keeping it concealed. And the

writer without his name will work under circumstances which are injurious to himself, and repressive of his energy. He will not be on his mettle, and will dare to be slovenly, inconsequential, and unjust. (Trollope 1865: 494–5)

we, the writers...while the custom [of anonymity] prevails, can write with much less sense of responsibility, and therefore much more copiously and easily; making more money and giving less thought – who, if ill-natured, can say savage things against our foes, if good-natured can do puffing and backing jobs for our friends, which we should hesitate to say and do in our own names. (Hughes: 168)

The reluctance to do down the profession and the mildness of the references to puffing (avoided by Trollope altogether) are striking. Morley tries to shift interest from the 'literary bravoes', by which term he refers to the puffers who are 'not numerous' in a 'respectable journal', to a better standard of argument and knowledge, virtues of higher literature: it is clear that he, too, is interested in establishing the profession, and enhancing its respectability, through signature:

Let us say as loudly as we choose, if we see good reason, that they are half-informed about some of the things which they so authoritatively discuss, that they are under strong class feeling, that they have not mastered the doctrine which they are opposing, that they have not sufficiently meditated their subjects, that they have not given themselves time to do justice even to their scanty knowledge. Journalists are too open to charges of this kind; but to think of them as a corrupt and shameless body, thirsting for the blood of better men than themselves, or ready to act as an editors' "instrument" for "money", involves a highly unjust and regrettable misconception. (Morley 1867: 288)

Thomas Hughes's description of the freedoms of the writer under anonymity is the third item in a paragraph in which he treats the similar freedoms of the editors, and proprietors (who were often publishers); many of these, too, resisted signature, and the loss of their privileges.

Another aspect of this dawning sense of professionalism, and the striving to establish the respectability of literary journalism seen in the anonymity–signature debate, is the self-derogation of Victorian critics and journalists privately. In 1894 T.H.S. Escott reviewed *Things I have Seen, and People I have Known*, an autobiography in two volumes by G.A. Sala, a well-known journalist connected with the rise of the penny press, and the editor of the *Daily Telegraph*. But neither the penny press nor the *Telegraph* merit mention by Sala, and Escott complains of the implication that journalism is beneath the dignity of public attention.

> If a regard for the etiquette of his calling had caused Mr. Sala to draw the veil of anonymity over his long connection with a well-known London newspaper, one might have understood this reserve. But seeing that these volumes are dedicated to the proprietor of the print in question, this hypothesis is inadmissable. (Escott: 532)

It would be mistaken to take Sala's reticence as typical so late in the century, and Escott's objection is perhaps a measure of its atypicality. Even in the early 1870s confidence in the standard of contemporary journalism is revealed by Leslie Stephen through his criticism of the commonly venerated early *Edinburgh Review*:

> Every one who turns from the periodical literature of the present day to the original *Edinburgh Review*, will be amazed at its inferiority. It is generally dull and, when not dull, flimsy. The vigour has departed; the fire is extinct....as a rule, one may most easily characterize the contents by saying few of the articles would have a chance of acceptance by the editor of a first-rate periodical to-day; and that the majority belong to an inferior variety of what is now called 'padding' – mere perfunctory bits of work, obviously manufactured by the critic out of the book before him. (Stephen 1878: 219–20)

The whole of the article bristles indignantly, throughout the implied comparison of the *Edinburgh* with contemporary periodicals, and a portrait of the strengths of the Victorian journals emerges as clearly as the weaknesses of the *Edinburgh*. It is typical of Leslie Stephen's high opinion and defence of the profession and of the journalism of his day.

But the unease seen in the references to G.H. Lewes's varied and numerous periodical contributions by Francis Espinasse is echoed but transformed by the disdainful references to his journalism by

two of Lewes's friends privately. In 1851 John Chapman, editor of
the *Westminster Review* confided to his Diary, 'But Lewes is a "bread
scholar" and lacks that enthusiasm of thought, and earnest purpose
which I must alone seek for in Contributors to the Westminster'
(Haight 1940: 203) and Frederic Harrison, a journalist like Chapman
and Lewes, sniffs disapprovingly in an obituary of Lewes in the
Academy:

> It is strange to find men to whom Mr. Lewes was merely a journ-
> alist and a critic, and who seem never to have heard of the
> *Problems of Life and Mind*. It is as if Bacon were to be known by his
> Essays, and Hume by his History of England. (Harrison: 543)

Both Harrison and Lewes wrote philosophy while closely implicated as critics in the periodical press for the whole of their
working lives, and it is perhaps the philosopher's shame at the
journalist's fertility that Harrison voices. Moreover, the *Academy*, in
which the obituary appeared, depended for both its contributors
and its readers on the universities, and Harrison would have been
sure to find approval for the following hierarchy of status:

> If, as some writers have reminded us, Mr. Lewes began life as a
> journalist, a critic, a novelist, a dramatist, a biographer, and an
> essayist, it is as well to remember that he closed his life as a
> mathematician, a physicist, a chemist, a biologist, a psychologist,
> and the author of a system of abstract general philosophy.
> (Harrison: 543)

These assessments of Lewes's criticism however, reflect more on
their author than on Lewes who, after 1859, seems to have taken
considerable care with the style of his articles, as he describes in his
Diary in February 1859:

> Latterly I have taken to rewrite almost everything except quite
> unimportant articles. This I formerly never did – or only quite by
> exception. But I find it necessary: the defect of my style is its
> want of largo: it is too brief, allusive, hurried. In re-writing the
> defect is in some degree remedied. (Kaminsky: 193–4)

But lest it is thought that philosophers and journalists were alone
in their castigation of periodicals, we must consider the adverse

opinion of a literary personage who kept relatively clear of the journals professionally, D.G. Rossetti. Although, as a poet, Rossetti's absence from periodicals other than the *Germ* might be expected, some poets such as Coventry Patmore and Swinburne, and of course Arnold, did write criticism which they published initially in the periodicals, and certainly some poets, including Tennyson, Arnold, Morris and Browning, published poems in journals. Despite Rossetti's disengagement, it is probable that he had second-hand knowledge of the journalist's life from his brother William Michael, the art critic quoted above, whose assurance of revision of periodical pieces for book publication isn't in the event borne out in the review of Palgrave. Perhaps the disapproval of periodical publication implied by WMR's public assurance of revision is echoed in DGR's letter to Thomas Gordon Hake in September 1872:

> Your idea of George's possibly finding an outlet in light literature does not seem promising to me, I confess. I have known more or less most of the men who have ultimately made a mark in this sort of work – the periodical kind – in my time; and know what an uphill drudgery it is, how almost entirely dependent on happy-go-lucky chances, how beset with contemptible companionships, and moreover how early an apprenticeship must be served to be admitted into the rather pitiful mystery of it. Men begin very young by some such step as sitting up all night in a newspaper office to receive late telegrams, or doing shorthand in a reporter's gallery. *Without* this sort of thing you more or less remain an outsider, and only great influence or quite exceptional powers will then serve you. *With* this, you may aspire eventually to push your way much as in a scramble at the Gallery door of a theatre, through little better company and language. I do not think it is a sphere suited to anyone who has health, gifts, and inclination for an active life, such as George eminently possesses.
> (Doughty and Wahl: III 1064)[17]

Rossetti's low opinion of the 'pitiful mystery' of journalism is coupled with his distaste for its social sphere, both of which James Hannay, of the *Pall Mall Gazette*, attempted to make respectable in 1866, at a dinner party for another journalist. Hannay's efforts echo the grand tone of the early quarterlies of the century, their literary assumptions, and the style of their prose, but in his consciousness of the widening breach between literature and journalism, he attests to the development of separate professions and the low esteem with which they were both regarded. He is poised between attitudes of the beginning and end of the century. Over a hundred years later we smile at his grandiose claim, but even Escott, who relates it after thirty years, presents it confidently to dramatise the rapid rate of change. Hannay, Escott reports,

> delivered an admirable oration...denouncing the "trumpery distinctions", as he called it, "drawn by pretentious blockheads between journalism and literature. Both," he said "were affluents or effluents of one and the same mighty stream, and both flowed from the same historic fountain-head – namely, the Greek and Latin classics." (Escott: 537)

The relation between literature or criticism and journalism which figures implicitly in Rossetti's letter and explicitly in Escott and Hannay, arises in many of the meditations on the nature of periodical criticism of the period. The Victorians' view of their own literature, their predisposition in favour of poetry and drama, and their serious underestimation of the novel,[18] indicate their blind spots. But I want to suggest that the low status of periodical literature is associated with many of the same factors which figure in the feeble welcome Victorian critics accorded the novel. With Dickens's popularisation of serial publication, the novel joined forces with the periodical, and the union between them was strengthened in 1860 when the *Cornhill* offered serialisation of two novels per monthly number in addition to magazine essays. Both the novel and the periodicals attracted the epithet 'lighter' rather than 'higher' literature, the latter category being reserved for classical rather than English literature according to Hannay; for poetry and drama in Arnold; for science, psychology and philosophy according to Frederic Harrison; theology according to Hutton; and political pronouncements according to Trollope who deems that anonymity is justified in political journalism and unnecessary in 'magazine articles' (Trollope: 493, 496).

These locations of higher criticism and literature are gendered, and all pertain to areas of knowledge associated with men – politics, science, psychology, philosophy, classics, drama and poetry, while the novel is clearly associated in the period with women readers and authors. It is particularly interesting that Lewes and Stephen, two of the most professional journalists and more in touch with readers and the publishing market, are those most committed in their criticism to the novel as a genre. In a *Cornhill* piece on Defoe's fiction and journalism (Stephen 1868: 294), Stephen links them through a comparison of lying, or the status of fact in both, and finds lies or fiction palatable in journalism, and facts acceptable in fiction. But for most early and mid-Victorian critics the novel, like the periodical, was deemed a lighter form, and had to take a place in a scheme of values dominated by earnestness. George Eliot's work, earnest and intellectual, rather than the work of Jane Austen, Dickens or Thackeray, propelled the novel as a genre into the thoroughly respectable 'higher' category of literature, so that later in the century even the most serious periodicals did not fail to review fiction respectfully. For many Victorian critics the periodical, like the novel, was ephemeral and transitory, qualities which leave John Sterling in 1828 somewhat breathless:

> The English press is the most powerful literary engine in Europe, as it is also the freest. It has absorbed nine-tenths of the minds of this country. The being of an Englishman has no great cycle which it would accomplish between the cradle and the grave; but its longest revolution is performed between the quarterly publications of a review, and this comprises various minor periods, each complete in itself, – monthly, weekly, tridiurnal, and daily. Pamphlets find no sale in the land of Swift and Steele. Metaphysics, political economy, and cookery, are discussed in the reviews and magazines, and all the thinking of the country has become a matter of shreds and patches. Truth and science are things of trimestrial immortality; the noblest subjects, "which the gods love", "die young" in monthly magazines....Great libraries sleep amid their dust, while newspapers are worn to bits by the successive fingers of a hundred readers. (Sterling: 695)

But Leslie Stephen in an essay on Scott written in 1871 ingeniously and comfortably tucks the ephemeral criticism into the ongoing process of evaluation of works of art and a commonplace of earlier literary criticism; that he uses a metaphor from science to do so gives it authority in the eyes of his original readers:

> When naturalists wish to preserve a skeleton, they bury an animal in an anthill and dig him up after many days with all the perishable matter fairly eaten away. That is the process which great men have to undergo. A vast multitude of insignificant,

unknown, and unconscious critics destroy what has no genuine power of resistance and leave the remainder for posterity. Much disappears in every case. (Stephen 1871: 292)

The twentieth-century modernists' development of literary criticism, with an 'art' or 'scientific method' of its own, is usually traced to Henry James, whose efforts to create a poetics of the novel pervade his fiction and criticism. But James, who initially published much of his fiction and criticism in the periodicals of the 1870s and 1880s was only one of many Victorian critics deliberating on the nature of literature and criticism in the periodicals. The ubiquitous and articulate Victorian critical discourse addressing its own nature and means of production reveals tellingly the cultural, economic, aesthetic, and ideological underpinnings of Victorian criticism – its origins in the sway and bustle of the market-place as well as in the tower.

Notes

1. Research for this article was undertaken with the aid of a British Academy Grant.
2. See Orel, for example.
3. A pioneer in this respect is *Victorian Periodicals Review* (1968–) and the other projects originating in the Research Society for Victorian Periodicals.
4. See Shorter, and Stephen 1876. Stephen's 1876 usage of 'aesthetic criticism' should be compared with Walter Pater's more renowned and earlier one in the Preface to *Studies in the History of the Renaissance* (1873) where he uses the term to distinguish his subjective criticism from Arnold's focus on 'the object as it really is'. Stephen's essay directly relates to the dialogue between Arnold and Pater. Pater's phrase points to the common usage of 'criticism' in a value structure where moral 'truth' is prized above all else. His attempt is to distinguish criticism of aesthetic questions from its common use and to foreground aesthetic criteria.
5. A nineteenth-century counterpart to Madden and Dixon, and Uffelman is badly needed.
6. For more on authorial choice of alternative periodical spaces, see 'The Discourses of Journalism' and 'Oscar Wilde and the *Woman's World'*, Chapters 4 and 7 in this volume.
7. For details on Lewes and the press, see Ashton.
8. See Maidment (1982a) on Ruskin.
9. The record of Pater's library borrowing only shows that by April 1866 Pater began reading for 'Winckelmann' which appeared in the *Westminster* the following January. See Inman (1981) 105–47.

10. Thomas Huxley wrote to Charles Kingsley probably in 1863 that he preferred publishing an agnostic paper on prayer in 'my favourite organ, the wicked *Westminster*' (Huxley: I, 247) than in *Fraser's* which at that time was too conservative.

11. Reviews for the brisker weeklies such as the *Spectator* and the *Saturday Review* between 1865 and 1870 varied between one and one and a half folio pages, and one and two folio pages respectively.

12. I have italicised Froude's phrases which are silently incorporated into Skelton's review.

13. Compare the distinction between periodicals and books offered by American publishers in '*Harper's New Monthly Magazine*: American Censorship, European Decadence and the Periodicals Market in the 1890s', Chapter 6 of this volume.

14. See Wiener (1978), Klancher, Shevelow, and Rose for more on periodical readership.

15. The history of anonymity and signature has long been available piecemeal, and I shall not duplicate that material. See particularly Maurer, and Everett.

16. On authority in nineteenth-century writing, see Small.

17. In 1872 D.G. Rossetti's opinion of periodical critics, like Swinburne's in *Under the Microscope*, would be adversely influenced by the fleshly-school controversy. See Murray.

18. See Fryckstedt on the status of the novel in 1866.

Works Cited

Allott, K. (1950). 'Introduction', *Victorian Prose*, ed. K. and M. Allott. Harmondsworth. pp. xvii–xliii.

Anon. (1897a). 'Notes and News'. *Academy* 52(4 Sept.), 182–3.

Anon. (1897b). 'Richard Holt Hutton'. *Academy* 52(18 Sept.), 221–2.

Ashton, R. (1991). *G.H. Lewes. A Life*. Oxford.

[Bagehot, W.]. (1855). 'The First Edinburgh Reviewers', *National Review* 1(Oct.), 253–84.

[Bagehot, W.]. (1859). 'Tennyson's *Idylls*', *National Review* IX(Oct.), 368–94.

Carruthers, Ian. (1970). 'E.S. Dallas as a Reviewer of Contemporary Literature'. Unpublished dissertation, University of London.

Cook, E.T. (1910). 'The Jubilee of the *Cornhill*'. *Cornhill Magazine* 28(Jan.), 8–27.

De Quincey, T. (1840). 'Style'. *Blackwood's Magazine* 48(July), 1–17.

Doughty, O. and J.R. Wahl, eds (1965, 1967). *Letters of D.G. Rossetti*. 4 vols. Oxford.

Escott, T.H. (1894). 'Thirty Years of the Periodical Press'. *Blackwood's* 156(Oct.), 532–42

[Espinasse, F.] 'Herodotus Smith'. (1852). 'The Periodical and Newspaper Press: No. V. *Blackwood's Magazine*', *The Critic* 11 (1 March), 113–14.

Everett, E.M. (1939). *The Party of Humanity: The 'Fortnightly Review' and its Contributors 1865–1874*. Chapel Hill.

Fryckstedt, Monica Correa. (1989), *On the Brink: English Novels of 1866*. Uppsala.

Haight, G., ed. (1954). *The Letters of George Eliot*. Vol. 2. Oxford.
Haight, G. (1940). *George Eliot and John Chapman*. New Haven.
Harrison, F. (1878). 'G.H. Lewes'. *Academy* 14(7 Dec.), 543–44.
Hatch, R.B. (1970). 'This will never do'. *Review of English Studies* 21 n.s., 56–62.
[Hogben, J.]. (1899). *Richard Holt Hutton of 'The Spectator'*. Edinburgh.
Hughes, Thomas. (1861). 'Anonymous Journalism', *Macmillan's Magazine* 5(Dec.), 157–68
Huxley, Leonard, ed. (1900). *Life and Letters of Thomas Henry Huxley*. 2 vols. London.
Inman, B.A. (1981). *Walter Pater's Reading*. New York and London.
Jerrold, Walter. (1907). *Thomas Hood: His Life and Times*. London.
Kaminsky, A.R. (1968). *George Henry Lewes as Literary Critic*. Syracuse, NY.
Klancher, J. (1987). *The Making of English Reading Audiences, 1790–1832*. Madison.
Madden, L., and D. Dixon. (1975). *The Nineteenth-Century Periodical Press in Britain. A Bibliography of Modern Studies 1901–1971*. VPN (*Victorian Periodicals Newsletter*) Supplement.
Maidment, B. (1982a). 'Readers Fair and Foul: John Ruskin and the Periodical Press', *Samplings and Soundings*, eds J. Shattock and M. Wolff. Leicester. pp. 29–58.
Maidment, B. (1982b). 'Interpreting Ruskin, 1870–1914', *The Ruskin Polygon*, eds J.D. Hunt and Faith M. Holland. Manchester. pp. 158–71.
Maitland, F.W. (1906). *The Life and Letters of Leslie Stephen*. London.
Marchand, Leslie A. (1941). *The Athenaeum. A Mirror of Victorian Culture*. Chapel Hill.
Maurer, Oscar. (1953). 'Leslie Stephen and the *Cornhill Magazine*', *Studies in English* 32, 67–95.
Maurer, Oscar. (1948). 'Anonymity vs. Signature in Victorian Reviewing', *Studies in English* 27(June), 1–27.
Merritt, Travis R. (1968). 'Taste, Opinion and Theory in the Rise of Victorian Prose Stylism', in *The Art of Victorian Prose*, eds G. Levine and W. Madden. New York. pp. 3–38.
[Morley, John] The Editor. (1882). 'Valedictory', *Fornightly Review* 32(Oct.), 511–21.
[Morley, John] The Editor. (1867). 'Anonymous Journalism', *Fortnightly Review* 8 o.s.(Sept), 287–92.
Murray, C.D. (1983) 'The Fleshly School Revisited', *Bulletin of the John Rylands Library*. 176–207, 206–34.
[Oakeley, Frederick]. (1853). 'Cardinal Wiseman's *Essays* – Periodical Literature', *Dublin Review* 34(June), 541–66.
Orel, Harold. (1984). *Victorian Literary Critics*. London.
Rose, J. (1992). 'Rereading the English Common Reader: a Preface to a History of Audiences', *Journal of the History of Ideas* 53 (Jan.–Apr.), 47–70.
Rossetti, W.M. (1867). *Fine Art, Chiefly Contemporary*. Cambridge.
Saintsbury, G. (1896). *History of Nineteenth Century Literature*. London.
Shevelow, K. (1989). *Women and Print Culture*. London and New York.
Shorter, Clement. (1897). *Victorian Literature: Sixty Years of Books and Bookmen*. London.

Skelton, J. (1895). *The Table-Talk of Shirley.* 3rd edn. Edinburgh.

Skelton, J. (1894). 'Reminiscences of James Anthony Froude – I', *Blackwood's Magazine* 156(Dec.), 756–76.

[Skelton, J.]. (1866). 'Mr Swinburne and his Critics', *Fraser's Magazine* 74(Nov.), 635–48.

Small, Ian. (1991). *Conditions for Criticism. Authority, Knowledge and Literature in the Late Nineteenth Century.* Oxford.

Stebbing, Henry. (1878). 'The *Athenaeum* in 1828–30,' *Athenaeum* (19 Jan.), 88–9.

Stephen, Leslie. (1903a) 'Some Early Impressions: III Journalism', *Cornhill Magazine* 92(Nov.), 611–22.

Stephen, Leslie. (1903b). 'Editing', *Atlantic Monthly* 92(Dec.), 750–63.

[Stephen, Leslie]. (1878). 'Hours in a Library. No. XVIII: The First Edinburgh Reviewers', *Cornhill Magazine* 38(Aug.), 218–34.

[Stephen, Leslie]. (1877). 'Charlotte Brontë', *Cornhill Magazine* 36(Dec.), 723–39.

[Stephen, Leslie]. (1876). 'Thoughts on Criticism, by a Critic', *Cornhill Magazine* 34(Nov.), 556–69.

[Stephen, Leslie]. (1871). 'Hours in a Library. No. III: Some Words about Sir Walter Scott', *Cornhill Magazine* 24(Sept.), 278–93.

[Stephen, Leslie]. (1868). 'Defoe's Novels', *Cornhill Magazine* 17(March), 293–316.

[Sterling, J.]. Theodore Elbert. (1828). 'The English Periodical Press: [A Fragment from the Travels of Theodore Elbert, a Young Swede]', *The Athenaeum and Literary Chronicle*, 2:44 (27 Aug.), 695–6.

Strahan, A. (1877). 'Essays and Notices', *Contemporary Review* 29(Feb.), 516–34.

Swinburne, A.C. (1872). *Under the Microscope.* London.

Swinburne, A.C. (1875). 'Preface', *Essays and Studies.* London.

Trollope, A. (1865). 'On Anonymous Literature', *Fortnightly Review* 1(July), 491–8.

Uffelman, Larry K (1992). *The Nineteenth-Century Periodical Press in Britain. A Bibliography of Modern Studies. 1972–87.* VPR Supplement.

Wiener, J. (1978). 'Circulation and the Stamp Tax', *Victorian Periodicals: A Guide to Research*, eds J. Don Vann and Rosemary T. Van Arsdel. New York. pp. 149–73.

Woolford, John. (1982). 'Periodicals and the Practice of Literary Criticism, 1855–64', *Samplings and Soundings*, eds J. Shattock and M. Wolff. Leicester. pp. 109–42.

2

From Critic to Literary Critic: the Case of *The Academy*, 1869

In the last decade, after intensive policing, the boundaries of English literature, like those of Germany and the Soviet Union, have fallen, and exiled elements such as language, history, philosophy, gender and anthropology have moved in to transform the nature and definition of the subject.[1] Interdisciplinarity, intertextuality and plurality now occupy the place of what was formerly understood as a more unified subject. Moreover, the cumulative critique of modernism, by structuralism rooted in anthropology; by post-structuralism rooted in philosophy, rhetoric, and linguistics; and by postmodernism, has not only embraced catholicity and diversity, but has excluded judgement and, in the case of postmodernism, has yoked low and high culture in a discursive continuum. At a stroke, over the last two decades, critical space has been created for the study and inclusion of periodicals within the categories of 'literature' and 'Eng. Lit.'. To students of Victorian periodicals, the twentieth-century preoccupation with definitions of literature and non-literature by modernists such as René Wellek, Austin Warren and F.R. Leavis, and the related obsession with standards and hierarchies of individual works and authors, have called attention dramatically to the institutionalisation and specialisation that the field of literature has undergone since 1900. In its contrast with the prevailing nineteenth-century understanding of literature as a general category, which both Victorian periodical reviews and the catholic writing practice of Victorian critics show, the modernist view of literature seems constrained, and implacably hostile to the inclusion of journalism in the field. For this reason among others, the study of Victorian criticism (often tellingly margainalised by its nomenclature as 'non-fictional prose') in the modernist period has been relatively sparse.

Its insecure and uneasy position may be seen in the variety of ways in which modernist critics and scholars have discussed the nature of Victorian criticism and, implicitly, its transition and fragmentation from general into literary criticism, history, philosophy, sociology and science. Most prominent in 'Eng. Lit.' has been the close analysis of the language of criticism to discern a critical vocabulary and shifts of strategies; less successful has been discussion of the literary criticism of individual critics, because in all cases this involves the artificial isolation of the work which is deemed literary from the majority of the author's work which is deemed nonliterary. While mid-Victorian periodicals indicate the existence of specialist critics in other areas, such as music, visual art, and gender politics (James Davison, Francis Palgrave and Eliza Lyn Linton respectively), very few critics who habitually wrote on imaginative literature did so exclusively. While there was quite a lot of what was retrospectively termed literary criticism in the periodicals, not many defined their activity as particularly *literary* except in the nonspecialised sense of the word prevalent in the period. I propose to look at the burgeoning of specialism in the periodicals around 1870, before the onset of the specialist little magazines of the 1890s; I shall focus on the early years of *The Academy* which began as a monthly in October 1869, to see how literary criticism and particularly criticism of English literature fared in a more specialised setting.

The Academy's attempt to specialise in the field of the criticism of literature is manifest in the changing format and content of its General Literature section which is also eloquent on the subjects of English literature and the nature of literary criticism. But it is important to realise that *The Academy* did not differ *radically* from the mixed matter of other Victorian periodicals; it had other much more highly specialised sections, and it retained the wide spectrum of other periodicals of its day. I wish here to stress its breadth as well as its specialisation for a moment, and to relate this common characteristic of the bulk of Victorian periodicals – their catholicity, plurality, generality – to the usage by critics and editors of the words 'literary' and 'literature'. If in this period the words were very occasionally used to refer to imaginative literature exclusively, they predominantly referred to the *entire* range of verbal discourse to be found in the periodicals. *The Academy*'s category of General Literature articulates this tension between the criticism of literature and of reading matter more generally.

Matthew Arnold uses 'literary' in this wider sense in 'The Literary Influence of Academies' in 1864, where his illustrations include Edmund Burke, Jeremy Edwards and Francis Palgrave, and the usage persists, if not dominantly, in the *Times Literary Supplement*. Even when Arnold uses the phrases 'literary criticism' and 'current English literature' at the end of 'The Function of Criticism', he is distinguishing literary criticism from criticism of religion and politics which are linked by Arnold because of their participation in another discourse, that of controversy; he is not however confining 'contemporary literature' to fiction, poetry and drama, but implicitly opening it out, as part of his claim for and interest in non-fictional prose, to include history and philosophy. Certainly, throughout 'The Function of Criticism' the word 'criticism' is used in relation to a great range of subject matter, and 'poetry' refers rather, to literature in the narrower sense. How entirely this latter sense of the word literature has come to dominate our usage is repeatedly evident in the resistance by students to reading Victorian criticism and the periodicals because they are not 'literature'. Arnold's insistent generality, of range and audience, caused him to cease writing for *The Academy* within a year because of the narrowness of its readership. While his generality of view indicates the nature of *most* Victorian periodicals including those in which the great bulk of Arnold's work first appeared, it is the enemy of the move toward specialisation and the kind of specialisation that *The Academy* was attempting.

In an *Academy* review of 'St. Paul and Protestantism' in 1870 H. Lawrenny comments drily that Arnold's essay contains 'enough eloquence to make it a favourable example of the literary chaos in which we shall be plunged when everybody has all his faculties cultivated at once' (Lawrenny: 283). Moreover, he dislikes Arnold's imprecision and multiple postures of perfection and disinterestedness:

> It would be unprofitable to follow Mr. Arnold through his analysis of St. Paul's doctrinal system. Science is wronged, art is wronged, and religious faith would be wronged, if it had any concern in the matter, when serious questions are arbitrarily dismissed, or discussed by canons taken at haphazard as the argument proceeds. It is enough to say that Mr. Arnold's softened explanation of the doctrines, "calling," "justification," "sanctification," as a not too literally understood "dying with Christ," "resurrection from the dead," and "growing into Christ,"

contains nothing which has not been said, in one contest or another by orthodox Puritan divines, and little which has not been anticipated by the rationalizers of Christian dogma.... Every man has his theological proclivities, and Mr. Arnold writes a paper on St. Paul to air his own, because the perfect man can write a clear and creditable paper about anything: but the perfection of the man and of the theologian are two, and not the least curious point about the present volume is the gradual triumph of the latter. The perfect man is too tolerant to condemn those who merely disagree from him, but the moral precepts he lays down as to *how* discordant views shall be held, are inevitably deduced from his own tenets, and if he allows himself to enforce them with some acrimony, because morality is common ground, he departs not the less surely from the sweet reasonableness of the artist, who sees "beauty" in sharp outlines; the humane culture of the poet, whose imagination knows neither true nor false while feeling the "charm" of contrast and conflict amongst excellencies, and the miscellaneous perfection of the critic who has no time to believe anything himself till he has done justice to the innumerable arguments for and against any possible thesis. (Lawrenny: 283)

The dialogue between Arnold's views and Mark Pattison's donnish emphasis on scholarship and specialisation which the *Academy* and its editor, Charles Appleton, represent is significant. It indicates that the nature of Victorian criticism of literature is fundamentally bound up with the nature of Victorian periodicals of which it is part; and also with the functions and character of English studies and the lower and higher education of the time. My argument concerning method is one that restores Victorian criticism to its form of production; it resists both the surgical extraction of criticism from the structure of which it is a part, and its subsequent isolation or relocation so that its function, readership and occasion – its part in the continuing dialogue which Victorian periodicals enact – are obscured if not obliterated.

Modernist critics were not the sole perpetrators of this practice. Victorian authors often heavily revised and regrouped their contributions to periodicals by theme and genre for book publication, and Collected Essays served to create specialisations that the general periodicals did not offer. Arnold's *Essays in Criticism* (1865) were selected from two types of serial activity, his Oxford lectures and his periodical work, and 'The Function of Criticism' was conceived as functioning in all three spheres: as the Introduction to the book, a culmination of his preceding lectures, and the follow-up article to 'The Literary Influence of Academies'. In one respect the periodicals themselves covered their tracks. The annual issue of bound volumes of each periodical without the advertisements (which were not normally paginated in the sequence of editorial copy) encouraged readers then and now to disregard the ephemeral and commercial dimension of periodical publication and purveyed the illusion of timelessness and immateriality; the appearance of bound volumes fostered their association with *books* and with the status of 'literature', and denied their journalistic origins. They invite us to regard them more as sun-bleached marble temples than brightly painted structures frequented by the original worshippers.

Right through the nineteenth century, alongside the weeklies, monthlies and quarterlies which contained review articles on imaginative literature along with a marked and predominent interest in some combination of news, politics and religion, existed a narrower kind of periodical which remained resolutely bookish though not confined to imaginative literature. I am thinking here of periodicals such as the *Literary Gazette* (1817–62), the *Reader* (1863–6), and *The Academy* to which Mark Pattison and William Michael Rossetti moved from the *Reader*.

The title of *The Academy* points in two directions, to the French Academy and to the universities; that both of them are pertinent to criticism and the criticism of English literature in the periodicals can be seen in an anonymous article, 'Concerning the Organization of Literature', which appeared in March 1864 in *Macmillan's Magazine*. Its anonymity in a periodical which made a point of signature is immediately noteworthy, as the editor of the periodical at the time, David Masson, was Professor of English Language and Literature at University College London, and the number included signed pieces by Arnold; that is, the anonymity of the piece may stem from its involvement with a sensitive area of current debate involving highly placed public institutions, and with individuals, one of whom may have been the author of the article or the castigator of the author here protected by anonymity. As Francis Espinasse, a maverick critic who in 1851–2 had published a revelatory series in *The Critic* under the pseudonym Herodotus Smith (i.e. learned but ordinary?), in which he unceremoniously removed the veils of anonymity of (other) contributors and editors of the larger nine-

teenth-century newspapers and periodicals, has latterly been identified as the author, we may conclude that here anonymity did the
protective job of the pseudonym in *The Critic.* We should note that
Espinasse judged that he must have recourse to protection for this
subject, which on the face of it seems quite safe, just as he did for
more unorthodox public revelations.

The occasion of Espinasse's piece is the recent proposal by Lord
Stanhope that the British organise an equivalent of the French
Academy and in his essay Espinasse provides an interesting sketch
of the state of literature and writers in England. In two places he
suggests that the desirable creation of an academy is linked with
the inadequacy of periodical criticism:

> The deficiencies, oversights, and caprices of newspaper and
> periodical criticism are to some extent compensated for and cor-
> rected by the elaborate examination to which the Academy sub-
> jects the literature of the day.... The literary and socio-economical
> criticism of the periodical and newspaper press does much; but,
> from the very nature of the case, it must be hurried, or perfunc-
> tory, or limited. It would be something to have, in one Academy
> in England, as France has in these two Academies, the men of the
> highest proved and realized intellect collected, and formed into a
> conspicuous, honourable, and honoured body. ([Espinasse]: 430,
> 432)

Here is concern with the standards of criticism rather than Walter
Bagehot's slightly guilty acceptance of the limitations of the periodical essay or Leslie Stephen's suspect self-congratulation which
emerge when both write about the first Edinburgh reviewers.

Not long after Espinasse's piece, and prompted by it and Stanhope
but also by Renan's defence of the French Academy,[2] in June 1864
Arnold delivered in Oxford 'The Literary Influence of Academies'
which then appeared in August in the *Cornhill,* that urbane and well-
paying periodical. Arnold, whose writing is both more combative
and not so much in the practical sphere as Espinasse's, also however
makes the link implicitly between our inferior prose ('How much
greater is our nation in poetry than in prose!' [Arnold: 159]) and the
Academy which, in its role of 'intellectual tribunal' will correct
English eccentricities. Explicitly he fulminates against the 'brutalité'
(which he translates as provincialism!) of English newspapers
and identifies the marred styles of English prose criticism. The

immediately subsequent essay, 'The Function of Criticism', can be seen as a continuation of the theme.

The assumption of the title *The Academy* for the new monthly in 1869, with Arnold writing the opening article and presumably participating in the 'intellectual tribunal' has its ironies; it is not entirely surprising to see that just beside Arnold's review of De Senancour's *Obermann* is an italicised notice which reads in part 'Readers are reminded that the mention of New Publications, Articles, etc., in our lists is intended as a guarantee of their importance' (Anon. 1869: 1).

But the title of the periodical also points to the origins of the editor and contributors. Although the articles are signed, the name of the editor, a young Fellow at St John's, does not appear on the title-page, and like the *Saturday Review*, most contributors were similarly male university teachers or graduates. The first number of *The Academy* shows it to be highly organised and specialised. It is divided into six sections, each of which contains signed reviews followed by a variety of smaller items: letters (if any), 'Intelligence' which contains publishing titbits, 'Contents of the Journals' which is confined to those from the continent, and titles of selected articles and new publications. The sections consist of General Literature and Art; Biblical Criticism etc.; Science and Philosophy; History, Geography etc.; Oriental Philology; and Classical Literature etc.

The first section of literature and art consists of nine and a quarter pages of the 32-page number, a high proportion not to be maintained in subsequent numbers. Out of six reviews only one, on Clough, involves British art or literature, manifesting a marked orientation to continental literature by the academic editors and readers, similar to the subsequent list of journals. The link of literature with art is one which recurs in the Espinasse article, which begins by discussing the Guild of Literature and Art, and ends by suggesting that the Board of Trustees of the British Museum be a germinal English Academy. The reiterated link between forms of art which normally appear distinct to twentieth-century critics calls attention to the notable traffic between literature and visual art in the period: the dual practitioners such as William Morris and D. G. Rossetti, the narrative dimension of visual art, and pictorial elements of literature.

'Selected Articles' is a list of six, three from the *Westminster Review, Cornhill, and Fortnightly Review* which show the dialogue among the periodicals in the period, as there is one on Clough to compare with their review of Clough, and one on the work of Arnold, who is a leading contributor; the other three titles, from a German periodical, show the same interest in the continent as the reviews and list of journal contents. Moreover, 'New Publications' includes no English literature except the Tauchnitz edition of collected Shakespeare, and a glossary of words and phrases found in Furness, Lancashire. This profile – the link of literature with art, the lack of attention to English culture, the stress on continental literature, and, when work of English origins is treated, the choice of linguistic or indisputably great subjects – indicates the shaky status of English culture and literature among critics and dons. Few if any of them had formally studied the subject in a sustained way and many were undecided about the place of English literature in education, as the debate in the periodicals and universities from the 1860s shows.

The other sections of the first number of *The Academy* are much shorter, but an indication of the degree of specialisation running through them all is given by the 'Science and Philosophy' section (the second longest, with five and a half pages) which, after a review by T.H. Huxley, contains two and a quarter pages of technical and sustained summaries of scientific papers and lectures (See Figure 2.1). This section burgeoned in later numbers, and before the reorganisation of the periodical after the first year, when it became fortnightly, it seemed to get out of hand. Two other periodicals were beginning to specialise at this time: *Nature* appeared for the first time a month after *The Academy*, and H.R. Fox Bourne notes that *The Athenaeum*, under a new proprietor and with new contributors after C.W. Dilke's death in 1869, began to rely on increasing specialisation among its reviewers:

> While special departments, such as science, art, music and the drama, were of necessity entrusted to regular hands, indeed, the reviewing of books, now more than ever the principal business of "The Athenaeum", was distributed over a very large staff, the plan being to assign each work to a writer familiar with its subject and competent to deal with it intelligently. (Bourne: II 317)

In subsequent issues in the first year of *The Academy*, the 'General Literature and Art' section continues to publish a preponderance of reviews by distinguished reviewers of non-British work on a breadth of subjects. Included in this category are reviews of books on broadly literary subjects such as *Slavonial Language and Literature in all Dialects,* and Welsh bibliography, as well as pieces on a biography of Alexander Smith, the Spasmodic poet, and on Tennyson's *The* or in common language, "matter." Some observers deny that this migration really occurs, contending that the passage of the white corpuscles through the vascular walls is an optical illusion, and that pus cells are formed *outside* the blood-vessels. Dr. Caton states that, having undertaken many observations on winter frogs, he was unable to satisfy himself of the occurrence of the migration of the white corpuscles; but at length, on examining strong and healthy frogs in spring, he clearly saw the passage of white corpuscles, as described by Cohnheim. Experiments made upon the transparent parts of fishes led to a negative result; but in tadpoles the process could be seen with great ease; indeed he states that he here observed the apparent migration of red as well as white cells, even when there was no local inflammation.

Relation of Tactile Sensibility to the Mobility of Parts. — MM. Kottenkamp and Ullrich have undertaken some investigations to determine the sensitiveness of different parts of the skin (*Zeitschrift für Biologie*, Band vi. p. 37). They fastened pins, at different distances, into pieces of wood, and then applied them to the skin, as a measure of the acuteness of touch, and no answer was deemed correct unless not only two pins were distinctly felt, but the direction of the line uniting these, in regard to the axis of the limb, whether longitudinal or transverse, could be accurately stated. Taking the upper arm, fore-arm, hand, and finger respectively, the acuteness of sensibility could be expressed by the numbers 1 : 3·5 : 29 : 160; and they lay down this proposition, that the delicacy of the sense of touch in a given region of the skin is represented by the sum of two factors, of which one indicates the mobility of the articular axis, whilst the second is proportional to the distance of the part from that axis.

Botany.

Structure and Affinities of the Passifloreæ. — Dr. M. T. Masters read an important paper on this subject before the Linnean Society at their meeting on Nov. 17th. Jussieu and St. Hilaire held that there is no true corolla in the passion-flower, but two calycine whorls, because both organs drop at the same time. But the mode of development and the internal structure clearly demonstrate that the inner whorl is a true corolla. The flower-tube is, according to Bentham, composed of a union of the calyx and corolla; Dr. Masters, on the other hand, believes it to be an expansion of the axis. Its development is comparatively late. The form of the corona was traced from its simplest form in *Turnera* to its most complicated arrangement in some *Modecca* and *Passifloras*; in all cases it is a mere projection from the flower-tube, and is of late development, and morphologically of little importance, though essential to the individual life of the plant. The inner portion of the tube is a glandular secreting substance. The anthers are invariably two-celled. The pistil is singularly uniform, one-celled, made up of three united carpels, with three parietal placentæ, and three stigmas. The arrangement of the reproductive organs favours cross-fertilisation. The anthers, originally introrse, become, when fully developed, distinctly extrorse, and it is thus rendered difficult for the pollen to fall on the stigma of the same flower: it falls on to the rays of the corona, on which insects alight in search of the honey concealed at the base of the tube, and carry the pollen away to other flowers. Some species are more easily fertilised by pollen belonging to a different species than by their own: hence hybrids abound. Dr. Masters connects the *Passifloreæ* rather with the *Turneraceæ*, *Samydaceæ*, *Violaceæ*, and *Sauvagesieæ* than with the *Cucurbitaceæ*, with which they have usually been associated; his main argument being the truly hypogynous character of the stamens. In geographical distribution the order is essentially tropical, occurring between 30° N. and 30° S. latitude. The true passion-flowers are almost exclusively American, and chiefly Brazilian. The *Passiflora incarnata*, or original passion-flower of the Jesuits, is one of the few North American species, and has probably been introduced there, being closely allied to *P. edulis* of Brazil. Types of the order more or less divergent from *Passiflora* occur in Peru, India, the Indian Archipelago, with a solitary outlier at Hongkong, Australia, the Pacific Islands, New Zealand, and Africa.

Chemistry.

Synthesis of Indigo. — The synthesis of indigo has at last been achieved by MM. Emmerling and Engler. Their results have been communicated by Prof. Baeyer to the Berlin Chemical Society, and are published in the latest number of their *Berichte*. Acetophenon (the methyl keton of benzoic acid) was converted by means of hydric nitrate into mononitroacetophenon. This azotised body was *reduced and dehydrated simultaneously*, which was done by heating the mononitroacetophenon with a mixture of powdered zinc and dry calcic hydrate (quicklime). The indigo sublimed over, and was recognised as such by its characteristic iodine-like vapours, and also by its yielding with strong sulphuric hydrate the "Indigo-Küpe." The authors could not obtain enough of the substance for the purposes of analysis, but they are continuing their experiments with the view of obtaining this artificial indigo in estimable quantities.

The Aerolitic Shower at Hessle. — This meteoric fall, the first recorded to have taken place in Sweden, occurred at 12.20 p.m. on 1st January, 1869, in the neighbourhood of Hessle, three Swedish miles from Upsala. Prof. Nordenskjöld, who announced the shower last year, has now issued (*Poggendorff's Annalen*, No. 10, 1870) a detailed account of the physical and chemical characters of the stones, and the phenomena attending their descent. They were strewn over a line of country lying 30° E. of S. towards 30° W. of N. Some fell within a few yards of peasants leaving church, another fell close to a fisherman on the Mälar bay Lårsta-Viken, dug a hole 3 to 4 inches deep in the ice, and rebounded; when picked up, it was still warm. The noise accompanying the fall, which was heard in Stockholm, is described as resembling some very heavy thunderclaps, followed by a rattle like the passing of waggons at a gallop, and ending with first a noise like an organ tone and then a hissing sound, the whole lasting some minutes. The sky was cloudy, and though apparently unseen at Hessle itself, a luminous meteor was noticed by observers at a distance. The stones vary greatly in size, some weighing nearly 2 lbs., the smallest (and the little ones were numerous) only 0·07 gramme. Though of sufficiently loose structure to break in pieces when thrown with the hand against the floor or frozen ground, it is remarkable that nearly all the specimens are intact, and that some of the stones weighing 2 lbs. which struck the ice of the Lårsta-Viken, failed to penetrate it, though its thickness on that day did not exceed a few inches. These facts support the statements of eye-witnesses as to their remarkably small downward velocity. These meteorites present no unusual aspect, and resemble in particular those of Assarun and Clarac, Haute-Garonne, which fell on the 9th December, 1858. Their exterior is black; within they are bright grey, and sufficiently porous to cling to the tongue, whence it is concluded that their mass has not undergone fusion, as would be required by the theory of Laplace. Chemical analysis proved them to be composed of about 20 per cent. of nickeliferous iron (chamoisite, Fe_3Ni); some schreibersite, and rather less than 1 per cent. of what was probably chromite; a variable amount of iron monosulphide (troilite); a trace of carbon, probably in the form of a hydrocarbon; traces of salts soluble in water; about 10 per cent. of labradorite or anorthite; 37 per cent. of olivine; and 23 per cent. of shepardite. These silicates, it should be remarked, were not isolated for examination, but are assumed to be present from calculations based on the results of an analysis of the mass. The researches of Prof. Maskelyne and Dr. Laurence Smith have shown the existence of shepardite as a mineral species to be highly improbable.

The most interesting feature of the Hessle fall is the association with the stones described above of others mainly composed of carbon. The peasants noticed that some of those which fell on the ice near Arnö soon crumbled to a blackish brown powder, which formed with the snow water a mixture resembling coffee-grounds. A similar powder was found on the ice at Hafsåviken in masses as large as the hand, which floated like foam on water, and could not be held between the fingers. A small amount secured for examination was seen under the microscope to be built up of small spherical granules. It contained particles extractible by the magnet, and, when ignited, left a reddish brown ash. Heated in a closed tube, it gave a small amount of a brown liquid distillate. A quantity dried at 110° had the following composition : —

		Equivalent Ratios.
Carbon	51·6	8·600
Hydrogen	3·8	3·800
Oxygen (calculated)	15·7	1·962
Silicic acid	16·7	0·371
Iron protoxide	8·4	0·233
Magnesia	1·5	0·075
Lime	0·8	0·029
Soda and trace of lithia	1·5	0·048
	100·0	

The combustible constituent of this body appears therefore to have the formula —

$$n. \ C_2H_1O_1.$$

It was noticed, moreover, that the stones found in the same district with this carbonaceous substance were, as a rule, quite round, and covered on all sides with a black, dull, and often almost sponge-like crust. The iron particles on the surface of the smaller stones were usually quite bright and unoxidised, as though the stone had been heated in a reducing atmosphere. The author believes that this carbon compound frequently, perhaps always, occurs in association with the meteorites, and attributes its preservation in this case to the fall of the stones on snow-covered ground.

Isotrimorphism of Stannic and Titanic Oxides. — Stannic oxide, resulting from the action of steam on stannic chloride at a red heat, has been shown by Daubrée to take a crystalline form, not identical with

Figure 2.1 *The Academy.* Detail of 'Scientific Notes'.

Holy Grail. However, reviews of *Tales of Hindu Devilry* and two books on India, one by a District Officer of the north-west provinces, show that subjects such as anthropology, geography, history, mythology and politics also fall within the category at the time. Clearly 'General Literature' is very general, English literature as a national literature would appear to be less established than French or German literatures, the novel is neglected and poetry is favoured, and the bibliographical and philological traditions established within the study of the subject are apparent.

In October 1870, in a piece entitled 'Our First Year', a change of format and emphasis is announced by the editor:

> During the past year we have made it our first duty to establish our competence to treat of those weightier matters which had hitherto been most neglected by English critics. But the purely scientific portion of the ACADEMY being now completely organized, we shall concentrate our attention during the ensuing year on the best means of meeting the wishes of those, who desire a more authoritative organ of criticism than has hitherto existed upon the Fine Arts, and a variety of other subjects of more general interest. Hitherto this department has occupied but one-third of the whole Journal. So soon, however, as the present exceptional depression of the book-trade both at home and abroad shall have ceased – if possible at the beginning of the new year – we intend to publish a number of the ACADEMY every fortnight, and without diminution of our scientific departments, to devote one-half of each number to General Literature. Amongst the new subjects which we hope to introduce, will be Old English Literature; Geography and Travel; Biography, Letters, &c.; Music, Painting, Architecture and Sculpture; Law and Political Economy; as well as some branches of Natural Science which from want of space have been hitherto neglected.
>
> The extension of our space will also enable us to attend to another suggestion, by providing even in our more difficult articles such explanations, that the unlearned reader may derive some instruction from at least a portion of them. ([Appleton]: 1)

Although Old English literature is singled out here, in practice a notable change is the occasional reviewing of major contemporary novelists. 'Our First Year' is followed immediately by a review of *Edwin Drood,* and the following issue, for November, before any changes take place, reviews only literature in the first section. Included is George Waring's fairly detailed piece, occasioned by a series of *Essays on Chaucer* in German and treating the subject of the basis for the canon; this in turn stimulates a scholarly exchange between F. J. Furnivall and Waring, attesting to the contemporary vigour of philological and medieval studies in the field of English and the presence of, for example, a Chair of Anglo-Saxon at Oxford since 1795. The tone of the exchange, with only a slight edge, is notably more temperate and less Corinthian or adjectival than most Victorian critical debate. With some exceptions, this moderation and seriousness of tone approaches Arnold's precepts of Hellenic disinterestedness (if not his practice) which appear so evident in the stated aims of *The Academy*, particularly in the emphasis on the cosmopolitan, the opposite of the provincialism with which Arnold inexorably charged the British.

> The ACADEMY was set on foot in answer to a widely felt and constantly expressed dissatisfaction with the existing organs of literary and scientific criticism. A critical journal was demanded which should neither praise indiscriminately nor blame from pique or prejudice; one on which the general reader might rely for guidance through the waste of superficial and ephemeral literature by which he is surrounded and through which he has neither the time nor perhaps the ability to guide himself; a journal which should systematically survey the European literary and scientific movement as a whole, and pass judgment upon books not from an insular, still less from a partisan, but from a cosmopolitan point of view; a journal, lastly, in which only permanent works of taste and real additions to knowledge should be taken into account, and in which the honesty and competence of the reviewer should be vouched for by his signature. ([Appleton]: 1)

Their claim to a strict and explicit disinterestedness also figures in their perception of the separation from their original publisher, John Murray:

> In accordance with our original plan, we have reviewed the most important theological literature of the year, Catholic, Anglican, Protestant, even Jewish and Mohammedan, in a spirit of complete neutrality. We have offered no opinion as to the truth or falsehood of religious belief, or of any form of it; not because we

are indifferent to these questions, but because we considered from the first that we should be performing a more useful part, by quitting the arena of religious polemics, and treating theology purely as a branch of learned literature. That we have not altogether failed in our effort to combine complete freedom of statement with tenderness toward the feelings of every class of believers, may be gathered from the approval with which the ACADEMY has been received by the whole religious press of this country, ranging from the ultramontane *Tablet* on the one hand, through every phase of Anglican or Protestant opinion, to the *Jewish Chronicle* on the other.

Before leaving this point, it may be well to touch lightly on a delicate subject, on which, had it not been open to misconstruction, we should have preferred to be silent. It is this. We have felt it to be our duty to the public to transfer the publication of the ACADEMY to a new firm. This change, while carrying with it the obvious advantage of greater facilities of communication with the Continental world of letters, has really grown out of our theological position. Mr. Murray, to whom the ACADEMY will always be indebted for its introduction to a wide circle of readers, did not call in question the fact of our theological impartiality, but disapproved of it. The Editor, on the other hand, felt that the adoption of the theological principles of the *Quarterly Review,* or of the organ of any given class of the English public, would have involved the surrender of one of the fundamental characteristics of the ACADEMY, one, too, which we had pledged ourselves to maintain. Under these circumstances, Mr. Murray has come forward in the most honourable manner, and offered to resign all his interest in the copyright of the Journal. Holding the principle at issue to be an important one, we have accepted his offer: and we now bid him, not ungratefully, a courteous farewell! ([Appleton]:1)[3]

It would appear that the issue was 'delicate' in at least two ways: it was sensitive commercially as the transfer of ownership of one business to another necessarily involves a number of nice and legal points, copyright being only one; and insofar as the commercial arrangements of the press were one of the many aspects of its existence which were normally carefully excluded from public gaze, attention to them with *reasons* as well was unusual. But the other important sense of 'delicate' lies in the application of disinterestedness to theology, which with politics represents an extremely testing case, and the association of such 'disinterestedness', politically a Broad Church position at best, with a particular faction within the universities. Their very evenhandedness, notwithstanding the editor's explanation, was, as Murray registered, a theological position.

After January 1871 'General Literature' is separated from art and contains longer reviews, but the notion of an 'intellectual tribunal' seems to have faltered, in that 'Selected Articles' are only intermittently covered; all these smaller topics are absorbed into a shorter section called 'Literary Notes', although new publications and selected articles are still listed in some of the other sections. 'General Literature' goes on to contain a higher proportion of English literature than formerly but eschews popular novels; praises *Middlemarch* articulately, but favours poetry of which there is more notice (of the work of Morris, Swinburne, and Tennyson) than fiction. It also still manifests a catch-all function: Alfred Wallace reviews 'a new history' of the mutineers of the *Bounty* in February 1871. New categories such as Archaeology and Music appear, and Classical Literature disappears; Oriental Philology expands to Philology. By 1880 the 'General Literature' section is quite different; it is called 'Literature' but it is more general, including novels as a sub-category along with school books, recent economic literature, and current theology.

What can be plainly seen in *The Academy* in this first decade is the *strain* of the general nature and audience of Victorian periodicals, and an impossible if laudable attempt to bolster up the degree of expertise on all fronts within the format of a general publication. *The Academy* shows a distinct shift within its 'General Literature' section from a focus on French and German literature to more prominence for and appreciation of English literature; but the selection of English literature reviewed and the uncertain conception of the 'General Literature' or even 'Literature' indicates the dilemma of the 'literary critic', the reasons for the preponderance of the 'general critic' and the transitionary state of the study of English literature, a matter contemporaneously under discussion.

Debate of the subject in periodicals was considerable and stretches from Edward Freeman's 'The Study of English' in the *Saturday Review* in 1860 through the acrid exchanges between John Churton Collins and Oxbridge in the 1880s. In 1886 the *Pall Mall Gazette* and the *Quarterly Review* published replies to a questionnaire on English circulated to men of letters, and John Morley and

Leslie Stephen both produced articles about it. Although two Chairs of English Literature were established at the inauguration of University College and King's College in London in 1828 and 1835, and London professors such as Henry Morley and David Masson published work on the fledgling academic subject, the status of English literature at the time was low. When A. J. Scott was appointed to the post of Principal at Owen's College in Manchester, he was also made Professor of English Language and Literature, of Grammar, of Logic, and of Mental and Moral Philosophy. Oxford University did not establish an English school until 1894 and the *Review of English Studies* appeared in 1927. At Oxford, English was made one of four parts of the Pass Degree in 1873; in 1877 the Regius Professor of History objected to the proposed Professor of English Literature being attached to the school of Modern History; he told the commissioners 'I think that to have the History school hampered with dilettante teaching, such as the teaching of English literature, must necessarily do great harm to the School' (Palmer: 71). A.S. Napier, a philologist, was appointed to the Chair of English which was the only outcome of the bid in 1877 to establish the teaching of English in the University, and at Oxford Anglo-Saxon and philology continued to dominate until 1894.

This movement from criticism of books in general to criticism of literature, discernible in reviews in the *Academy* and from general critic to literary critic, is party to a variety of cultural transformations at the time: the specialisation of knowledge, the growth of professionalism, state education, literacy, and the periodical press, all of which have attracted academic attention [4] and all of which the *Academy* project inscribes.

Notes

1. See, for example, Anita Levy, *Other Women: The Writing of Class, Race, and Gender, 1832–1898*, Princeton, 1991.
2. Renan's essay is a review of *Histoire de l'Académie française* by Pellison and d'Olivet, published in Paris in 1858.
3. A similar tension arose in 1877 between the *Contemporary Review* and its offspring, the *Nineteenth Century*. See Chapter 3 'Theories of Formation: the *Nineteenth Century*', pp. 51–62. The theological diversity of *The Academy* confirms its male discourse and readership.
4. Of particular relevance here are Roll-Hansen, Baldick, Klancher, and Heyck.

Works Cited

Anon. (1869). 'Notice', *Academy* 1(9 Oct.), 1.
[Appleton, C.]. (1870). Editor, 'Our First Year', *Academy* 2(22 Oct.), 1.
Arnold, M. (1864). 'The Literary Influence of Academies', *Cornhill Magazine* 10(Aug.), 154–72.
Bagehot, Walter. (1855). 'The First Edinburgh Reviewers', *National Review* 1(Oct.), 253–84.
Baldick, Chris. (1983). *The Social Mission of English Criticism*. London.
Bourne, H.R. Fox. (1887). *English Newspapers*. 2 vols. London.
[Espinasse, Francis]. (1864). 'Concerning the Organization of Literature', *Macmillan's Magazine* 9(March), 426–36.
Heyck, T.W. (1982). *The Transformation of Intellectual Life in Victorian England*. London.
Klancher, J. (1987). *The Making of English Reading Audiences, 1790–1832*. Madison.
Lawrenny, H. (1870). [Review of] '*St. Paul and Protestantism*', *The Academy* 1(13 Aug.), 282–3.
Morley, John. (1897). 'On the Study of Literature', London, 1887 [13pp.], and in *Studies in Literature*. London. pp. 189–228.
Palmer, D.J. (1965). *The Rise of English Studies*. Oxford.
Renan, Ernest. (1903). 'L'Académie française', *Essais de morale et de critique* (1859). Paris. pp. 333–51.
Roll-Hansen, Diderik. (1957). '*The Academy*: 1869–79. Victorian Intellectuals in Revolt', *Anglistica*, 8.
Stephen, Leslie. (1887). 'The Study of English Literature', *Cornhill Magazine*, 8 n.s.(May), 486–508.
Stephen, Leslie. (1878). 'Hours in a Library. No. XVIII. – The First Edinburgh Reviewers', *Cornhill Magazine* 38(Aug.), 218–34.

3

Theories of Formation:
The *Nineteenth Century*, 1877

Despite the implication in the prospectus of the *Nineteenth Century* which appeared in *Athenaeum* on 10 February 1877, the transfer of editor, distributor and writers from the *Contemporary Review* to the *Nineteenth Century* was not legitimised, gradual or peaceful, but cataclysmic and concentrated, an eruption of the press in which the constituent elements were momentarily hyper-visible and palpable. The 'story' in the contemporary press, in pamphlets by the principals, and in twentieth-century criticism by A.W. Brown, Patricia Srebrnik and Priscilla Metcalf has all the characteristics of a 'good' news story – intrigue, complexity and suspense, and longevity as far as news goes. To view the formation of the *Nineteenth Century* and our constructions of it as phenomena of cultural production, I want to look at some aspects of this transfer of cultural power which relate to our own methods for the study of modern printed texts – the issues of literary authority and the interaction of gender and contents.

The resulting serial text – the *Nineteenth Century* – first appeared in March 1877, a monthly costing two shillings and sixpence. It proved among the most radical of its period, insofar as it printed side by side philosophically and theologically divergent writing, deist and atheist, by bishops and scientists. Its heterogeneity makes it comparable to the *Fortnightly Review*. Although the rhetoric of this editorial stance is familiar to readers and viewers today in the form of the argument for 'balance', the editorial organisation of most Victorian periodicals depended on apparent homogeneity, and some form of sectarian readership to which it appealed and which assured sales. Even the *Fortnightly* was at times geared to Comtism and the Philosophical Radicals. Atypically, as A.W. Brown notes (Brown: 186), the *Nineteenth Century* formally sought to deny itself an editorial position other than an open space for the best work from divergent positions on questions of philosophy, theology and science. (This is not to say it it assumed no other positions, but that they were unacknowledged.[1]) This open-space policy of the *Nine-teenth Century* can be said to exploit the revelations of signature: of name and employment; and although the policy of heterogeneity could have been visible without signature, signature underlined the diversity for the reader, and proved an important means of adver-tising and promoting the magazine, on the one hand through care-ful selection of renowned authors, and on the other the *making* of stars through formats[2], or the choice of controversial topics which catapulted their relatively unknown author to fame.[3] Nor was there a correspondence column in the *Nineteenth Century*; the debate in the main[4] was closed to outsiders.

It is interesting in this connection that the author of a piece in the first number of the *Nineteenth Century*, haunted by the contem-porary dissension in the Church of England and calling for a 'really high-class Church paper' to be created, offers the following foot-note on Correspondence sections:

> The practice of continuing the "silly season" in the form of cor-respondence, throughout the year is now becoming positively prejudicial. Party spirit is more fanned and fed by these irrespons-ible communications than by any other form of published utter-ances. That the communications are frequently very foolish does not prevent their being read and even approved of.... It would be well if the good example of the *English Churchman* were more generally followed, and the best current articles on Church matters from leading papers substituted for this undesirable correspond-ence (Ellicott: 61).

The controversy over the *Contemporary Review*, and the emergence of the *Nineteenth Century* and its uneasy sibling, the reconstituted *Contemporary Review*, involved an interplay of economies – financial, theological, philosophical and journalistic – on which I want to comment briefly. Financially, Strahan, who was the publisher and principal owner of the *Contemporary*, had a troubled history of poor financial management which resulted in his loss of two-thirds of the shares of the journals and the management of the business arrange-ments for them (Srebrnik: 154), while Knowles – previously Strahan's employee – took on, and very successfully, the sole ownership and editorship of his new creation, the *Nineteenth Century*, which sold 20 000 copies of the first number. Theologically, the break between Strahan and his editor and authors represented the incompatibility between Evangelicals – committed to conversion and intolerant of aspects of what the opposition wished to say – and all the rest. Although very diverse[5], 'the rest' shared a common and articulated defence of diversity because the *Contemporary Review* editor and contributors had their own cultural formation, the Metaphysical Society, to match Evangelical networks.

Not only did this rupture between management/owner and journalist employees entail theological positions, but also the culture of an intellectual élite, largely university educated, who regarded themselves broadly as philosophers, ranged against that of industrial capitalists typically educated outside the universities. Not least, one of the principal reasons for the spectacular success of the *Nineteenth Century* in its initial struggle with the *Contemporary* in 1877 lay in the economy of journalism. The 'philosophers' included among their number (in the Metaphysical Society) ten editors of contemporary magazines, while the remainder of Strahan's periodicals were in the theological sphere and unable to muster influential support outside it. Management was effectively stripped of its support by an editor and authors who whipped the periodical out of its management stable, renamed it, and located it elsewhere. They even retained the *Contemporary Review*'s distributor who for several months distributed the two periodicals together.

I want to look now at some of the more particular cultural formations within these economies. The Metaphysical Society antedated Knowles's tenure at the *Contemporary Review*[6] and the Society wound up in 1880, decades before either of the two journals. And if the influence of the Metaphysical Society was greater over the *Contemporary Review* between 1870 and 1877 when it was edited by Knowles, than it was over the *Nineteenth Century* which was created when the Society was beginning to falter, the format of the *Nineteenth Century* approximates that of the Society, whose diverse members (numbering forty as in the French Academy) read papers to the group who then undertook formal discussion. This format Knowles developed further in the *Nineteenth Century*, into the Symposium for example, in which various contributors addressed themselves to a common topic and to each other's stated positions about it. Moreover, the Society provided a steady source of suitable articles for the journal, and a stock of authors to draw on for specific projects. Eight out of the eleven pieces in the first number were by members of the Society. Additionally, the ten member editors and others allied to journalism proved a formidable network for the initial organisation and launching of the new *Nineteenth Century* project. They included the editors of the *Spectator*, the *Economist*, the *Fortnightly*, and the *Dublin Review*, and others who lent their names to the list of supporters in the prospectus (such as Tennyson and the Dean of St Paul's), or agreed to write for the early numbers (such as Gladstone). Although the Society had a small and exclusive membership, it included a broad spectrum of religious and other groups – High Church, Catholics, Broad Church, Evangelical Anglicans and Non-Conformists, as well as rationalists, scientists, and factions of Liberalism. This breadth commanded a broad spectrum of readers first for the *Contemporary* and then after February 1877 for the *Nineteenth Century*. One of the Society's youngest members, Henry Sidgwick, was active in the establishment of higher education for women, and it may be due in part to his position that two of the one hundred-odd names on the prospectus for the *Nineteenth Century* are Mrs Owen[7] and Helen Taylor.[8] For the Victorian protagonists Strahan and Knowles the public debate pivoted about the merits of the star system that signature permitted. In the February 1877 *Contemporary*, the one issue Strahan edited before the advent of the *Nineteenth Century* in March, an unsigned essay, 'Editing', addresses Strahan's immediate problem: how an editor stripped of his 'stars' copes with the forthcoming star-studded *Nineteenth Century*. 'Editing' offers three arguments: financially, the star system is unaffordable; secondly, it disallows young, untried authors; and thirdly it provides a false sense of authority when experts write outside their fields: 'a false authority waits upon many a public utterance of an expert. He is off his beat, but his voice carries all the weight that belonged to it in other ranges of knowledge or opinion' (Anon. 1877a: 520).

The anxiety of the anonymous author of 'Editing' is part of a more general concern voiced by many and diverse Victorians concerning the implications of the loss of the authority of God. That consciousness of loss of authority contributed to the concomitant debates about anonymity versus signature, and the fear of the loss of the house 'voice' of a journal (allegedly attached to anonymity) and the onset of the pluralism of signature and relativism. Strahan's concern as an Evangelical, however, is not the right of readers to form their own opinions without strong guidance from periodicals, but that the guidance stems from *false* authority. The logic of his position is that of the editor of a more sectarian journal than the *Nineteenth Century* was to be. Nevertheless, the author of 'Editing' does indicate the way that the star system, though apparently and openly pluralist, is at the same time authoritarian, and he rightly feared the financial success of the appeal of experts to readers. The front cover of the *Contemporary Review* for April 1877, the month after the first *Nineteenth Century* appeared, shows that initially Strahan attempted to compete for stars. The list of contents that appears on the cover begins with 'Renan on Spinoza', and the authors' names which follow are in bold type. Arthur Waugh in 1902 in *The Critic* praises the *Nineteenth Century* as 'the most widely read of the monthly reviews' and the periodical which probably 'enjoys the most weight' (Waugh: 36), but he also charges the star system with exclusiveness: 'Although a good article has always had its chance, it has been no part of Mr Knowles's editorship to "discover" new writers; he has sought, and sought with conspicuous success, for the best acknowledged experts, and has made it his business to give the public the views of the men upon whom it has learnt to rely' (Waugh: 36). Is this true? In regard to 'men' perhaps, but not to women: after the first fifteen months, the *Nineteenth Century* published a number of articles by women, most of whom were not well known.

Where do our twentieth-century interest in literary authority and that of the nineteenth century touch? The visibility of the 'stars' indicates that less-visible group behind the *Nineteenth Century*, the Metaphysical Society, to which many of the stars belonged or with whose members they associated. My point is that the apparently individual stars are themselves a collective, and that they provide both real intellectual (and class) coherence *and* diversity for the new journal. For us, they articulate usefully the interaction between the social group and the individual in the cultural production of journalism. In our work as critics and historians, we need always to keep the group and the social dimension of journalism in view. The problem is described by Jerome McGann in terms of textual bibliography:

As the very term 'authority' suggests, the author is taken to be – for editorial and critical purposes – the ultimate locus of a text's authority, and literary works are consequently viewed in the most personal and individual way. Furthermore, just as literary works are narrowly identified with an author, the identity of the author with respect to the work is critically simplified through this process of individualization. The result is that the dynamic social relations which always exist in literary production – the dialectic between the historically located individual author and the historically developing institutions of literary production – tends to become obscured in criticism. Authors lose their lives as they gain such critical identities, and their works suffer a similar fate by being divorced from the social relationships which gave them their lives (McGann: 81).

Authors and texts are parts of a process of cultural production in history, and we need to examine our understanding of the implicit assumptions about literary and historical authority in our work, and how they operate to shape our perceptions of the press. The question of the relation of women to the *Nineteenth Century* is raised by the two female names in the prospectus list, and the more general issue of gender in the two periodicals and the Society follows. The Society had no female members; George Eliot was ineligible, a factor which might have contributed to the absence of George Henry Lewes from the membership. John Stuart Mill, while asked, refused to join, as did Herbert Spencer, a friend of the Leweses. The gendered character of the social formations it drew on – the gentleman's club, the political party, the public discussion forums – seems evident in Metcalf's account of the meetings (Metcalf: 215ff). The subjects of debate – science, religion and philosophy – were also tied to institutions of nineteenth-century culture which excluded women: scientific research, the Church and higher education, and to a significant degree these subjects dominated the *Contemporary Review* during Knowles's association with it, and very few women writers published in it. These same subjects were those *excluded* from the *Cornhill Magazine*, conceived as a family publication,[9] and by implication were defined as subjects best confined to male writers and readers. This the *Contemporary Review* under Knowles largely did. It is noteworthy that although the *Contemporary Review* possessed a section on 'Contemporary Literature' which included occasional reviews of fiction from its inception in 1866,[10] this section was withdrawn after the September 1870 issue, six months after Knowles became editor. Between April 1870 and January 1877 less than ten articles out of a total of some 750 discussed fiction, a genre associated with women readers and women authors.[11]

The discourse of gender more generally shows the exclusion of women in another, discordant, light. Not only were women constructed as subjects, necessarily excluded from such topics as the *Nineteenth Century* addressed, women in this last quarter of the century were also perceived as unwelcome censors and inhibitors of serious discourse of all types. This is evident in 1885 in George Moore's response to institutional censorship; his anger is expressed in a gendered metaphor, 'Literature at Nurse'. Likewise, an essay by Gleeson White in an aesthetic little magazine, *The Spirit Lamp*, in June 1893 uses the same kind of gendered language to distinguish, wittily, the freedom of the male press from the discourse of the family: 'Custom and Mrs Grundy are too strong. In the privacy of print one may advocate heresies forbidden in the publicity of home life' (White: 81–2). This journal was initially produced by Oxford undergraduates for other undergraduates, an all-male readership.

A.W. Brown and Walter Houghton both identify politics as the principal area which distinguishes the *Nineteenth Century* from the *Contemporary Review* under Knowles, and it is true that three out of the eleven articles in the first number of the *Nineteenth Century* are primarily political, equalled only by three on religion. What is also a distinct additional element of both the new *Contemporary Review* and eventually the *Nineteenth Century* is dramatically increased attention to literature and the arts. The *Contemporary Review* takes its opportunity to pre-empt the *Nineteenth Century* here by including in the February 1877 number, after years of neglect of English literature under Knowles, a main article on George Eliot's novels *Middlemarch* and *Daniel Deronda*, and by adding a new feature of 19 pages called 'Essays and Notices' which contains short essays – 'Editing' among them – and promises to include reviews of novels in future. In defence of this policy of noticing 'lighter' reading than theology, philosophy and science, it argues that some English novels are weighty and deserve serious consideration: 'In George Eliot and others, we see the novel carrying (one might almost say) the whole weight of modern culture, or at least a good part of it' (Anon. 1877b: 528). The anxiety about the status of fiction in a periodical discourse formerly so exclusively male reveals itself in the parenthetical phrase in the middle of the claim and the qualification at the end. What can be seen here is the process of the intrusion of the vernacular, popular genre into a periodical in which scholastic notation and classical languages and subjects had formerly predominated. This had resulted, I am suggesting, in a readership of those equipped by culture with these skills – educated men of the upper classes. With the entrance of literature and the arts to the *Contemporary* and later the *Nineteenth Century*, the potential for women writers, and their number, increases, along with the accessibility of the two periodicals to women readers.

The Spirit Lamp signals another subject prohibited from family publications. In May 1893 in its prospectus for its new monthly format, *The Spirit Lamp* openly declares what had been discernible from the first, that it saw itself as a purveyor of 'the new culture', that is, the culture and discourse of the gay male community. In 1877 homosexual discourse arises as a subject in both the *Nineteenth Century* and the *Contemporary Review* in their March numbers: in articles by Matthew Arnold in the still-male space of the first *Nineteenth Century* issue where he notes the 'passionate friendship' of Falkland for 'a young man as promising and as universally beloved as himself',[12] and by the Revd J. Tyrwhitt (author of 'The Greek Spirit in Modern Literature'), an entire article of exposure and denunciation specifically focused on the writing of Arnold and J.A. Symonds. In the more Evangelical and now familial space of the *Contemporary Review*, Tyrwhitt writes:

> These pages are a rebellion against nature as she is here, in the name of nature as described in Athens. And the word nature now brings us unavoidably on awkward ground. Mr. Symonds is probably the most innocent of men; we certainly cannot look upon him in any other light. He might not return the compliment, for everybody who objects to suggestive passages of a certain character is now called prurient by their authors, and this reproach we propose to incur. The emotions of Socrates at sight of the beauty of young Charmides are described for him by Plato, in the dialogue which bears the name of the latter. Socrates' purity, and indeed his asceticism of life are freely and fully vindicated elsewhere by Plato, and will never be disputed here. The expressions put in his mouth are, no doubt, typically Hellenic. But they are not natural: and it is well known that Greek love of nature and beauty went frequently against nature. The word is used equivocally in this book – for the outward shows of creation, and for the inward impulses of man; and it is assumed that because the former are generally beautiful, the latter are invariably to be followed. Neither are good, for what is good? They are both here, and must be taken for what they are.
>
> Other assertions seem to be made rather, it must be said, in the spirit of the persecutor; that is to say, in order to inflict moral outrage instead of physical (Tyrwhitt: 557).

Tolerance of homosexuality varies with the gender of the space. The textual play of difference, of male presence and female absence and presence respectively and complications of the gendered subject are visible in the two essays.

The *Nineteenth Century* countered the new section of the *Contemporary*, interestingly by also producing a 20-page end-section, but one on science, written by 'The Editor' with the assistance of a star, T. H. Huxley. The one article on literature in *Nineteenth Century* I(i) is on Turkish stories. If one looks at the dailies of the period, the overwhelmingly dominant subject in leaders and news is the Eastern Question – the conflict between Russia and Turkey – the Armistice, and the unsuccessful conference of powers to attempt a treaty. The coverage of literature here is linked to the political rather than the literary economy. Moreover, this attention to antiquarian foreign language, and exotic literature, with its emphasis on recondite fiction, inaccessible to the 'unskilled' reader, continues to characterise some *Nineteenth Century* articles on literature, but by August 1877, in its sixth issue, the *Nineteenth Century* introduces an occasional end-section on 'Recent Literature' by Henry Morley, which next appears in November 1877. In August too (the reason for lighter reading!) appears its first article on contemporary English literature, a piece on Harriet Martineau's *Autobiography*, and in December Matthew Arnold's 'A Guide to English Literature'. Meanwhile, a good selection is offered of articles on subjects other than religion, theology and science – many of which seem targeted to include women readers, such as Henry Irving's notes in April and May 1877 on Shakespearean character roles, followed by an article in June 1877 by a woman author, Juliet Pollock, 'For and against the Play'. 'Teaching to Read' appears in May 1877 and 'Medical Women' in July. After June 1878 the *Nineteenth Century* includes regular female contributions, some by stars such as Florence Nightingale who writes on the people of India. Articles in the *Nineteenth Century* were still footnoted, and the great majority still addressed to political, theological, philosophical and scientific questions of the day, but even some of these were now written by women.

In the *Nineteenth Century* and the post-1876 *Contemporary Review* we see the reaches of the higher journalism admitting the novel, an entire genre, to its contents – as they were even then adding science and psychology as disciplines separate from natural philosophy.

With the addition of fiction in English comes its female readership and authors. It is, I think, a moot point whether the *Nineteenth Century* would have made this move had the February *Contemporary* not made literature a conspicuous part of the new agenda. In case its readers (and the editor and readers of the *Nineteenth Century*) did not understand the significance of the new section of the *Contemporary*, in its April number, tipped-in to the advertisements on a half-sheet of yellow paper, is an announcement promising monthly sections on Contemporary Literature, Contemporary Science, and Contemporary Arts. For both periodicals, the growth market of readers of novels and their publishers was not one to ignore. Intellectually, the inroads of the novel on the classical subjects were undeniable.

It would seem from the absence of a correspondence section in a periodical structured around controversy that the scope for debate was limited. By introducing in the second number of the *Nineteenth Century* a formal structure of controlled debate, a Symposium, Knowles highlighted the open platform element of the journal, the spice of controversy, while spreading it over two or more numbers so that it functioned as a serial to which readers could look forward. The topics themselves, as well as the format, might engage the interest of women as well as men readers: the influence upon morality of a decline in religious belief; the soul and future life; and is the popular judgement in politics more just than that of the higher order? In this, and in the 'Noticeable Books' format where reviewers took the initiative in book selection, Knowles's *Nineteenth Century* might be said to move away from journalism centred on the editor to journalism which gave a measure of control to the contributors. The dissemination of authority seems an apt description.

So far, critics discussing these periodicals have not noted the absence of attention to the English novel, nor have they linked the issue of literary authority with that of gender.[13] One future project of interest would be to look closely at the voices of authority in the text of the first number of the *Nineteenth Century*, and the (considerable) space it gives to doubt as well as conviction. As Arthur Waugh enviously points out in 1902, in its early years the *Nineteenth Century* exclusively printed the work of Tennyson, the Poet Laureate. If Gladstone eloquently defended the idea of authority and Christian authority in the second item of I(i), in the first item Tennyson leaves us with the doubt that Strahan and Co. wished to exclude:

For some, descending from the sacred peak
Of hoar high templed Faith; have leagued again
Their lot with ours to rove the world about;
And some are wilder comrades, sworn to seek
If any golden harbour be for men
In seas of Death and sunless gulfs of Doubt. (1)

The occasion of a Poet Laureate and a Prime Minister contemplating the inroads of doubt and change is characteristic of the new *Nineteenth Century* – 'stars' in structured opposition, in accord in tolerating whatever their intellectual peers might wish to say.

Notes

1. In, for example, 'The Un-islanding of England: press debates on the Channel Tunnel in 1882', an unpublished lecture delivered in Manchester in July 1992, Ann Parry argued that Knowles mounted a concerted campaign against the tunnel in the pages of the *Nineteenth Century* while abiding by the letter of 'balance'.
2. The 'Modern Symposium' begun by the *Nineteenth Century* in the second issue is an example.
3. See for example E.K. Clifford on 'The Ethics of Belief' in the last *Contemporary Review* edited by Knowles in January 1877.
4. It is possible, for example, that Millicent Garrett Fawcett's article in August 1878, 'The Future of Englishwomen: a reply', which followed Alexandra Orr's 'The Future of English Women' (June 1878), was unsolicited.
5. For example, Cardinal Manning and Thomas Huxley.
6. It began in 1869 and he started his editorial stint at the *Contemporary* in 1870.
7. Marienne E. Owen, author of an article listed in *Wellesley*, in *Cornhill* (August 1866), on criminal women.
8. Feminist; author of periodical articles but not in the *Nineteenth Century*; daughter of Harriet Taylor and stepdaughter of J.S. Mill.
9. This nomenclature singled out journals which women might read with impunity.
10. See Fryckstedt on the first year of the *Contemporary*, where it is among the few journals to give space to reviews of English fiction.
11. See Shevelow and Tuchman.
12. Arnold is careful to include literary authority for his celebration of the friendship of the two men, by citation of Ben Jonson's poem 'To the Immortal Memory and Friendship of that Noble Pair, Sir Lucius Cary and Sir Henry Morison'.

13.   Shevelow examines women and the *eighteenth-century* periodical;
      Tuchman, gender and cultural production of the nineteenth-century
      novel.

Works Cited

Anon. (1877a). 'Editing', *Contemporary Review* 29(Feb.), 517–20.
Anon. (1877b). 'Essays and Notices', *Contemporary Review* 29 (Feb.), 516–34.
Arnold, Matthew. (1877). 'Falkland', *Nineteenth Century* I(March) 141–55.
Brown, Alan Willard. (1947). *The Metaphysical Society: Victorian Minds in
      Crisis, 1869–1880.* New York.
Ellicott, C.J. (1877). 'The Church of England, Present and Future',
      Nineteenth Century I(March), 50–71.
Fryckstedt, Monica. (1989). *On the Brink: English Novels of 1866.* Studia
      Anglistica Upsaliensia 69. Stockholm.
Houghton, Walter. (1972). 'Introduction': *Nineteenth Century*, in *The
      Wellesley Index to Victorian Periodicals 1824–1900.* Vol. II. Toronto and
      London. pp. 621–6.
McGann, Jerome. (1983). *A Critique of Modern Textual Criticism.* Chicago.
Metcalf, Priscilla. (1980). *James Knowles.* Oxford.
Moore, George. (1885), *Literature at Nurse.* London.
Shevelow, Kathryn. (1989), *Women and Print Culture.* London and New
      York.
Srebrnik, Patricia. (1986). *Alexander Strahan, Victorian Publisher.* Ann Arbor.
Tennyson, Alfred. (1877). ['Those that of late had fleeted far and fast'],
      Nineteenth Century I(March), 1.
Tuchman, Gaye. (1989). *Edging Women Out. Victorian Novelists, Publishers,
      and Social Change.* London and New York.
Tyrwhitt, J. (1877). 'The Greek Spirit in Modern Literature', *Contemporary
      Review* 29(March), 552–66.
Waugh, Arthur. (1902). 'The English Reviews: A Sketch of the History and
      Principles', *The Critic* 40(Jan.), 26–37.
White, Gleeson. (1893). 'In Praise of Idleness', *The Spirit Lamp* 4(June 6),
      81–2.

4

The Discourses of Journalism: Authorship, Publishers and Periodicals

The interrogation of authorship by Roland Barthes and Michel Foucault, and latterly by postmodernist theory, is not only indebted to the technology and nature of twentieth-century media for its inception; it also affects the terms in which scholars now study the media, enabling a transfer of 'details' of publishing history from the margins of bibliography and footnotes to the foreground of critical writing, *into* the text. In this chapter I scrutinise three authors (Matthew Arnold, Walter Pater and Oscar Wilde) whose names and naming, like those of all authors, have functioned in the construction of unified subjects. This construction of authorship not only tends to posit a seamless and coherent entity (e.g. 'Hardy') but also circulates notions of self-determinism, untrammelled individualism, unique genius and personal psychology. It denies the constituting and defining factors of language, history, culture. I am trying to reinsert these factors and to challenge the notion of the free, unique artist. I examine the construction of authorship in the late nineteenth century by comparing the publishing patterns, opportunities, censorship, and choices of these three interacting male writers.

This chapter has had a number of previous lives, each instructive and formative: it began as a study of Pater's work in the 1880s, and was called at this early (lecture) stage 'Pater, politics, and publishing in the 1880s'. Then, it acquired the title 'The Discourses of Journalism' and took Arnold into its framework. Penultimately, after I spent time reading some of the Wilde archives I added Wilde. I then gave it as a lecture in its new form at a Pater conference, and when it appeared in print, it was in a Paterian context in a book derived from that conference. Its place here, in a context of publishing history and theory, in an altered form which cites the authors as examples of publishing patterns, is perhaps most

63

appropriate. This evolving of the work, from the notion of an individual author's publishing history and career management to a scrutiny of the discourses of journalism and the cultural formations themselves involving comparative work with individual authors traces cultural history and discourse during the period in which I undertook the work. The essay inscribes its history.

*   *   *

T.S. Eliot's essay on Pater, first published in 1930 stresses the continuities between Arnold and Pater rather than the disruptions. Eliot undervalues Arnold's deep attachment to Christianity (and perhaps Pater's) and suppresses Pater's many challenges to Arnold's ideas. I would like to suggest that Pater attacked two of Arnold's key positions in the 1870s and 1880s, that of the inferiority of romanticism and the superiority of poetry. To these notions rooted in Arnold's construct of a classical tradition, Pater counters positions which derive from identification with modern literary forms and writing: he defends romanticism and assesses it from a position consciously and unapologetically within it; prose, he claims is 'the special art of the modern world' (Pater 1888: 730). The relationship between Pater and Arnold was largely one of disagreement and rivalry, voiced in public dialogue in print, in the press and in books, as well as in private conversation. In 1876 and 1888, in 'Romanticism' and 'Style', Pater's essays which begin and and end *Appreciations,* his volume of collected essays published in 1889, he is, among other things, continuing the public dialogue with Arnold.

As for Arnold, the second series of *Essays* in *Criticism* appeared in November 1888, a month before 'Style' and a year before *Appreciations.* In his *Essays* Arnold foregrounds his introduction to Humphrey Ward's 1880 anthology of English poetry as the first essay, now newly entitled 'The Study of Poetry': Arnold's 1880 essay republished in 1888 does constitute a genuine referent of Pater's claims for prose in his essay on 'Style' in the December 1888 issue of the *Fortnightly:* insofar as Pater himself had contributed to the Ward anthology which Arnold's then untitled essay served to introduce, Pater was familiar with Arnold's position, and was addressing it. In November 1889 Pater's 'Style' is placed analogously as the flagship of *his* collection.

Enter Wilde. According to Frank Harris, editor of the *Fortnightly* in which 'Style' appeared in December 1888, Pater, Arnold and

Wilde *discussed* style in 1886 or early the following year at a London dinner party where Harris commissioned the essay from Pater (Harris 1919: 212). Pater's defence of prose and Arnold's of poetry in the 1880s are related counterstatements which, with Oscar Wilde's interventions, inscribe a contest in the late nineteenth century between adherence to models from classical literature (which privileges poetry, nobility and the grand styles) and a challenging recommendation of contemporary literary forms (prose and its new popular form, the novel).[1] The apparent meanings of the ideological alliance between Pater and Wilde and their differences with Arnold on this question are disrupted however by an eloquent if unnoted harmony between Pater and Arnold: their common publisher (Macmillan) and periodical (*Macmillan's Magazine*). These parallel publications can be contrasted with the provenance of Wilde's work published by the small house of Osgood McIlvaine, and originally in the tolerant space of the *Nineteenth Century* and the *Fortnightly Review*. These aspects of production yield ideological meanings. Moreover, it may be that Eliot's *choice* as well as construction of Arnold and Pater as subjects is in part due to their implication in the problematic of culture and religion in the nineteenth century. Eliot's predisposition to matters of faith in 1930 leads him to exclude Wilde and to minimalise the ideological contest in the 1880s and early 1890s just as Frank Harris's bohemianism insures Wilde's prominence and exposure of the discontinuities.

Both Arnold's *Essays in Criticism* (November 1888) and Pater's *Appreciations* (November 1889) were published by Macmillan, and both included a large number of essays originally in *Macmillan's Magazine* or in books published by Macmillan. If these essays and books seem to have common origins and to be parts of the same discourse, that cannot be said for essays which were included in the *Nineteenth Century* in 1889 and 1890, signed Oscar Wilde, and published in book form by Osgood McIlvaine in 1891 as part of *Intentions*.[2] The first, 'The Decay of Lying', published in January 1889, prominently quotes notions of Arnold's and Pater's, either to reject them outright or to extend them beyond recognition. The second, 'The True Function and Value of Criticism', in two parts or acts printed in July and September 1890, openly confronts Arnold's earlier pronouncements in 1864–65 in 'The Function of Criticism at the Present Time' and the first series of *Essays in Criticism*. The wit, pace and form of Wilde's essays distinguish them markedly from the contemporary work of Pater and Arnold:

they combine argument and aphorisms with an unembarrassed, even exploitative topicality. The Platonic dialogue, W.S. Landor's *Imaginary Conversations*, Frederic Harrison's 1867 'Culture: a Dialogue' (an analogous and influential critique of Arnold), and Wilde's persistence from 1880 with writing drama contribute to his essay's distinctive and unexpected dialogue form, which offers an alternative metaphor for the site of criticism. Wilde displaces Arnold's pulpit and Pater's academy with the aesthetic drawing-room, and the setting of the public occasion and audience favoured by Arnold and Pater with the private. These qualities together make Arnold's and Pater's contemporary work appear rarefied and even constrained compared with Wilde's, and suggest that Wilde's work is part of a different periodicals discourse.

If the definition of the 'text' is extended beyond content and style to include the discourse and its readers, then the differences between Wilde's text and that of Arnold and Pater emerge more clearly. The flamboyance of Wilde's writing is indicative of the degree of freedom afforded by the periodical in which it appeared; indeed, through Wilde's exploitation or more neutrally, utilisation, of that freedom, its capaciousness is revealed. Although neither Arnold nor Pater tested its limits as strenuously as Wilde, they also availed themselves of the freedom of James Knowles's *Nineteenth Century* which prided itself on tolerant untrammelled eclecticism, and fostered oppositional expression through the format of the symposium. The definition of the 'text' includes the periodical of which (Wilde's) writing is a part.

While 'signature', the signature of *individual* authors, that is, figured importantly in James Knowles's programme for his journal, the other signature, clear to the editor and the periodical reader of the day, is the 'signature' of the journal itself; its significance if not its identity is now obscured to us. Moreover, the production process whereby writing is translated from the ephemeral of the periodical essay into the permanence of the book engineers the obscuring of the ephemeral characteristics and, most important, origins, even to the original readers of the book. The corporate institutional authorship of work is obfuscated, and authorship is shifted to a context which foregrounds the individual; the discourse of the book is now that of art, the collected work, with its emphasis on individual performance, genius, memorability, here the tarnished image of the artist-as-critic.

I write 'collected' work because that is how the production process is perceived by the consumer. But for the author it is selected work, and what is deselected, left to the limbo of ephemera is, for our purposes, as important. In this process of selection and omission the 'text' by the *critic* is constructed by the writer. Another process of this construction is characteristic of this system of production: it is the systematic revision of the ephemeral writing to provide it with a 'finish' allegedly not required by periodical publication. Disallowed as a characteristic of a form of publication associated with constraints of time and with the undignified labours of Grub Street authors, whose livelihood depends on meeting deadlines, 'finish' comes to be exclusively associated with another form of production, leisured and gentlemanly, which may result in art which, by implication, is defined as 'not journalism'. Finish often involved the careful suppression of topical allusions in order to enhance the illusion of timelessness of the new 'art' text. This was often Arnold's purpose in the relatively few revisions of his periodical texts for book publication. In the course of restoring the periodical texts of Arnold's work to readers in his edition of the *Collected Prose Works*, R.H. Super stresses

I hope it has been apparent how much of Arnold's writing – which was almost all journalism on its first appearance – is ... embedded in the ephemera of his day...

   Arnold's relation, not with the monuments of Victorian literat- ure, but with the multitude of forgotten and fallen leaves – seeing him read his daily newspaper and comment upon it, then seeing that newspaper take up his comment, until as with the *Saturday Review* and the *Daily Telegraph*, a tradition of mutual banter is set up. (Super 1966: 637)

Wilde, like Pater and Arnold, selected essays to reprint in book form: *Intentions* (1891) consisted of four pieces, 'The Decay of Lying' and 'The True Function and Value of Criticism' from the *Nineteenth Century*, one other from the same periodical, equally uncom- promising, now entitled 'The Truth of Masks', and 'Pen, Pencil, and Poison', from the *Fortnightly Review*. A liberal and erudite periodical from its inception in 1865 when it was modelled on the *Revue des Deux Mondes*, the *Fortnightly* was edited in 1889 by the young Frank Harris, and open to publication of Wilde's libertine, provocative and lighthearted defence of the aesthetic perfection of the life of a murderer and forger. *Intentions* is a text to keep in view beside Arnold's *Essays* and Pater's *Appreciations*, with Wilde's selection from his critical essays characterised by inclusion of work from the two journals in the heights of the élite culture which offered the widest moral parameters in the British press of the day. Wilde excluded and never reprinted in his lifetime, for example, numerous reviews and articles from the daily *Pall Mall Gazette* and his contributions to *Woman's World*, the *Court and Society Review*, *Queen*, and *The Speaker*. He constructs himself in *Intentions* as the irreverent and youthful upstart who takes on and displaces the ageing gurus. Arnold's death in April 1888 may have freed Pater and Wilde from critical constraints (would Wilde mock and attack Arnold at 66 so directly had Arnold been alive?), but Arnold *hors de combat* may also have consolidated his influence among critics and readers more generally.

By contrast a great part of the selections by Arnold and Pater for their respective books in 1888 and 1889 stemmed from a relatively staid periodical aimed at a family audience.[3] *Macmillan's* habitually carried fiction, which signalled its lighter magazine format and its intention to include women unequivocally among its readers. Unlike the *Nineteenth Century* or the *Fortnightly Review*, *Macmillan's Magazine* was implicated in its publisher's book publication; originally conceived as a vehicle of trailers for forthcoming books of the firm, the magazine addressed the moral tolerance not only of its own immediate audience but that of the large circulating libraries such as Mudie's and retailers such as W.H. Smith; these possessed considerable economic and moral authority through their power to purchase books in bulk from publishers or not. An anonymous review of Macmillan's cumulative catalogue which appeared in *The Bookman* in 1891 makes plain this moral dimension of Macmillan's list in its diction, with value accorded to Macmillan's 'honourable career', its 'steadfast' adherence to 'principles', and its efforts to 'raise' the publication of books, while the alternatives of 'bad books', 'startling successes' (material) and 'big sales' are rejected. The association of the publication of aesthetically fine books with this high moral posture endorses the 'worth' of the publications.

This volume has been executed in a manner which is worthy of the honourable career it records. Some publishers may have achieved more startling successes than any even of Messrs.

Macmillan, but big sales of bad books the latter have never aimed at. None have done more to raise the whole manner of the publication of books. They have been steadfast to two great principles: first, never to publish a book which they did not think worth reading; next, always to give all books fair opportunity so far as printing and binding were concerned. Looking over this catalogue, it is with growing surprise one notices how very few of the titles are unfamiliar.... Every one knows that it is almost always a pleasure to handle a Macmillan book – the binding is invariably tasteful, and some of the new sizes introduced by the firm peculiarly neat. (Anon. 1891: 34)

The ideological link between Macmillan's and Smith's, renowned for its refusal to circulate 'immoral' books, is revealed by the case of Wilde's novel *The Picture of Dorian Gray* which Macmillan refused to publish and Smith to distribute.

Arnold's second series of *Essays in Criticism*, comprising ten essays, includes only two from non-Macmillan origins. Both are on controversial topics, and they appeared in the same two journals which harboured Wilde's work. *Essays* reprints one item from the *Nineteenth Century;* predictably, it is the most morally vulnerable in the opinion of Lord Coleridge who provides a 'Prefatory Note' to this selection of essays that Arnold made before his death. 'C' suggests that Arnold's review of Edward Dowden's biography of Shelley (it is the most recent essay in the volume, having appeared in January 1888), is only part of what Arnold would have wished to say – while he would not wish to have retracted what he does say, he would have said more about Shelley.

The other non-Macmillan essay, on Tolstoy, is from the *Fortnightly Review* published only a month before the piece on Shelley, in December 1887. We know that Tolstoy too was a morally delicate subject at the time, probably unfit for inclusion in *Macmillan's Magazine*, as an irate reviewer of *The Picture of Dorian Gray* in the Tory *St James' Gazette* of 24 June 1890 indicates: Tolstoy's 'Kreutser Sonata' serves the reviewer as an example of Puritan prurience which is one form taken by authors like Wilde who derive pleasure from treating a subject merely because it is disgusting (Jeyes: 3–4). These essays which originate outside of *Macmillan's* pages inscribe its familial audience and the limits of respectable morality as well as identify their subjects and the sites of their publication as marginalised and suitable for male readers, in a different discourse.

Pater's selection from his published work for *Appreciations* is far more eclectic in a variety of ways than either Wilde's or Arnold's. The essays are drawn from three decades, two from the 1860s, four from the 1870s, and five from the 1880s; partly in consequence the essays cohere less. Where Arnold's book overwhelmingly addresses poetry and Wilde's criticism and theory, Pater's volume includes essays on each of three genres – four on prose, four on poetry, and three on drama; there are also two on critical terms – 'style', and 'romanticism' and 'classicism'. These two are carefully positioned at the beginning and end of the volume, and the title of the last essay is even changed by Pater from 'Romanticism' to 'Postscript', to enhance the illusion of unity and discernible structure. Similarly, the sources of the essays show a greater range: four from the *Fortnightly Review*, three from *Macmillan's Magazine*, two from the *Westminster Review*, one from *Scribner's Magazine*, and one from T.H. Ward's anthology, *The English Poets*, published by Macmillan. The faceted eclecticism of *Appreciations* in part results from Pater's decision to give fiction his serious attention in the 1880s; he is forced to dig more deeply into the past than Arnold or Wilde to provide criticism suitable for translation from emphemera to art.

Both Pater and Arnold include essays in their books which first appeared in T.H. Ward's anthology of English poets (1880, 1883), but the roles these essays play are contrasting: they reveal the centrality of poetry to Arnold's literary production in the period, and Pater's parallel preoccupation with imaginative and critical prose. Arnold's three contributions to Ward (his niece's husband) were the introduction (later titled 'The Study of Poetry'), and pieces on Keats and Gray. These were all written especially for the selections of poems which they preface in Ward. Two other essays on Romantic poets in Arnold's volume treat Wordsworth and Byron; these served as introductions to editions of their poems edited by Arnold and published by Macmillan in 1879 and 1881 respectively. With his review of Dowden's life of Shelley in 1888 Arnold could be said to have completed a personal project, that of reconsidering his earlier views on the Romantic poets stated in 1864 and 1865. Just as 'The Study of Poetry' genuinely states the programme of the 1888 volume, 'The Function of Criticism at the Present Time' itself served as the keynote to the first series of *Essays in Criticism* in 1865. The essays Arnold did for Ward were part of a larger, previously conceived reconsideration of Romantic poetry, a project which Arnold continued to pursue after Ward's anthology appeared.

The coinciding of Arnold's interests with Ward's volumes is not accidental. Darrel Mansell strives to distinguish between the conception of Ward's project – with its twin emphases on the teaching of English poetry and the dispersal of authority implicit in the plurality of critics – and Arnold's well-known predilections for classical and European literature, and for authority. However true these differences, it is also true that Ward's project is itself significantly Arnoldian. As early as 1864 Arnold recommends 'that a practice, common in England during the last century, and still followed in France, of printing... a notice by a competent critic, – to serve as an introduction to an eminent author's works, might be revived among us with advantage' (Arnold 1960–77: III, 258), and in 1877 he responds positively to his publisher's suggestion that he undertake a selection of Wordsworth and provide a preface. This appeared in September 1879, the same month Arnold probably began to prepare his introduction for Ward; Arnold's parallel selection of Bryon's poems in 1881 immediately followed the publication of Ward's volumes 3 and 4 in December 1880, in which Arnold's Keats and Gray essays appear. All three, Arnold's selections from Wordsworth and Byron and Ward's anthology, were published by Macmillan. The close interrelatedness of the projects is indicated by the common publisher; the family link between Arnold and Ward; and the Oxford associations of Arnold (graduate and former Professor of Poetry), Ward (graduate and recent Fellow of Brasenose College), and most of the critics Ward employed in his anthology. These selections of Arnold's and Ward's anthology are a product of the same formation.

Comparison of Humphry Ward's proposal to Macmillan with Arnold's suggestion in 1865 shows that both took their idea from French models, possibly the same model, as Sainte-Beuve had already attracted Arnold's attention in 1864 in 'The Literary Influence of Academies'.

The idea, which I wish to carry out is one which I think will mark off such a book from all similar collections in English, namely, that each poet or group of poets should be undertaken by a separate writer, who would select from his work, and write a short *critical* introduction, varying from a single page to ten or twelve. This idea has been [?]ted in a most admirable collection of French poetry, called 'Les poètes français', published in 1861 by Gide and now (I believe) issued under Hachette's name. That collection occupies four volumes. I should propose that the present book should be in three...

I have already enlisted a good many friends to help in the work ...I should say that Mr. Matthew Arnold has expressed himself strongly in favour of the scheme, & has promised to help if he can possibly find time. If I can induce him to write the general introduction, as Sainte-Beuve did for the French Collection, I think we would not fear for the success of the book. (Ward: 1879)

Ward's anthology slots easily into Arnold's endeavours at the time, allowing Arnold to lend his name and authority to Ward by agreeing to write the introduction. The flattery of the parallel with Sainte-Beuve and the authority it implied may also have induced Arnold to agree. Ward's project, a version of which Arnold is simultaneously engaged upon, is a variant of one proposed by Arnold fifteen years earlier, and now nurtured by a publisher common to both. Prompted to publish *because* Arnold endorsed it, Macmillan recognised its compatibility with aspects of his current list, while Arnold endorsed it out of recognition of its origins and those (familial and academic) of its youthful proposer.

Pater is also a Macmillan author, publishing with the press in the 1880s a combination of fiction and criticism, *Marius the Epicurean* in 1885, *Imaginary Portraits* in 1887, the third edition of *The Renaissance* in 1888, *Appreciations* in 1889, and numerous articles including chapters from *Gaston de Latour* in the *Magazine*. Ward's original proposal to Macmillan of February 1879 shows Pater as volunteering to take eight out of the twenty-seven poets in volume III: Coleridge, Robert Southey, Samuel Rogers, Keats, Milman, John Keble, W.S. Landor, and possibly E.B. Browning. In the event, he only takes on Coleridge, and in 1883 for the second edition Rossetti, now dead and thus eligible for inclusion. Southey and Rogers are undertaken by Henry Taylor, Keats by Matthew Arnold, Keble by A.P. Stanley, Landor by Lord Houghton, and E.B. Browning by W.T. Arnold. It is interesting that in theory Pater was willing to concentrate on nineteenth-century poetry to this degree in early 1879, and that circumstances intervened to prevent him. Poetry does not appear to be prominent in *Appreciations*, insofar as two of the four essays on poetry date from 1868 and 1874; the other two are derived from Ward, and one of those, on Coleridge, which Pater dates in the volume '1865, 1888' is created in 1888 by combining the Ward essay and his 1866 *Westminster Review* article on Coleridge's prose. Three out of the four essays on poetry were written over a decade before *Appreciations* appeared. Moreover, the introductory and concluding essays of the volume – which are both theoretical – discuss modern European *prose* texts; in this respect they parallel 'Amiel' and 'Count Leo Tolstoi', the only two parts of Arnold's 1888 *Essays* which do not treat Romantic poetry. However, where Arnold's first essay, from Ward, foregrounds poetry and anticipates the majority of the essays which follow, Pater's 'Style' is recent, it foregrounds prose, and it marginalises the essays on poetry, including those from Ward, which follow. What the poetry essays in *Appreciations* show is Pater's willingness to discuss recent literature in English, such as that by Rossetti and Morris. The list of poets Pater volunteered for Ward's third volume, which included contemporaries and near contemporaries such as Keble, Landor and E.B. Browning bears this out. In this respect Pater, and Wilde after him, differ from Arnold who clearly confines his published literary criticism on English literature to work by the previous generation, as he does in 1888.

Beside pieces on poetry and prose, Pater selects three essays on different types of Shakespearean drama for inclusion in *Appreciations*. This choice of subject typifies the apparent moral and intellectual respectability of the essays in this volume. Pater's essays from the *Fortnightly* do not probe its perimeters of tolerance as Wilde's do, and on the whole the distinction between the *Fortnightly* and *Macmillan's Magazine* do not emerge as clearly as they do in Arnold's selection. The *Appreciations* essay which is to attract controversy was one of Pater's earliest reviews, originally entitled 'Poems by William Morris' which appeared anonymously in the *Westminster Review* in 1868, a period when Huxley was to call it 'the wicked *Westminster*' (Huxley: I 247). The Morris essay attracted adverse criticism then and in 1873, when part of it appeared as the 'Conclusion' to Pater's Renaissance essays. Although Pater removed it from the 1877 second edition, here republished it twice in 1888/9, in the third edition of *The Renaissance*, and in a different form as 'Aesthetic Poetry' in *Appreciations* (1889), as a companion piece, perhaps, to the Ward introduction to Rossetti. But because it again provoked criticism, it was withdrawn a second time by Pater, this time from the 1890 edition of *Appreciations*. If Oscar Wilde at this time sought to be provocative, exploiting the spectrum of latitude in the press, and Arnold was also, even as an elder critic, willing to reprint the Shelley and Tolstoy reviews, Pater emerges in his criticism of the period as the most sensitive to the prevailing morality of the readers of his books, most anxious to construct a reputation of rectitude to survive him.

The significance of the critic constructed by Pater is not only illustrated positively by what *Appreciations* includes, but also by the critical journalism not reprinted. All the articles published between 1873 and 1888, and excluded, reveal facets of Pater's critical practice and reserve. Certain topics are carefully avoided, such as classical Greek culture and French fiction. Thus, the succession of pieces from 1875 on, 'The Myth of Demeter and Persephone' (1875), 'A Study of Dionysus' (1876), 'The Bacchanals of Euripides' (1878), 'The Beginnings of Greek Sculpture' (1880), and 'The Marbles of Aegina' (1880), are not only excluded from *Appreciations* which, in the event, is confined to English literature: the Greek essays *remain* uncollected by Pater, who is aware of the common association among his peers of classical Greece with homosexuality, and aware too of his own vulnerability on this score. These Greek studies, with others, were only collected posthumously.[4]

Pater's suppression of this material takes on increased significance, even poignancy, when one notes that in 1889 he republished his treatment of the *revival* of Dionysus in a *French* setting, in the apparently protective guise of fiction, as one of the four *Imaginary Portraits*. Indeed, the whole of that volume suggests that prose fiction for Pater was liberating, and incurred less risk of personal liability. However, the suppression of the explicitly classical Greek essays registers the strength of presence of the vociferous moral majority among readers and institutions such as the Church, the academy, and the critics; particularly vulnerable it would appear are collected prose essays, availing themselves of the authority art offers the ephemera of journalism in the form of printed books. In the light of this, Matthew Arnold's definition of Hellenism, characterised by sweetness and light, may be read, even in its earliest forms, as carefully excluding the homosexual aspect of Greek life while leaving the hearty manliness to Hebraism. This is a delicate distinction, and his advocacy of disinterestedness, most commonly read as an allusion to the affray of journalism and political life, may well exclude covertly this form of engagement in and with Greek life.

Pater's decision to risk the inclusion of 'Aesthetic Poetry' in 1889 is of interest in light of what replaces it in the second edition of *Appreciations* in 1890. Pater chooses a review he published anonymously in *Macmillan's Magazine* in 1886 on a French novel, Feuillet's *La Morte*.[5] The Victorian press shows that readers were kept well informed through reviews about noteworthy writing of all kinds in Europe and nineteenth-century writing in Britain shows marked familiarity with its European counterparts. However, it is equally true that French fiction, associated with sordidness, moral laxity, and realism had for some time been labelled as unsuitable reading for a major group of novel readers, respectable women. It would be reassuring to such readers that Pater's review had appeared in *Macmillan's* (had they known it), but significantly its author chooses to publish it anonymously in just such a family magazine. When Pater made his selection of work for *Appreciations* he may have judged that having restored the 'Conclusion' to *The Renaissance* (1888), it was safe in 1889 to reprint the entire essay from which it was drawn, but having incurred criticism again, he substituted in 1890 – perhaps wryly – this moderate and 'approved for the family' review of a French novel.

Pater's fear of castigation was not the result of individual neurosis or simply personal experience. In theological circles and the closely-related academic world, the indignation and litigation following the publication of *Essays and Reviews* in 1860 was swift, long-lived, and well-known. In the wider national sphere, while *La Traviata* was performed in London in 1857, the libretto was 'unavailable' and the novel banned. Censorship, the tyranny of the majority, was a live issue in the mid 1880s, and fiction – associated with light literature and women readers – was predictably a prime site of conflict.

If the issue of censorship is implicit in Pater's selection and deselection process, novelists whose work was its victim, such as George Moore and Wilde, protested openly and vociferously. In 'A New Censorship of Literature', an article in an evening daily newspaper, the *Pall Mall Gazette*, in December 1884, and in a pamphlet *Literature at Nurse* (1885), George Moore exposed the refusal of the circulating libraries to stock *A Modern Lover* and subsequently *A Mummer's Wife*; he claimed that the consequential failure of fiction in this position was disastrous for contemporary English literature as well as for the author and publisher of the works refused. In noting that the reaction of the press to the pamphlet was cool, Pierre Coustillas quotes a review in the *Academy*, a journal written by and for men in the universities, which disapprovingly links the realism of George Moore's novels with that of Emile Zola's (Moore 1976: 18); in 1888 the septuagenarian Henry

Vizetelly, the publisher of Moore's pamphlet, was fined and imprisoned for three months for publication of Zola's *La Terre*. In February 1891 Wilde included a riposte to the critics of his novel, *The Picture of Dorian Gray*, in an article he published in the *Fortnightly*, 'The Soul of Man Under Socialism'; while his claim there is stylistically emphasized by hyperbole and italics, his contention that 'There is not a single real poet or prose-writer of this century, for instance, on whom the British public have not solemnly conferred diplomas of immorality' (Ellmann: 273), refers to a contemporary climate that all of his *Fortnightly* readers would recognise. When one considers poets and novelists of the nineteenth century, many did attract the charge of immorality: Wordsworth, Coleridge, Keats, Shelley and Byron, but also Dickens, Thackeray, Charlotte and Emily Brontë, Elizabeth Gaskell, George Eliot, Moore, Meredith, Hardy, Gissing, William Morris, D.G. Rossetti and Swinburne.

Pater's careful behind-the-scenes regulation of what should be published on diverse occasions in different discourses, and Moore's and Wilde's explicit interventions to alter public opinion and behaviour provide two models of responses to censorship. The explorer, editor and translator Richard Burton provides a third. He withdraws the potential object of controversy from the public domain by publishing for private subscribers; and in order to protect himself and his associates from charges under the Obscene Publications Act of 1857, he invents a false Indian company under whose imprint he publishes his edition of *The Book of the Thousand Nights and A Night* in 1885. His edition of the Arabian Nights is copiously annotated, and its long 'Terminal essay' is largely devoted to the subject of pederasty; undoubtedly learned, the project is bound up with exploration and anthropology of the period, and detailed sexual exotica is presented in the notes under guise of the interest of cultural relativism. The 2000 subscribers to the first edition undoubtedly included a majority interested in this material. In the introduction Burton roundly defends this medieval Islamic work from charges of immorality and, contrasting it favourably with modern hypocrisy, identifies a French novel as a genuine purveyor of vice! No doubt he is appealing to his readers' knowledge of another, more familiar literature labelled exotica by the same censorship. But he too is attesting in 1885 to the existence of censorship, and the pressure emanating from its formation, such as the law. He also shows that in 1885 French fiction was still commonly regarded as an object of censorship:

The morale is sound and healthy; and at times we descry through the voluptuous and libertine picture, vistas of a transcendental morality, the morality of Socrates in Plato. Subtle corruption and covert licentiousness are utterly absent; we find more real "vice" in many a short French roman, say La Dame aux Camélias, and in not a few English novels of our own day than in the thousands of pages of the Arab. Here we have nothing of that most immodest modern modesty which sees covert implications where nothing is implied, and "improper" allusion when propriety is not outraged; nor do we meet with the Nineteenth Century refinement; innocence of the word not of the thought: morality of the tongue not of the heart, and the sincere homage paid to virtue in guise of perfect hypocrisy. (Burton: xvii)

We should therefore not be surprised that beside work on Greek culture, Pater does not select any of four reviews of French fiction for *Appreciations* in 1889. He also leaves out a number of anonymous reviews of the work of friends which appeared in periodicals such as the *Oxford Magazine*, and newspapers such as the *Pall Mall Gazette* and the *Guardian*, none of which are represented in his selection. The absence of these reviews seems to derive primarily from their function of the anonymous puff, as their authority would undoubtedly diminish were their authorship acknowledged, but there is also the factor of where these reviews appear: these periodicals and newspapers lack the status of periodicals in which the selected articles originate. In particular, the newspapers in the 1880s and 1890s are identified with the vulgar mass medium, the 'new journalism', not the non-professional man of letters at leisure to write the amusing or learned paper within the domain of letters.

Unlike Arnold and Wilde, Pater does not resort habitually to the latitude offered by the *Nineteenth Century*, making only four contributions to it in his lifetime, two book reviews in the late 1880s and two papers on the great French churches in 1894. Both of the reviews were not only signed but understood to be entirely the reviewer's work, with the initiation of the review and the choice of book his. The first of Pater's reviews of Noticeable Books appeared in April 1889 and treated a French novel; the second, published in December, proved to be Pater's most explicit manifestation of interest in politics. Pater sees the potential of the space James Knowles offers, but avoids being associated with such a libertine journal. Two other decisions by Pater support this. In the June following the signed

Ferdinand Fabre review in April, he reviews another novel by Fabre, but in a different periodical, one which is allied to the Anglican Church and which permits anonymity; it offers Pater double protection: non-exposure to the reading public, and the respectability of the Church for the many colleagues and critics privy to the authorship of unsigned journalism. That Pater chose an Anglican weekly like the *Guardian* to place a review of French fiction suggests an element of wit as well. Pater's wish in the latter part of his career to identify himself and be identified with religious rather than libertine formations is also indicated by his decision to place essays on Plato and classical Greece in the *Contemporary Review*, the journal whose religious constraints its editor, James Knowles, left to create the unconstrained *Nineteenth Century*. Pater's association with homosexuality and paganism in the 1860s and 1870s, and the popular association by the 1880s of homosexuality with Plato meant that publication of these essays was potentially damaging to Pater. The appearance of such work in the *Contemporary Review* might forestall adverse response. The only other essay Pater placed in the periodicals before the publication of *Plato and Platonism* in February 1893, 'A Chapter on Plato', appeared in *Macmillan's Magazine*, another journal calculated to attest to the respectability of the material.

The last category of significant omissions from *Appreciations* is politically topical material, in particular two essays which deal with the question of English literature and English in the university syllabus, which appeared in the *Guardian* and the *Pall Mall Gazette*. These may be thought too slight for inclusion, but fused in the way Pater constructed the essay on Coleridge, a suitable piece might have resulted, but for a different book. These pieces have no place in a collection of appreciations which identifies itself in its title as an aesthetic project pertaining to high culture. The contemporary debate about English is ruled out.

Pater's publishing tactics to avoid unwelcome exposure is well illustrated by his intervention in the debate following the appearance of *The Picture of Dorian Gray* complete in one issue of *Lippincott's Monthly Magazine* of July 1890; Ward Lock & Co. published an expanded version the following April, incorporating a preface of epigrams which Wilde published in March in the *Fortnightly*, no doubt as a trailer for the novel. He followed it up with *Intentions* in May. Yet the bulk of the reviews of *Dorian Gray*, and Wilde's public response to them – in letters to the press and in his essay 'The Soul of Man Under Socialism' which appeared in the

Fortnightly in February 1891 – were reviews of the periodical version, so sensational was the novel. A friend and former teacher of Wilde, Pater had been sent the novel in manuscript by Wilde for comment. We might expect that Pater would be one of the supportive reviewers. Certainly, Wilde himself might have such an expectation, as he had produced at Pater's delicate request (Evans: 106) a highly appreciative review of *Appreciations* in the *Speaker* just ten weeks before *Dorian* first appeared; its last paragraph concluded 'But in Mr. Pater, as in Cardinal Newman, we find the union of personality with perfection. He has no rival in his own sphere, and he has escaped disciples. And this, not because he has not been imitated, but because in art so fine as his there is something that, in its essence, is inimitable" (Wilde 1890a: 320). More praise for Pater was incorporated by Wilde in the novel itself as published in July 1890 and in *Intentions* which appeared in May 1891. The significance of this sequence is that, although requested by Frank Harris to write a review for the *Fortnightly* (Harris 1919: 215), Pater did not review the novel when it first appeared, when his favourable view might have been of value to Wilde (Harris 1918: 123).[6] Nor did Pater review it promptly when it appeared in volume form in April, or after *Intentions* was published in May. Only in November, seventeen months late, did Pater publish a review. However, few reviews of Wilde's novel *were* published, and Pater's reticence was unquestionably shared by other critics.

The debates of Pater, Arnold, and Wilde on the nature of the subject of literary discourse are implicated in the wider contemporary discussion of the institutional role of literature: whether the classical model was to continue to prevail with its constituent validated literary forms, or whether the subject was to be defined so as to have its roots in the vernacular language and its indigenous, modern form: 'The future of poetry is immense' Arnold proclaims at the opening of 'The Study of Poetry'. Wilde and Pater demur: 'imaginative prose', Pater declares in 'Style', 'being the special art of the modern world', and the *decay* of lying of more concern to Wilde than Arnold's search for truth. If the ideological alliances are clear, their material forms show that Arnold and Pater share a periodical discourse and a publisher which are repudiated by and repudiate Wilde. The positions of the three critics on the late Victorian spectrum of gender and discourses of gender figure significantly in the equation. Self-censorship as well as external censorship is evident. This examination of a cluster of critical writing in the late nineteenth century

reveals the processes of authorial management of publication and the
construction by authors of themselves as critics. In the interplay of
debate and cultural formations, detail of the relationship between the
history of periodical and book publication and kinds of discourse
emerges. Insofar as the construction of the twentieth-century canon
has marginalised Wilde's interventions, it reproduces the effect of
Victorian publishers, publications, and critics.

Notes

1. See Dowling, who suggests other antecedents for 'Style' as well,
    namely Newman's 'Literature' in *The Idea of a University*, George
    Moore's *Confessions*, and Flaubert: it has long been noted that sections
    of Pater's review of Flaubert's correspondence (25 August 1888) are
    embedded in 'Style' (December 1888).
2. In 1892 Osgood McIlvaine published *Tess of the d'Urbervilles*, Hardy's
    most controversial novel to date, published also in the US by Harper
    & Bros. For more on this London publishing house and its links with
    American publishing, see '*Harper's New Monthly Magazine*' in this
    volume.
3. See Parry's different estimate of *Macmillan's Magazine* (Parry 1989: 19).
4. In 'Pater's Reshuffled Text' Shuter shows (504) that Pater used
    passages from 'The Marbles of Aegina' in *Plato and Platonism*.
5. See Monsman (27) on this review.
6. Harris claims that Pater refused his request out of awareness of
    personal danger, and finally wrote a review out of a sense of duty.
    While the *Fortnightly* continued to publish Wilde's most controversial
    work after *The Picture of Dorian Gray* appeared, it never published a
    review of the novel.

Works Cited

Anon. (1891). 'Macmillan and Co', *Bookman* 1(Oct.), 34.
Arnold, M. (1960–77). *The Complete Prose Works of Matthew Arnold*. Ed. R.H.
    Super. 11 vols. Ann Arbor.
Arnold, M. (1888a). 'Shelley', *Nineteenth Century* 23(Jan.), 23–39.
Arnold, M. (1888b). *Essays in Criticism. Second Series*. London.
Arnold, M. (1887) 'Count Leo Tolstoi', *Fortnightly Review*. 48 old series
    (Dec.): 783–99.
Arnold, M., ed. (1881). *Poetry of Byron*. London.
Arnold, M., ed. (1879). *Poems of Wordsworth*. London.
[Arnold, M.]. (1871). 'A French Elijah', *Pall Mall Gazette* (24 Nov.), 10.
Arnold, M. (1865). *Essays in Criticism*. London.
Arnold, M. (1864a), 'The Literary Influence of Academies', *Cornhill
    Magazine* 10(August), 154–72.
Arnold, M. (1864b). 'The Function of Criticism at the Present Time',
    National Review 19(Nov.), 230–51.

Barthes, Roland. (1979). 'The Death of the Author' (1968), *Image-Music-Text*. London.

Burton, R., ed. (1885). *The Book of the Thousand Nights and A Night*. Vol. I. London.

Courthope, W.J. (1874). ['Modern Culture',] *Quarterly Review* 137(Oct.), 389–415.

DeLaura, David. (1966).'The Wordsworth of Pater and Arnold', *Studies in English Literature* 6, 651–67.

Dowling, Linda. (1984). 'Pater, Moore and the Fatal Book', *Prose Studies* 7(Sept.), 168–78.

Eliot, T.S. (1935). 'Religion and Literature', *Faith that Illuminates*. Ed. V.A. Demant. London, [29]–54.

Eliot, T.S. (1930). 'Arnold and Pater', *Bookman* 72(Sept.), 1–7.

Ellmann, R., ed. (1969). *The Artist as Critic*. London.

Evans, L. (1970) *Letters of Walter Pater*. Oxford.

Foucault, M. (1977). 'What is an author?' (1968), *Textual Strategies*. Ed. Josue V. Harari. Ithaca and London.

Gagnier, R. (1987). *Idylls of the Marketplace: Oscar Wilde and the Victorian Public*. London.

Harris, F. (1919) 'Walter Pater', *Contemporary Portraits*. 2nd series. New York, pp. 203–26.

Harris, F. (1918). *Oscar Wilde. His Life and Confessions*. 2 vols. New York.

Harrison, F. (1867). 'Culture: a Dialogue', *Fortnightly Review* 80 old series (Nov.), 603–14.

Huxley, L., ed. (1900). *Life and Letters of Thomas Henry Huxley*. 2 vols. London

[Jeyes, Samuel, H.]. (1890). 'The Picture of Dorian Gray'. *St. James Gazette* (24 June) 3–4.

Landor, W.S. (1826). *Imaginary Conversations of Literary Men and Statesmen*. 2nd edn. London.

Mansell, Darrel. (1986). 'Matthew Arnold's "Study of Poetry" in its Original Context', *Modern Philology* 83. 279–85.

Moore, G. (1888). *Confessions of a Young Man*. London.

Moore, G. (1976). *Literature at Nurse* (1885). Ed. Pierre Coustillas. Hassocks, Sussex.

Moore, G. (1884). 'A New Censorship of Literature', *Pall Mall Gazette* (10 Dec.), 1–2.

Monsman, G. (1980). *Walter Pater's Art of Autobiography*. New Haven.

Newman, J.H. (1873). 'Literature', *The Idea of a University Defined and Illustrated*. 3rd edn. Basil Montague Pickering. pp. 268–94.

Parry, A. (1989). 'The Intellectuals and the Middle Class Periodical Press: Theory, Method and Case Study', *Journal of Newspaper and Periodical History* 4.3, 18–32.

Parry, A. (1986). 'The Grove Years 1868–1883: A "new look" for *Macmillan's Magazine*?' *Victorian Periodicals Review* [Spec. No. Macmillan's] 19, 149–57.

Pater, W.H. (1891). 'A Novel by Mr. Oscar Wilde', *Bookman* 1(Nov.), 59–60.

Pater, W.H. (1889a). 'Noticeable Books: *Toussaint Galabru* by Fabre', *Nineteenth Century* 25(April), 621–3.

Pater, W.H. (1889b). 'The Bacchanals of Euripides', *Macmillan's Magazine* 60 (May), 63–72.

[Pater, W.H.]. (1889c). 'Ferdinand Fabre: an Idyll of the Cevennes', *Guardian* (12 June), 911–12.

Pater, W.H. (1889d). 'Noticeable Books: *A Century of Revolution* by W.S. Lilly'. *Nineteenth Century* 26(Dec.), 992–4.

Pater, W.H. (1888a) 'The Life and Letters of Flaubert', *Pall Mall Gazette* (25 Aug.), 1–2.

Pater W.H. (1888b). 'Style', *Fortnightly Review* 50 old series (Dec.), 728–43.

[Pater, W.H.]. (1886a). 'Four Books for Students of English Literature', *Guardian* (17 Feb.), 246–7.

Pater, W.H. (1886b). 'English at the Universities', *Pall Mall Gazette* (27 Nov.), 1–2.

Pater, W.H. (1880a). 'The Beginnings of Greek Sculpture', *Fortnightly Review* 33 o.s. (Feb., March), 190–207, 422–34.

Pater, W.H. (1880b). 'The Marbles of Aegina', *Fortnightly Review* 33 o.s.(April), 540–8.

Pater, W. H. (1877, 1888, 1890). *The Renaissance. Studies in Art and Poetry.* London.

Pater, W.H. (1876). 'The Myth of Demeter and Persephone', *Fortnightly Review* 25 o.s. (Jan., Feb.), 82–95; 260–76.

Pater W.H. (1873). *Studies in the History of the Renaissance.* London.

Shuter, W. (1989). 'Pater's Reshuffled Text', *Nineteenth-Century Literature* 43. 500–25.

Super, R.H. (1966). 'Vivacity and the Philistines', *Studies in English Literature* 6. 629–37.

Ward, T.H. (1880, 1883). *The English Poets.* 4 vols. London.

Ward, T.H. (1879). MS letter to Macmillan (24 Feb.). Macmillan Archive 59927. British Library.

Wilde, Oscar. (1891a). *Intentions.* London.

Wilde, Oscar. (1891b). *The Picture of Dorian Gray.* London.

Wilde, Oscar. (1891c). 'The Soul of Man Under Socialism', *Fortnightly Review* 55 o.s. (Feb.), 292–319.

Wilde, Oscar, (1890a). 'Mr. Pater's Last Volume', *Speaker* 1(22 March), 319–20.

Wilde, Oscar. (1890b). 'The Picture of Dorian Gray', *Lippincott's Monthly Magazine* 46(July), 3–100.

Wilde, Oscar. (1890c). 'The True Function and Value of Criticism', *Nineteenth Century* 28(July, Sept.), 123–47; 435–59 (title in *Intentions:* 'The Critic as Artist').

Wilde, Oscar. (1889a). 'The Decay of Lying: a dialogue', *Nineteenth Century* 25 (Jan.), 35–56.

Wilde, Oscar. (1889b). 'Pen, Pencil, and Poison: A Study in Green', *Fortnightly Review* 45 n.s. (Jan.), 41–54.

Wilde, Oscar. (1885). 'Shakespeare and Stage Costume', *Nineteenth Century* 17(May), 800–18 (title in *Intentions:* 'The Truth of Masks').

5

The Old Journalism and the New: Forms of Cultural Production in London in the 1880s

As a cultural form journalism may be seen as the commercial and ideological exploitation of the transient and the topical, a ceaseless generating or production of 'news' and novelty, involving a plurality of discourses, including literary and political. It has normally been seen by critics, however, as 'subliterary'; and the retrospective foregrounding of the novel as the dominant literary form of the nineteenth century must be predicated on the exclusion of the nonfictional prose that appeared so prodigiously in periodicals and newspapers in the forms of essays, reviews, leaders, and 'correspondence'. The 'New' Journalism was named in an article in the *Nineteenth Century* in 1887 by Matthew Arnold, a practitioner for more than thirty years of what by implication was the 'Old' Journalism, whose long-term project was to elevate his journalistic practice into 'criticism' and thus to the authority of literature. He places unsurprisingly the New Journalism at the bottom of a hierarchy of cultural forms, at the top of which is art, which, by his definition, outlives the specificities of history and is accessible only to the cultivated. In tainting the *Pall Mall Gazette* and journalism like it with the epithet *New* (a pejorative term for Arnold and much of his audience) and, by implication, designating a sector of the press Old and trustworthy, Arnold created a 'history' and a tradition that posit a decisive and anomalous transformation in the nature of journalism associated with the *Pall Mall Gazette* in the 1880s. I argue that the Old Journalism was by no means monolithic or stable in character or forms, that the *Pall Mall Gazette* shared this instability of ideology and form, and that in none of its forms was it aimed at a mass readership. Nor was this phase of journalism founded in the 1880s in the expected form of the cheap daily morning newspaper but appeared in the relative freedom of a 'quality' London evening paper and monthly and weekly periodicals, to some of which Arnold was a regular contributor. In short, transformations of journalism in the 1880s do not fit into the social, economic, and cultural hierarchies of Matthew Arnold's definition of the New Journalism. Nor do they accord with his apocalyptic notion of history, which posits sudden change.

THE OLD JOURNALISM

To indicate the difficulties of the notion of an Old Journalism counterpart to the New, it may serve to look at the dialectical relation of pairs of journals in mid-century: on the one hand, the *Saturday Review* predicating its existence in its first number on the 'autocracy' of *The Times*, and on the other, the 'hatching' from one journal of a second, which in part derived its identity from its rivalry with and its appropriation of its parent, as in the case of the emergence of the *Nineteenth Century* from the *Contemporary Review*.

The circumstances of origin of both the *Saturday Review* (1855) and the *Nineteenth Century* (1877) are set out elsewhere; what I want to note is the way both present themselves as offering a serious alternative to the existing cultural hegemony, the alternative in both cases being perceived as an independence that suggests representation and service of a readership beyond the limits of the existing rivals.

In the first number of the *Saturday Review* appeared the following:

> Even the direct rivals of the *Times* in the daily press impliedly admit its autocracy....Each of them has a small special following of Tories, or Radicals, or old ladies, or footmen, and to these they sometimes appeal, but the greater part of their occupation consists in echoing the small cries of the *Times*. As for the weekly newspapers, they have degenerated into the toadies of the great daily journal...we don't much mind it ourselves. We would infinitely sooner live under the *Times* than under the French Empire, or the American democracy (Anon. 1855: 2–3).

It is clear from the acerbic tone and the conclusion of this paragraph, in which the new paper's antipathy to both the right and the left is indicated, that the *Saturday Review* is making a bid for existing readers of *The Times* as well as for new ones among the highly literate and cultured, and for comparable status to *The Times*. What it did offer to both kinds of readers was serious attention to literature, science, and art as well as to politics, which was the plain focus of *The Times* and which was excluded from the *Athenaeum*, its main rival. The *Saturday* presents itself then as reformative, its innovations of wider subject matter and independence firmly associated with 'the great daily journal' in the challenge to its autocracy.

The relation of the *Nineteenth Century* to its predecessor, the *Contemporary*, is similarly one of continuity and innovation, but both the initial and the final relationship of the one to the other is far closer than in the previous example. On the one hand, the new monthly 'which will be conducted on the absolutely impartial and unsectarian principles which governed the *Contemporary*' (Athenaeum: 205) can be regarded as a clone of the old, having the same editor, price, size, and many of the most eminent contributors (including Gladstone) but a new publisher and title, whereas the new periodical is the parent that has refashioned itself to conform to the narrower interest (in theology) of its backers, publisher, and new editor. This is a pattern of transformation that was also to characterise the *Pall Mall Gazette* (only for a period the carrier of the New Journalism) in 1880, in 1889–90, and again in 1893. James Knowles, former editor of the *Contemporary* and the new editor of the *Nineteenth Century*, calls attention to his previous connection in the advertisement for the latter, 'Edited by James Knowles. Late of the *Contemporary Review*', (Athenaeum: 205) but he also introduces in the second number a structure of debate, the Symposium, which enhances the controversial impartiality of debate, an important factor in his departure from the parent journal, and which serves to distinguish it further from its now narrow forebear.[1] It may be observed that both the *Nineteenth Century* and the *Saturday Review* twenty-two years before it sought intellectual readers from among the new clerisy for publications that stressed respectively a more erudite, broader, and impartial orthodoxy and a complementary exhaustive pluralism. Significant transformations and innovation are evident in these journals, which inscribe social and cultural change in generated formations.

Nor are these phenomena anomalous in the long history of the Old Journalism; they are common occurrences. The entire history of the press is characterised by markers, or transformations, of equal significance to the changes in the newspaper press of the 1880s to which Arnold attached the epithet *new*.

Another aspect of the Old Journalism of the 1860s and 1870s that is of interest in connection with the New Journalism is the relation between the advocacy of signature and the disruption of the monolithic authority of a periodical, its fictional 'unity' such as that claimed by *The Times* and the earlier nineteenth-century quarterlies. Two anonymous writers of midcentury, in the weekly *Saturday Review* in 1855 and in the monthly *Cornhill* of 1862, and Leslie Stephen take pains to reveal the collective endeavour of the daily newspaper where, on the whole, a kind of anonymity was to continue far longer than in other sectors of the press.

The *Saturday* sceptically considers claims by *The Times* for its own unity.

The recent manifesto will have it that a daily journal, if not the labour of a single pen, is an emanation from a body of men, fused into the nearest possible approximation to unity. The most complete *solidarité* is suggested as existing between the producers of the leading articles – they have but one will, but one style, but one calibre of talent. A lively representative is provided for this mysterious entity in its Editor. He moves about in the world, and absorbs the intelligence which may be floating in the atmosphere of society; while the contributors are kept in bottles of smoke in the back-office, to be summoned forth like the genie in the *Arabian Nights*, when their giant energies are required for service.... A very little common sense will show the most cursory observer that the leading articles of a great newspaper cannot be written by less then six or eight gentlemen, who, as it is, are probably a great deal overworked for the perfect accuracy of their reasoning, and the perfect felicity of their illustrations. The power of selecting some one member of a literary staff for the treatment of a particular topic, must of course be vested in some one person, and this it is which constitutes the unity of a newspaper. The conductors of a daily journal who should attempt to secure a closer uniformity than this, would obtain it at the cost of the most important elements of intellectual power. There is no reason to believe the *Times* when it insinuates that such a blunder is committed in its own case. It strikes us that a man must have singularly little discrimination who cannot detect a variety of hands in the articles of the Leading Journal. The writers who rule us are clearly characterized by different degrees of ability, different degrees of taste, and, we must add, different degrees of morality....

We are not for a *loi de la signature*, which, for the excessive protection afforded by the present system, would substitute an excessive proscription. Still less would we imitate Mr DRUMMOND in giving publicity to the names which gossip associates with the Leading Journal – a course to be avoided for this reason among others, that you may chase, like Mr. DRUMMOND himself, egregiously to mistake your man.... We say to a confiding public – do your best to resolve the 'we' into 'I'.... Consider, above all things, that each of your literary rulers has been selected to govern you, not for his Absolute Wisdom, but for his peppery style and his fertility of allusion. Does Absolute Wisdom necessarily accompany these qualifications? Is Absolute Wisdom exactly compressible into a column and a bit, and does it assume those dimensions not less than three times a week. (Anon. 1855: 3)[2]

Leslie Stephen also comments on the editorial 'we' in his biography of his brother, James Fitzjames Stephen, in connection with Stephen in the *Pall Mall Gazette* and G.S. Venables of the *Saturday Review*. First Stephen:

The inexperienced person is inclined to explain it ['we'] as a mere grammatical phrase which covers in turn a whole series of contributors. But any writer in a paper, however free a course may be conceded to him, finds as a fact that the 'we' means something very real and potent. As soon as he puts on the mantle, he finds that an indefinable change has come over his whole method of thinking and expressing himself. He is no longer an individual but the mouthpiece of an oracle. He catches some inflection of style, and feels that although he may believe what he says, it is not the independent outcome of his own private idiosyncrasy. Now Fitzjames's articles are specially remarkable for their immunity from this characteristic....a large part of the 'Pall Mall Gazette' represented the individual convictions of a definite human being. (Stephen, L.: 216)

It is clear that Stephen is divided. About Venables Stephen remarks:

> One of his fancies... was a prejudice against the editorial 'we'. His remarks would take the form of a series of political aphorisms not so much expressing personal sentiment as emanating from wisdom in the abstract. They seemed to be judicial utterances from the loftiest regions of culture, balanced, dignified, and authoritative, though of course edged by a sufficient infusion of scorn for the charlatan or the demagogue. (Scott: 27)

Although Stephen is reluctant to cede the 'we' (he writes as an autocratic editor himself), I conclude that that is what he is moving toward.

The Cornhill article that appeared anonymously in July 1862 makes a forceful effort to demystify journalism for a family audience that is assumed to be ignorant of the subject but, significantly, interested in it. Conceived as a family magazine – which epithet would appear to include women in its intended readership – *Cornhill* consequently barred religion and politics. Journalism, because of its heady sense of an expanding readership among the middle classes, however, is regarded as suitable for exposé and familiarisation. This article offers a full, astute, and utilitarian analysis of the Old, higher journalism. Of leaders, or 'intellectual mincemeat' (Stephen, J.F.: 53), the author opines:

> The best leading articles that are written are nothing more than samples of the conversation of educated men upon passing events, methodized and thrown into a sustained and literary shape. They seldom or never rise above this level....The faculty of composing leading articles is merely a form of technical skill, like the handiness of a mechanic, the fluency and readiness of a barrister, or the delicate touch of a musician. (Stephen, J.F.: 55–6)

and of leader writers:

> They are, generally speaking, able and educated men, who, from some cause or other, have as it were been caught in some of the eddies of the main streams which are navigated in search of

wealth and distinction, or have reached comparatively early secure shelves which connect them with the business of life, and leave them a certain degree of leisure, and an appetite for some additional income. Our leading journalists are barristers waiting for business, or resigned to the want of it; clergymen unattached, who regret their choice of a profession which their conscience or inclination forbids them to practise, and which the law forbids them to resign; Government officials whose duties are not connected with party politics, and do not occupy the whole of their time; and in a few cases men of independent means, who have a fancy for writing, and who wish to increase their incomes. (Stephen, J.F. : 55–6)

Although the writer seems denigrating here, if ironic, it is clear that leader writers, authors of the form of journalism that he most exalts and respects, are drawn from other, establishment, professions or are 'independent'. The contempt of the leisured wealthy for the working journalist is more explicit in the hierarchy of the profession, contempt that emerges in his account of 'journalists, pure and simple' who are 'men who have no other occupation or position in life than those which they derive from newspapers, and no other prospect than those which lie in their success'. They are often of low beginning and without 'much other education than the newspaper itself supplies'. (Stephen, J.F.: 61) For these periodicals and all three authors the monolithic authority of the newspaper press is absorbing and challengeable; that the fascinating anatomy of the formation is revealed and exposed and celebrated and belittled is the inscription of the dialectic of the nascent profession in the mid-Victorian period.

If anonymity gradually lost ground during this period, signature *per se* was not a form of personalising that newspapers would readily adopt, although an increase in the personal in a different form was a characteristic that later came to be associated with the New Journalism in its use of interviews and personal detail. T.P. O'Connor writes:

The main point of difference is the more personal tone of the more modern methods. There was a day when any allusion to the personal appearance, the habits, the clothes, or the home and social life of any person would have been resented as an impertinence and almost as an indecency. (O'Connor: 423)

The author, a Gladstonian Liberal MP, and editor of the *Star*, writing in 1889, was particularly conscious of Parliamentary reporting in the past.

> You had no information as to how the speech was delivered or how received. You were told nothing of the personality of the persons who made the speech. There the long lifeless even columns were before you; the speech delivered in the dread void of the dinner hour to a select audience of the Speaker and the orator himself, filled the space in exactly the same kind of way as the speech that was punctuated by the ringing cheers of a crowded and deeply moved House. The words that came with the fierce fluency of an impassioned speaker were given in exactly the same way as the speech that was interrupted by hems and haws, or mumbled from an inarticulate throat. It was the same, of course, with public men throughout their whole life. (O'Connor: 423)

For the periodicals the argument for anonymity was often cast in terms of their desire to retain contributors from high places who without the protection of formal anonymity would no longer be at liberty to influence opinion covertly, if at all. And less eminent and more penurious contributors could use the system to write similar material for a variety of journals. But of course the implications for sales of named contributors also beckoned editors and proprietors. James Knowles's principled position of signature for his new *Nineteenth Century* later attracted the envious charge from the knowing perspective of a New Journalism publication, the *Review of Reviews*, that this was a policy of predatory 'tuft-hunting,' or attracting readers through names irrespective of the quality of their articles.

> Editing of the tuft-hunting variety seldom had a more successful exponent than Mr. Knowles. While other editors have sought for articles he has sought for names, and he has made a golden harvest out of the quest. He absolutely refuses to publish any anonymous or pseudonymous articles. Lord Tomnoddy's trivial inanities, if so be that they be signed 'Tomnoddy,' on this system are welcome, while the letters of 'Junius' or 'Ecce Homo' would be shown to the door. (*Index*: 24)

And Frederick Greenwood, founder of the *Pall Mall Gazette*, regretted what he regarded as the imposition of anonymity on the new venture: 'Anonymity was an inflexible rule for journalists then, and the public was slow to descry our galaxy of shining ones through the universal veil.' (Greenwood 1897a: 2)

It may be suggested that while the periodical press was moving, with reservations, toward signature and fragmented authority, the newspaper press came to occupy the middle ground between blanket anonymity and the vulgarity of named contributors: a kind of acknowledged collectivity that indicated the individuality of journalists by generic bylines (From our own Correspondent), regular columns, and occasionally outright signature; in the New Journalism these were supplemented with the foregounding of the editor and the personal details of individuals in the news as described by O'Connor above. An enhancement of the editorial power over the individual journalist's is evident in the greater extent of sub-editing in papers associated with the New Journalism (Massingham: 610), but at the same time, sub-editing attests to the collective nature of the enterprise. The entrepreneurial component of editing and publishing, the professionalisation of journalists and journalism, and the transition from the wealthy, educated, leisured reader to the working, literate reader of the middle classes are inscribed in the changing cultural formations of the periodical and newspaper press throughout the period. T.P. O'Connor, in his signed article on the New Journalism in the monthly *New Review* in October 1889, shortly after he began his stint as editor of the *Star*, attests to the self-consciousness of journalists about these changes.

A journal, whatever its views, should express them with the greatest lucidity and in the strongest and most striking manner it can command. We live in an age of hurry and of multitudinous newspapers. The newspaper is not read in the secrecy and silence of the closet as is the book. It is picked up at a railway station, hurried over in a railway carriage, dropped incontinently when read. To get your ideas through the hurried eyes into the whirling brains that are employed in the reading of a newspaper there must be no mistake about your meaning...you must strike your reader right between the eyes. The daily newspaper often appears to me to bear a certain resemblance to a street piano: its music is not classical, nor very melodious, and perhaps there is a certain absence of soul, but the notes should come out clear, crisp, sharp. (O'Connor: 434)

It is an excitement that Arnold recognises, resists, and discredits in a paragraph on the New Journalism in an article that he wrote on politics and Parliament in early 1887.

If we look more closely at the two examples of mid-century anonymity cited above in the *Saturday Review* and the *Cornhill*, an understanding of the ways in which anonymity functioned may result. The author of the *Saturday Review's* 'Our Newspaper Institutions' (1855) is Henry Maine, a jurist and one of the founders, with J.D. Cook, of the new weekly; the author of the *Cornhill's* 'Journalism' (1862) is James Fitzjames Stephen, also in law and a former student of Maine, who had introduced Stephen to Cook and professional journalism while Cook was editing the daily *Morning Chronicle*. Moreover, Stephen published three articles on journalism in 1859 in the *Saturday Review*, which he then abandoned between 1861 and 1863 for the *Cornhill*, enticed by better pay. But so closely was Stephen associated with the *Saturday Review* for most of his life that T.H.S. Escott wrote: 'He *was* the *Saturday Review*.' At the *Cornhill* Stephen was writing for Frederick Greenwood, the editor at that time but to found and edit the *PMG* in 1865. Stephen was a frequent contributor both to the early *Saturday Review* (from 1855 onward) and to the early *Cornhill*. The vigilant interest in the press maintained by the *Saturday Review* from its inception fostered Stephen's interest in it, led to the publication of his work about the subject, and directly contributed to the astute understanding of the press shown in the *Cornhill* article. My main interest here is to stress the continuities between different forms of journalism (a literary and political weekly, a monthly that eschewed politics, and two dailies); between the Old and New kinds, and between periodicals and newspapers; for in addition to the network of anonymous journalists revealed here, close links exist between the *Pall Mall Gazette* and the *Saturday Review* and the *Cornhill*, which Greenwood named as the daily *Pall Mall Gazette's* antecedents. And Stephen's frequent contributions to the *Saturday Review* and the *Cornhill* were succeeded by a significant commitment to the *Pall Mall Gazette* for which he wrote 'middles' intensively between 1865 and 1874.

THE NEW JOURNALISM

In his *Cornhill* article Stephen wryly drew attention to the way in which the press in 1862 legitimised cultural and economic hegemony:

In almost all the most influential papers, their tone [of the leaders] is conservative in the extreme upon all essential points, however they may favour political liberalism. It is easy to trace in every one proof of the fact that its author has a strong interest in the maintenance of all the chief principles and institutions of society, and a general conviction that alterations in them are rash... in a rich and intelligent country, a perfectly free press is one of the greatest safeguards of peace and order. Under such circumstances it is nearly certain that the ablest newspapers will be both read and written by and for the most comfortable part of society, and will err rather on the side of making too much of their interests than on that of neglecting them. (Stephen, J.F.: 57–8)

Fragmentation of this kind of complacency about the establishment press is signalled by, among other things, Greenwood's and W.T. Stead's challenges to the balance of the links between press and state in the *Pall Mall Gazette* and in 'Government by Journalism', [3] which appeared in the most outspoken and exposed of many articles written by Stead on aspects of this theme.

But the origins in 1865 of the *Pall Mall Gazette*, so closely associated with the development of the New Journalism in the 1880s, show the same alliance between the press and the status quo. Frederick Greenwood consciously modelled his new *Pall Mall Gazette* on the *Anti-Jacobin*, a weekly (fl. 1797–98), which appeared only when Parliament was sitting; founded by George Canning to combat radical views and initially edited by William Gifford, whose interest lay in literary parody and satire, it published the following considered view in 1801: 'We have long considered the establishment of newspapers in this country as a misfortune to be regretted, but since their influence has become predominant by the universality of their circulation, we regard it as a calamity most deeply to be deplored' (Williams: 18). *The Anti-Jacobin* attracted Greenwood through its liveliness and its 'quaintly graceful...old-fashioned form,' including its 'old-faced type, the lettering of the title, the italic capital head-line' (Greenwood 1897a: 1). Thus the *Pall Mall Gazette*, which was to develop some of the characteristics associated with the New Journalism and to occasion its denunciation, had its origins in a project that was in part regressive and conservative; the other principal model for Greenwood, more reformative than conservative but still looking to past achievements, was 'to bring into Daily Journalism that full measure of thought and culture which is now found only in a few Reviews' (Greenwood 1897b: 2). According to J.W.R. Scott, (Scott: 24) as well as Greenwood, these 'Reviews' were the *Saturday Review* and the *Cornhill.* Looking back in the *Review of Reviews* in 1893, Stead saw this as 'an attempt to wed literature to journalism' ([Stead] 1893: 143), a project that echoed the position of Arnold who contributed frequently to Greenwood's *Pall Mall Gazette.* All three models – the *Anti-Jacobin*, the *Saturday Review*, and the *Cornhill* – point to the continuation of the aim for an educated readership for the new paper, which was later to be associated with a 'clubland' readership as well as Arnold's 'demos'. Although various campaigns of the *Pall Mall Gazette* under Greenwood and Stead resulted in surges in readership figures, the normal figure lay between 20 and 30 000 of 'the political and literary classes' ([Stead] 1893: 146) at its height, after the price had dropped from 2d to 1d in 1882 and during Stead's stint as editor ([Stead] 1893: 154). It seems clear that many of the features (such as headlines, illustrations, and interviews) of this evening daily, which commentators other than Arnold (such as Greenwood, O'Connor, and Scott) came to associate with the New Journalism in their subsequent glosses on Arnold's epithet, did not as such enter into Arnold's definition. What seems to have triggered his alarm was the combination of the anomalous (and momentary) surge of the *Pall Mall Gazette's* circulation figures to 100 000 at the time of the week-long series of articles on 'The Maiden Tribute of Modern Babylon' in July 1885 and the subsequent agitation and legislation and Stead's high-pitched claim from prison on 'Government by Journalism' in May 1886. This momentary foray of the *Pall Mall Gazette* and its editor into the spheres of both mass readership and government in the face of Arnold's vehement opposition to the Gladstonian Liberals and Home Rule – the principal enemies in the article 'Up to Easter' in which the comments on New Journalism appear – and their habitual defence by Stead and the *Pall Mall Gazette* occasioned Arnold's attack. Arnold objects here to T.H. Huxley's claim in the previous number of the *Nineteenth Century* that 'the chief good is, in brief, freedom to say what he pleases' (Arnold: 629) and observes that in Ireland 'we might need a much more thorough repression of disorder than any we have had hitherto, but that much more thorough medieval measures were needed as well... whoever obstructs the repression of disorder, obstructs remedial measures' (Arnold: 631); in his glancing single long paragraph on the New

Journalism, a transference of tone and anxiety concerning the populous in Ireland to the restless 'demos' at home is evident. This is the group that Arnold inappropriately associates with the readership of the *Pall Mall Gazette*, which, under Stead, supported Home Rule. The passage, which follows in its entirety, shows the transference clearly and the origin of the association of the New Journalism with the masses before the publication of the halfpenny *Star* in 1888 and before the connection had in fact been made, although Stead's rhetoric in a number of articles had made the association. Whereas Arnold locates the 'critic' (read 'journalist') outside class and 'interest', as an 'alien' or part of the 'remnant' poised against the majority, Stead in 'Government by Journalism' writes provocatively from prison: 'an editor... must live among the people whose opinions he essays to express' (Stead 1886b: 654). Arnold writes:

> It has suited Mr. Gladstone and his friends to launch their new doctrine that no constraint must be put upon the Irish, and that there is no remedy for the disorder there until the national aspirations of the Irish are gratified. I have said that no reasonable man, who thinks fairly and seriously, can doubt that to gratify these aspirations by reconstituting Ireland as a nation politically, is full of dangers. But we have to consider the new voters, the *democracy*, as people are fond of calling them. They have many merits, but among them is not that of being, in general, reasonable persons who think fairly and seriously. We have had opportunities of observing a new journalism which a clever and energetic man has lately invented. It has much to recommend it; it is full of ability, novelty, variety, sensation, sympathy, generous instincts; its one great fault is that it is *feather-brained*. It throws out assertions at a venture because it wishes them true; does not correct either them or itself, if they are false; and to get at the state of things as they truly are seems to feel no concern whatever. Well, the democracy, with abundance of life, movement, sympathy, good instincts, is disposed to be, like this journalism, feather-brained....[4] (Arnold: 638–9)

In replies to Arnold's definition of the New Journalism, the case for the *Pall Mall Gazette's* accuracy and self-correction is the one consistent note. But even the month before Arnold's allegation of 'feather-brained' journalism, the *Saturday Review*, no friend of 'democracy', in an article titled 'The Old Journalists and the New,' singles out the authority of the new press for praise:

> Thanks to lavish expenditure and admirable management, the best of the contemporary journals are distinguished for their authority and impartiality. Partisans they are, no doubt; but, so far as facts go, they have found that frankness and honesty are the best policy. Indeed, they can hardly help themselves. Should they decline the explanation of an aggrieved opponent, who asserts that he has been misrepresented, it is sure to find publicity elsewhere, and thus permanent injustice is made practically impossible. (Anon. 1887: 579)

This article, which offers its own analysis of the New Journalism, puts its entire argument on the twin factors of technology and the cash to purchase it: 'The marvellous inventions of modern science are all in favour of the moneyed journals'. The cool regrets of this piece prompt me to suggest that one more factor might have contributed to Arnold's ire. It is that the *Pall Mall Gazette* campaigns, principally under Stead but also Greenwood, concerned themselves not only with Irish politics but also with the insalubrious such as divorce and child prostitution and slavery, subjects which, in their 'coarseness', went beyond the Dickensian exposure of shallow graves, debtor's prison, and workhouses. The *Pall Mall Gazette* strain of investigative journalism invokes the world of naturalism – the absorption in low life or the sordid – found in contemporary French novels by Zola and English novels by Gissing, Moore, and Hardy. Realism was a mode that Arnold never accepted, fixed as his attention was on the best that was thought and said; for him Chaucer lacked 'high seriousness'. In correspondence in 1886 he refers revealingly to both the American and the British press: from the United States he writes to Miss Arnold: 'The great relief will be to cease seeing the American newspapers... their badness and ignobleness are beyond belief', and he goes on immediately to link these qualities with the *Pall Mall Gazette:* 'They are the worst feature in the life of the United States, and make me feel kindly even to the *Pall Mall Gazette* by comparison with them.' To John Morley, former editor of the *Pall Mall Gazette*, he writes a terse P.S.: 'Under your friend Stead, the *P.M.G.*, whatever may be its merits, is fast ceasing to be literature.' In these remarks, with their invocation of nobility and literature in relation to the press, are inscribed the rhetoric and tenets of the high-culture hegemony now beginning to give way and the common contemporary identification of the New Journalism in Britain with American press methods. The increasing and public self-consciousness of journalists and journalism in the mid-century and after and the growth of a profession of journalism in the period highlight the confrontation between the hegemony of the clerisy and the competing ideologies of the emergent capital, electorate, and literate, which are significantly yoked by Arnold with the New Journalism. An alternative hegemony to that of Arnold and the clerisy is nascent here, promising alternative formations in the press. Moreover, although Arnold's besmirching of the New Journalism has dominated the tradition we know best, there existed at the time other critical discourses in which journalism was viewed more equitably.

The bouyancy and vigour of these groups in the period are manifest in the multiple forms that the *Pall Mall Gazette* took, the two look-alikes it generated, the *St. James' Gazette* in May 1880 when Greenwood was forced to leave the *Pall Mall Gazette* and the *Westminster Gazette* in January 1893 when E.T. Cook left; examination of the first issues of both shows similar and interesting claims to constitute the original publication under a new name, as in the case of the generation of the *Nineteenth Century* by the *Contemporary Review*. The most prodigious offspring, the lavishly illustrated monthly *Review of Reviews*, was created in 1890 when Stead left. A 'Character Sketch' of the *Pall Mall Gazette*, unsigned but apparently by Stead, appeared there in February 1893. In it the successive positions of the *Pall Mall Gazette* to date are limned:

This composite personality... has been almost Protean in its shapes. It has been a morning paper and an evening paper; it has been an eight-page, a twelvepage, and a sixteen-page paper. It has been a penny paper and a twopenny paper. It began as a kind of a Whig, and developed into a Conservative Jingo. It has been Cobdenite under Mr. Morley; Imperialist under his successor [Stead]; Ruskinian under Mr. Cook, and now it is Unionist and socialist under Mr. Cust. It has been the organ of the most antagonistic movements. Originally projected in jest as a paper written by gentlemen for gentlemen, it was for some years the daily champion of the Socialists of Trafalgar Square. At one time the sworn defender of the medical priesthood, with all

its shibboleths – vaccination, vivisection, and the C.D. Acts – it
became the enthusiastic champion of all the crusaders against all
the infamies of the doctors and of the police. It has been priggish
with the culture of the classes, and sensational with the passions
of the democracy. From being the cold cynical exponent of the
gospel of those whose motto is 'above all things no enthusiasm',
it became the eager and sympathetic exponent of every new fad
and the apologist for every new craze. ([Stead] 1893: 139)

Other forms its multiplication took were the publication of a
weekly distillation, the *Pall Mall Budget*, and of numerous 'Extras'
that consisted of reprints of single or successive articles associated
with one of the *Pall Mall Gazette's* campaigns. These appear to
provide a substantial additional income for the publisher and to
amount to increased circulation of a kind. Even the format of the
Pall Mall Gazette registers this consciousness of the proliferation of
the press; from 3 January 1881, shortly after Stead arrived to aid
Morley, a feature called 'Ideas from the Reviews', which echoed in
form the 'Epitome of [Political] Opinion' on pp. 2–3, appeared on
pp. 11–12 with the following rubic:

The multiplication of monthly magazines and reviews and the
increasing importance attaching to them as vehicles for the
responsible discussion of public questions and the ventilation of
new ideas have frequently been remarked. So many readers,
however, have neither time nor opportunity to master the contents of all the monthlies, that the following summary of the
thoughts embodied in the more important papers of three leading periodicals may, perhaps, be found useful. (Anon. 1881: 11)

The appropriation of this feature found commonly in weekly and
monthly journals of the period illustrates how the *Pall Mall Gazette*
had straddled the divide between the newspaper and the
periodical press from its inception; moreover, it brings into play
the sub-editing function to which producers of Victorian evening
papers (which summarised the news and opinions of the morning
papers) were accustomed. H.W. Massingham describes the process
of producing an evening paper as putting into framework and
focusing 'in a strong clear light the whole loose body of news and
opinion which the morning papers present' (Massingham: 608).
This form of short, pithy summary or commentary is seen pre-

eminently in the famous Occasional Notes columns of every *Pall Mall Gazette* number, the Notes consisting of a series of unheaded paragraphs, shapely and incisive, by different authors on various topics of the day. What these various forms – the Epitome, Ideas from the Reviews, and the Occasional Notes – share is the breaking up of the subject into short digestible units that contrast dramatically with the unbroken columns of type in morning dailies such as *The Times* and the *Daily Telegraph*. The incorporation of headlines of all kinds and of frequent illustrations in the form of maps, graphs, and line drawings also helped make the page accessible to less resolute reading at the end of the day and possibly by the family at home. These features suggest a potential readership that was to be articulated and pursued more fully later in the advertisements for *Review of Reviews* publications – 'Reading for the Million' (1895) – and for the Review itself – 'Best Magazine for Busy Men, Best for Busy Women' (1892). The conception and the format of the *Reviews of Reviews* as well are direct developments of the epitomising and informing of busy readers, which came increasingly to characterise the project of the *Pall Mall Gazette*, although the circulation figures of the *Pall Mall Gazette* at 30 000 per day set against the figure of 100 000 per month claimed by Stead for the *Review of Reviews* (Stead 1897: 1) suggest that the 6d monthly's circulation was far wider.

The last feature of the *Pall Mall Gazette* to which I want to draw attention is the Index and the extent to which it is indicative of the conscious interest of Stead and more generally this phase of the New Journalism in a particular segment of the readership, the journalist and the profession of journalism. In the *Leisure Hour* articles on 'The Great London Dailies' in 1892, Massingham singles out for special comment the archives of the *Pall Mall Gazette:*

[It] has not only a far better reference library than the 'Times', but it has a special kind of information bureau, presided over by a lady. In this a minute record is kept of notable events and speeches, and from it an army of facts and illustrations can be produced at a moment's notice to confound a political opponent, to show a statesman's record, and to instruct the public as to the progress of a great controversy. Out of this bureau has grown the series of 'Pall Mall' 'extras', without which... no politician's library is complete. (Massingham: 609–10)

After Stead left the *PMG*, the index disappeared.

I want to look briefly at the *Review of Reviews*, which began in 1890, before the onset of the *Daily Mail* in 1896, and survived until 1936. It was published initially by George Newnes who, beginning in 1881, published the highly successful and downmarket *Tit-Bits*, which the *Review* resembled only in the units in which its material was presented. Appropriating and legitimising the common practice of the day, *Tit-Bits* did not acknowledge the sources for its material, whereas Stead sought and obtained permission from his. *The Review* is notably oriented to the needs of the new profession of journalism and the exigencies of the methods of production for which rapid reference is essential. A paradigm of compilation, classification, and sub-editing, the *Review* manifests the same commitment to the improvement of access to sources as the *Pall Mall Gazette* indexes. Beginning in 1892, it published individual volumes of annual indexes to the periodical literature of the world, some of which included a Directory of Periodicals from which I quoted the account of James Knowles's 'tuft-hunting'; these give an excellent overview of the opinions of the first phase of the New Journalism about its predecessors and contemporaries, and the index of 1893 includes an article by its compiler, Miss E. Hetherington, on the indexing of periodicals. For some years, until February 1897, the *Review* included monthly lists of the contents of current periodicals. At the end of the May issue of volume I, for example, is a 15-page section of information clearly aimed at journalists. It contains a Diary for April (events, utterances and dates, Parliamentary record, and obituary), a classified list of 'The New Books and Blue Books of the Month', Contents of the Leading British Reviews, of the Current Quarterlies, Proceedings of Societies, Art in the Magazines, Music Magazines, The More Notable Articles in the Magazines, American Periodicals for April, and an Index to Periodicals.

The other group among the millions of which the *Review of Reviews* takes special notice is its women readers. Early in the run, in June 1890, 'Women and the Study of Contemporary . History. A Scholarship of £100 per Annum for three years' appeared, which describes its project as an effort to add to the numbers of female politicians. In the course of explaining the terms of the contest and the grant, the author of the article regrets the dearth of women readers of newspapers and women journalists, and points to particular features of the *Review of Reviews* – its character sketches and the monthly resumé of the 'Progress of the World' – which make it

more suitable for women readers than *The Times* or *Spectator*.
Knowledge of these two sections during six months is to constitute
the subject of a scholarship examination, success at which will be
rewarded by a three-year grant for study at Oxford or at home. More
equitable staffing of newspapers is envisaged: 'Some day, sooner or
later, the great Daily will be born which will represent both sections
of humanity in being staffed from top to bottom, half by men, half by
women. At present the supply of competent men for newspaper
work is far in excess of that of competent women.' ([Stead]. 1890: 471)
And the current situation of female readers of newspapers is detailed:

> The value of the present offer lies not so much in the benefit
> which it will bring to the one successful competitor as in the
> stimulus which it will give to the minds of the multitude of girls
> who, but for such a competition, might never have looked in the
> newspaper for anything but births, marriages, and deaths, the
> *Court Circular*, and personal gossip. ([Stead], 1890: 471)

The two women who shared the prize were both working women –
a journalist and a teacher.

Stead was not alone in believing that women were an untapped
source of newspaper reader. The February 1893 'Character Sketch'
of the *Pall Mall Gazette* in the *Review* included 'Mr. [E.T.] Cook's
Impressions' of the Magazine that he had just ceased editing. This
piece coincided with the launching in January of the second offspring of the *Pall Mall Gazette*, the *Westminster Gazette*, to which
Cook had moved. He writes:

> A general newspaper should be made interesting to everybody.
> The evening paper is mostly consumed in railway trains; we
> want the *Westminster Gazette* to be taken home. We shall try and
> have something every day to interest the city man; but we want
> him to say as he turns over some of its pages, 'I must take this
> home to show my wife and children'. And once taken home the
> *Westminster* will try and deserve to be read through. ([Cook]: 156)

The identity of these two groups of readers, journalists and lower
middle-class women, who lie within the compass of 'busy men' and
'busy women', perhaps offers the best gloss on the lower social and
educational limits of the readership aimed at by this phase of the
New Journalism.

It would seem that substantial continuities in cultural formations and transformations exist between the Old Journalism and this phase of the New and that the process of change is gradual rather than sudden. Applied to the journalism of the 1880s before the *Star*, it would seem that Arnold's definition is a misnomer. But this fear-inspired definition made by an establishment-based journalist did correctly anticipate the mass journalism to come in 1888, the year of Arnold's death. Moreover, discourses counter to Arnold's existed in the 1880s, which explicitly opposed disinterestedness and the impersonal – 'impersonal journalism is effete' (Stead 1886a: 663), Stead writes – and commended rather than castigated the New Journalism's 'crisp condensed laconic style of the telegraph'. (Stead [1892]: 23)

Notes

1. Moreover, he *retrospectively* involves the first number in the Symposium format by following up Gladstone's review of a book on the influence of authority on matters of opinion with an article on the same subject in the second and a reply in the third, and through the structure of the Contents page of volume one, which is organised by subject.

2. For an earlier metaphor of the press as government, see Bagehot, and compare Stead (1886b).

3. In his suggestion that the press has appropriated the functions of government, Stead echoes Bagehot's 'The First Edinburgh Reviewers,' another document of the Victorian press in which an attempt was made to mark off the journalism of mid-century from that of its immediate predecessor. Bagehot's piece, which appeared in a prominent position as the first article in the second number of the *National Review* (1855) was occasioned by the publication of the collected periodical essays of these reviewers; his review was recirculated through republication in 1878 and again in 1884 in Bagehot's own collected periodical essays, *Literary Studies*. In it Bagehot writes on the instruction by the press of 'the mass of influential persons, to the unelected Commons, the unchosen Council, who assist at the deliberations of the nation' (Bagehot 1884: 3–4).

4. Typical of the *Nineteenth Century* symposium format, this article is followed by one on a related subject – the Coercion Bill – and an article by Gladstone (on Apollo), as well as another shorter reply to Huxley and an article on 'The Fallacies of the French Press', another related subject.

Works Cited

Anon. (1887). The Old Journalists and the New', *Saturday Review* LXIII (23 April), 578–9.
Anon. (1881). 'Ideas from the Reviews', *Pall Mall Gazette* (3 Jan.), 11–12.
Anon. (1855). 'Our Newspaper Institutions', *Saturday Review* I(3 Nov), 2–3.
Arnold, Matthew. (1887). 'Up to Easter', *Nineteenth Century* XXI, 629–43.
Athenaeum (1877). Advertisement (10 Feb.), 205.
Bagehot, Walter. (1855). 'The First Edinburgh Reviewers', *National Review* I(Oct.) 253–84.
[Cook, E.T.] (1893). 'Mr. Cook's Impressions', *Review of Reviews* VII, 155–6.
Greenwood, F. (1897a). 'Birth and Infancy of the Pall Mall Gazette', *Pall Mall Gazette* (14 April), 1–2.
[Greenwood, F. (1897b). 'Prospectus [1865]', *Pall Mall Gazette* (14 April), 2.
Index to the Periodical Literature [for 1891.] (1892). *Review of Reviews*, London.
Massingham, H.W. (1891–2). 'The Great London Dailies: The Penny Evening Papers. – The "Pall Mall Gazette", *Leisure Hour* XLI(July), 607–10.
O'Connor, T.P. (1889). 'The New Journalism', *The New Review* I, 423–34.
Scott, J.W.R. (1950). *The Story of the Pall Mall Gazette*. London.
Stead, W.T. (1897). 'After Seven Years', *Review of Reviews* XV (Jan.) 1–16.
[Stead, W.T.]. (1893). 'The "Pall Mall Gazette"', *Review of Reviews* VII (Feb) 139–54.
Stead, W.T. (1892). 'How to Become a Journalist', *A Journalist on Journalism*, ed. with introd. E.H. Stout. London. pp. 20–6. Originally in *The Young Man* (Jan. 1891).
[Stead, W.T.] (1890). 'Women and the Study of Contemporary History', *Review of Reviews* I (June), 470–1.
Stead, W.T. (1886a). The Future of Journalism', *Contemporary Review* L(Nov), 663–79.
Stead, W.T. (1886b). 'Government by Journalism', *Contemporary Review* XLIX(May), 653–74.
Stephen, L. (1895). *Life of Sir James Fitzjames Stephen*. London.
Stephen, J.F. (1862). 'Journalism', *Cornhill* VI, 52–63.
Williams, R. (1970) 'Radical and/or respectable', *The Press We Deserve*, ed. R. Boston. London. pp. 14–26.

6

Harper's New Monthly Magazine: American Censorship, European Decadence, and the Periodicals Market in the 1890s

Startling differences between two late twentieth-century views of *Harper's New Monthly Magazine*, by Larzer Ziff and Barbara Perkins, suggested to me the theoretical problem of how meaning is constructed in periodical studies – from peaks in a given serial's circulation figures (Perkins) or in comparison with figures from other adjacent serials (Ziff). Is *HNMM* in the 1890s at the height of its great success as Perkins implies on the basis of high circulation figures; or, as Ziff argues in a comparative study which adduces ample evidence of systematic editorial censorship in a quartet of older monthlies, is *Harper's*, along with the *Atlantic*, *Scribner's*, and the *Century*, on its way out, victim of of a 'scrupulous avoidance of the startling' (Ziff, 123)? Against Ziff's contention may be set a facet of *Harper's* November 1893 number – the publication in a family magazine of two pieces associated with European decadence by British authors. I propose to view the cultural formation of which *HNMM* is a part, to set the hypotheses of Perkins and Ziff against a contents analysis of this issue, and to assess the functions of British writing about European decadence in an American family periodical.

For the publishing house of Harpers & Bros., the 'transatlantic connection' was first and last economic and commercial. Two conditions of the period made the publication of British writing in the United States extremely profitable: first, until 1891 the dearth of international copyright law, meaning that British material might be free or cheap, without the encumbrance of royalties, and second,

Figure 6.1 *Harper's New Monthly Magazine.* Cover.

that peculiar legacy of revolution – a vestigial, high cultural value attached to the ejected imperial power, at the expense of the native. Work by British authors sold exceedingly well in the new country. *All* of the fiction in the first number of *Harper's New Monthly Magazine* in June 1850 was British. But profit was not confined to periodical publication. Like many mid-century publishers in the US and Britain, Harper & Bros.' stable of periodicals – *Harper's Monthly, Weekly, Bazar,* and later Harper's *Young People's Magazine* – was accessory to their publication of books, and served their list in a variety of ways. New authors were attracted and auditioned in the periodicals, and works of successful authors were trailed in one or another of the journals prior to book publication; with British authors Harper's exacted two publications – periodical and book – very cheaply from the advanced sheets they procured, without paying royalties on book publication.

When the generously illustrated *Harper's New Monthly Magazine* began in 1850, it bid for a wide, comparatively popular, family audience of literate readers, and printed 7500 copies; within six months it was selling 50 000 copies monthly, with an average of 110 000 per month between 1850 and 1865. Although the *Magazine* abandoned its exclusion of American fiction soon after 1850, under a barrage of native protests, it stalwartly maintained perceptible links with Britain, both in continuing to include British authors and in paying regular attention to social and political – as well as cultural – events in Britain. In that sense even the monthly publication of the Harper firm functioned as a purveyor of British news, a role that the Harpers were to emphasise in an anonymous publicity pamphlet as late as 1889, when the encroachment of newspapers began to bite. From 1880 an English edition of *HNMM* appeared in the UK with English advertisements, published by Sampson Low who were Harper & Bros.' British agents at the time, and from May 1891 by Osgood, McIlvaine, their new agents.[1] I describe the edition as 'English', although for some time after 1880 it is described variously in correspondence between Harper and their agents and authors as 'European' and 'English', only eventually subsiding to the limited ambitions of the latter[2] in the Correspondence, but 'European' on the title page. Promulgating the transatlantic character of its contents, only the wrapper of the English edition sported parallel views of the New York harbour and skyline with that of London.

Bibliographically, some English writing in the early numbers appeared in the English edition alone. But this distinction soon lapsed, and the low profile of the succession of editors in Britain (R. R. Bowker to launch it, John Lillie from 1880, Andrew Lang from 1884 intermittently to November 1889, and unknown after this date), at the time and in subsequent accounts, suggests that the power base of *HNMM* remained firmly in the US with Henry Mills Alden the American editor, and Harper the American publisher.[3] Lang's account in his letters of his stint as English editor is filled with the frustration of powerlessness, from the beginning (20 April 1885 when he is 'horribly hustled with *Harper's* and can't attend to what interests me, books no one wants'), to the end (18 November 1889: 'I have ceased editing for Harper's, as they very naturally thought the game not worth the candle. The M.S.S. were never accepted, and I don't think I had 10 of ordinary magazine calibre all the time I had been occupied with them' Demoor 1989: 66, 102).

Why did the Harpers decide to publish in Britain in 1880? First, to increase circulation there by purveying American news and authors, as well as by attracting British readers with British authors, such as Hardy, Symons, and Pater whose fiction and essays *HNMM* subsequently published. At the launch in 1880, 10 000 copies of the English/European edition were printed, and in January 1893, 10 000 was still the basic circulation, although they were hoping to reach 25 000 a month for ordinary numbers and 35 000 at Christmas (*Archives.* Reel 2, Vol. 6, 520–2). For American readers, the British base of an edition and editor would upgrade the *Magazine's* links with British authors and news. Here, it is interesting to note the existence of American editions of British periodicals such as *Longman's Magazine,* so that when *Harper's Bazar* offers to publish 'White Heather' by the British author William Black, the agreement stipulates that the American edition of *Longman's Magazine* is not to precede the appearance of the *Bazar* instalments. In this way, Harper could more effectively publicise their publication in book form of the American editions of British writers, and thus at once gain better book-sales *and* attractive and cheap copy for their journals. One historian of the firm alleges that from the first the link of the English edition of *HNMM* with Harper's *book* list was perceived by British publishers:

From the beginning the *Magazine* was popular in England and soon outsold its competitors, including the American *Century* [formerly *Scribner's*] and the English *Illustrated Magazine*, which was started in 1883 to dislodge such rivals from overseas. In fact, the launching of an English edition of *Harper's Magazine* worried the London *Bookseller*, which suspected that Harper's next step would be to publish books in England as well. It queried, "What is to prevent the Harpers from competing with the Longmans for the control of the works of future Macaulays?" (Exman: 160 –1).

By 1904 Frederick Macmillan indicates that the use of magazine serialisation as a lure to secure book publication was still current practice:

> It is a very common plan with publishers of magazines to try to use them as a lever for getting books which would not otherwise come to them.... If the *Cornhill* and *Monthly Review* are serious in wishing to have your novel as a serial, they will no doubt give way about the book rights, if you stand firm. (Macmillan: f.80)

I think too that Harper used the British base of the *Magazine* to recruit British authors for *all* their periodicals. The draft of an 1889 contract with W.D. Howells shows that the firm attempts to bind him to give them first refusal of all his periodical work, for placement indifferently in the Harper journals as they see fit, despite differential rates of pay (Archives, Reel 3, 227b). This Howells refuses to do! Harper also gains advertising revenue from the English edition, as the prominence of advertising arrangements shows in the various contracts with Sampson Low and Osgood & McIlvaine, their English agents.

Additionally, until January 1892, when the Chace Act of copyright of 1891 took effect, the English edition of *Harper's NMM* was unaffected by copyright as the sheets were printed in the US [4]; so, through the English edition the firm recruited more British writing at cheaper rates than American, and continued to pay no royalties on book publication. J. Henry Harper's account in 1912 of the benign role played by Harper & Bros. in the campaign for international copyright in the US is contested by a later, disinterested historian who claims that 'The American firm which had benefitted most handsomely over the years from such piracy was

Harper & Bros. (West: 363). From the position of American campaigners for copyright, it was 'the perfidy of the Harpers' (West 361) which was uppermost:

> [Putnam] and his supporters in the industry were never able to overcome the influence in Congress of typesetters' unions, nor were they able to persuade the Harpers, who were the most active and successful of the genteel pirates, to support their cause. Indeed it was largely because of clandestine opposition by the Harpers that Putnam's last effort to get a bill out of the Judiciary Committee and onto the floor of Congress failed in 1872. (West: 361)

However, as soon as the Act came into effect, Harper offered to pay Thomas Hardy 15 per cent royalties for book sales in addition to the £298.8s stipulated in the original agreement for *Tess* (*Archive* Reel 2, A5, 451). By 1893 HNMM was reputed to pay its contributors well. The rates quoted to Howells in October 1889 for his 1891 contract were $50 per 1000 words for HNMM and $30 per 1000 for *Bazar*, *Weekly*, and *Young People* (*Archives*, Reel 3, 227a), with the differential being explained as 'an extra allowance for the English market'. In 1892 Richard Harding Davis's pay was $15 per column and $25 per column with illustrations. By this reckoning Peter and Symons would have received at least (in 1893) $350 and $325 respectively.

The difficulty that seems to remain with publication in the older American monthlies is censorship. Examples, numerous and well-known, include the publication in 1894–5 of *Hearts Insurgent* [*Jude*] in *HNMM*, and of *Tess* in 1891 when Hardy placed two chapters excluded by *Harper's Bazar* and the *Graphic* in other periodicals, one of which was Frank Harris's libertine *Fortnightly Review* – which also published Oscar Wilde's 'Prologue to *Dorian Gray*' in 1894. The Harpers also censored the periodical version of a novel by Alphonse Daudet translated by Henry James by simply omitting a doubtful chapter without consulting James, to whom it was explained in July 1890 that the chapter would be restored in Harper's book publication of the novel:

> We have never for a moment thought of omitting the chapter from the volume. As to the omission from the MAGAZINE ... we would not have sacrificed matter and illustrations for which we had paid so much without some weighty reason for doing so.

There were passages in the chapter which would give offence to a large number of our Christian readers. (Alden, quoted in Harper: 620)

There was nothing covert about this American censorship – it was an avowed and articulated policy within which journalists and authors worked. Alden writes unapologetically to a new contributor to *HNMM* on May 26, 1880 as follows:

> I will only ask you to bear in mind the audience of the Magazine, in the preparation of your article – just as I must in considering it ... You will have this consolation for any sacrifice you may make in adapting the matter to our Magazine – viz., that in that periodical you will bring your subject before a million of readers; & I would not have one of them wish to skip a paragraph. (Alden)

Hardy published repeatedly with Harper, well aware of the rules and constraints; he remained notably cordial in his dealings with Harper's agents in 1892 after the serial publication of *Tess* in the *Bazar* and was ready to place his next work with them for journal and book publication (*Archives*, Reel 2, A5 452). One reviewer of *Tess*, George Douglas in *The Albemarle*, reads the novel itself as a self-conscious intervention by Hardy in the ongoing debate about censorship and the future of fiction in Britain:

> an interest of a very special kind attaches to the book now under consideration. It is an open secret – a secret which any discriminating reader of the reviews may possess – that for some time past Mr. Hardy's views have been tending to a more out-spoken attitude towards social questions than the English fiction of our time has as yet ventured to assume. In his "faithful presentment of the pure woman, Tess", he has, in the fitting season, shown the courage of his opinions .... That he has taken a step so fraught with possibilities to the future of the English novel without due consideration, no competent judge will for one moment suspect; indeed, the book in which he has taken it has, throughout, the insistent force of a heartfelt utterance which has been long brooded over in silence. (Douglas: 71)

One must assume that Hardy put up with Harper's and its British partners Osgood McIlvaine because in his considered opinion these conditions of publication were the best available for the kind of fiction he wanted to write. Simon Gatrell comes to a similar conclusion, and points out that in April 1894, in respect of *Jude*,

> Hardy wrote to Harper to say that the serial he was writing for them was not after all conforming to the certification of inoffensiveness that he had given them, and offered either to cancel the contract, or to allow them to emend for the serialization as they saw fit. Harper chose to ask for changes, and Hardy made them, as he had made them for *TD* [*Tess*] and *GND* [*Group of Noble Dames*]. (Gatrell: 238)

William Dean Howells, the renowned author of realist fiction and distinguished journalist and critic, who contributed to *HNMM* from 1882 for over a decade, matter-of-factly recounts how censorship figured in his initial interview, and how it was achieved: 'Mr Harper skilfully led up to what a man might or might not say in the Harper periodicals. There appeared to be very few things ... [such as] the subject of capital punishment, ... at any approach to which it "rang a little bell." ... I tried to catch the tinkle of the little bell when it was not actually sounded' (Harper: 321–2; Ziff: 126). But for all Howell's practice of self-censorship apparently claimed here, and seized upon by Ziff, Howells' preceding sentence attests to 'the good business ... with which the House left me free to say what I pleased on whatever topic I chose to talk about' (Harper: 321). Certainly Howells' reiterated defence of realism and denunciation of 'the sentimental and romantic in fiction' in his *HNMM* column, 'The Editor's Study' (1885–91) attracted the charge from an English critic of *Criticism and Fiction* that in these pieces Howells had 'placed himself beyond the pale of decency' (Harper: 322). Howells' work for Harper does not seem to have suffered from external censorship.

If from the position of the late twentieth century, Ziff may adopt a position of indignation regarding the stated position on censorship of Harper & Bros., at the end of the nineteenth century, in its own period it can be argued that *HNMM* did carry as its principal staff critic a defender of the new naturalism. Even in retrospect J. Henry Harper, writing in 1912, is conscious of the controversy that Howells' criticism elicited: 'Howells is not invariably a favorite critic, because he is a man of very strong views as to the use or misuse of literary talents' (Harper: 328). If Howells denounced Dickens and Thackeray in the *Century* (November 1882) in the name of realism, he also embraced the work of Tolstoi and Flaubert (May 1889, 983) and of Zola. Another demonstration of tolerance by Harper & Bros. in these years is the divergence of published opinion in its journals and company practice. Denunciation of Hardy's conduct of the narrative of *Tess* (published in periodical and book form by the firm) is expressed anonymously in [Charles Dudley Warner's] 'Editor's Study' column of the June 1892 issue of *HNMM* ([Warner 1892]: 152–3). In August 1894 the same anonymous author in the same column attacks the vulgarity of the contemporary English novel.

> Because the English have graciously borrowed from us our feature of personal journalism, does courtesy require us to accept and adopt their style of personal and socially vulgar fiction? We think not. We will do almost anything to keep the peace and to keep the good-will of our English cousins, but it is asking too much that we should like a good deal of the fiction which is largely sold and much talked about in London, which our own publishers hesitate to reproduce in paper even, and which the English themselves would call "nasty" if it were produced elsewhere. It is hardly safe in these days to give an English novelist free access to the general American public through the pages of a popular magazine without careful scrutiny.' ([Warner 1894]: 476)

In December of the same year the first instalment of Hardy's *The Simpletons* (later *Hearts Insurgent* and then *Jude*) appeared in *HNMM*. The publishers appear to have permitted adverse criticism of their own policy and lists in their own periodicals. Moreover, for a certain period, between 1885 and 1889, two of the paid staff of *HNMM* – Howells, whose fiction and criticism appeared regularly, and Andrew Lang, the designated English editor – were in public debate about the merits of realism and romance, with Howells based in *HNMM's* 'Editor's Study' and Lang 'At the Sign of the Ship' in *Longman's Magazine*. That Alden took measures to prevent internal dissonance showing explicitly within the *Magazine* is shown in 1891 when he suppressed an attack by Howells on Lang, demurring that Lang was 'so good a friend of the Magazine in England' (Howells: 300 n. 3, quoted Demoor 1987: 420).

The terms in which censorship is defended by Alden are of particular interest to the theory of periodical reading. Both Henry

Mills Alden, editor of *Harper's NMM* for 50 years (1868/9–1919), and his contemporary Roger Burlingame, editor of *Scribner's*, distinguish between the means of acquiring access to a book – choice – and periodical material – often inadvertently stumbled upon by ignorant readers. 'The buyer of a magazine buys a variety of literature. He may buy it for one thing, yet have another, for which he also pays, thrust upon him. The buyer of a book on the other hand knows – or should know what he is getting in for' (Burlingame: 83; Ziff: 124). William Locker of the *Graphic*, in a letter to Hardy of 1889, also posits a periodical readership which unexpectedly stumbles on unwelcome material. He genders this readership explicitly, male at the point of acquisition, payment and club readership, and female at the family reading:

> I have now read "A Group of Noble Dames" and am sorry to say that in the main I agree with our Directors' opinion. In the matter of tone they seem to me to be too much in keeping with the supposed circumstances of their narration – in other words to be very suitable and entirely harmless to the robust minds of a Club smoking-room; but not at all suitable for the more delicate imaginations of young girls. Many fathers are accustomed to read or have read in their family circles the stories in the *Graphic*; and I cannot think that they would approve for this purpose a series of tales almost every one of which turns upon questions of childbirth, and those relations between the sexes over which conventionality is accustomed (wisely or unwisely) to draw a veil. (Quoted by Gatrell: 81)

To Hardy in 1894, Alden also invokes the American family circle as the protected audience whose 'purism' must be respected (Harper: 530; Ziff: 123), and distinguishes coolly between the 'artist's point of view' (Hardy's) and the editor's. However, one of Alden's assertions to Hardy – that 'purism ... is undoubtedly more rigid here than in England' (Harper: 530; Ziff: 123) – indicates a difference of editorial rhetoric (if not practice) in Britain and America, rather than the doubtful proposition that English readers were more tolerant than Americans. Nor is there good reason to believe that in this latter part of the century British publishers were more willing than their American counterpart to countenance publication of morally unorthodox material. *Tess* was turned down for serial publication in Britain by three publishers (Tillotson, John

Murray and Macmillan) before acceptance of a bowdlerised version by the *Graphic* and *Harper's*. Yet the text published by Harper in the United States was less bowdlerised than that appearing in Britain in the *Graphic*: 'when the proof-sheets of *Tess* in the *Graphic* were sent to America for *Harper's Weekly*, Hardy felt sufficiently certain of the capacity of American audience[s] to tolerate a greater degree of realism in sexual matters to omit the episode with the fake registrar' (Gatrell: 95). *Tess*, and Oscar Wilde's *Intentions* for example, rejected by British publishers, were taken on in 1892 and 1891 respectively by a new publishing firm in Britain, Osgood, McIlvaine, a venture backed and in part staffed by Harper & Bros. who employed the new company as their British agent.[5]

From the 1880s, British novelists and critics were articulating their impatience with the tyranny of the censorship imposed by circulating libraries in Britain (such as Smith's and Mudie's) on the morality of the English novel, with authors indebted to naturalism such as George Moore and Hardy particularly bitter. Moore's pamphlet *Literature at Nurse* in 1885 and Hardy's contribution to a forum on censorship in the *New Review* in 1891 suggest that the *practice* of British publishers was perceived by British authors as no better than that of publishers in the US. It could be said that in the last two decades of the century, the house of Harper in its periodicals is distinguished by publication of not only some of the most renowned works of American naturalism and its critical defence (by W.D. Howells), but also of Hardy's fiction and of British decadence (by Symons and Pater). As can be seen, the magazine format which *Scribner's* Roger Burlingame used to justify censorship also permitted inclusion of this range of risky work which the bulk of the contents obscured. The trailer for the contents of the November 1893 issue of *HNMM*, which carries Pater's recherché story 'Apollo in Picardy' and Symons's essay on decadence, indicates the proportion and nature of the other articles in the number (Figure 6.2).

Ziff's construction of the periodical history of the nineties pits four established journals characterised by 'pruning-hook editing' (Ziff: 132 from Ford: 173), of which *Harper's NMM* is one (the others being *Century*, *Scribner's* and the *Atlantic Monthly*), against the onslaught of the new mass journalism represented by *McClure's*, *Munsey's*, *Lady's Home Journal*, *Cosmopolitan*, and a revived *Saturday Evening Post* which catered for a mass rather than educated readership. It is presumably through this structure of comparison

HARPER'S MAGAZINE
∴ FOR NOVEMBER ∴

Mr. Edwin Lord Weeks will continue his narrative of a journey **From the Black Sea to the Persian Gulf** by caravan. The story given in this paper covers the adventures of the trip **From Tabreez to Ispahan,** and the author's admirable illustrations are novel pictures of caravan life, and of scenes in Persian cities, and in the country of the Kurds.

In **London in the Season,** Mr. Richard Harding Davis will treat London as a show town, describing scenes on the Row, in the Parks, and in the House of Commons. The article is picturesquely illustrated by Mr. W. Hatherell.

Mr. Julian Ralph will describe life **Along the Bayou Teche,** the new enterprise in the plantations, the old mansions, the Acadian country and people; and all these features will be characteristically illustrated by Mr. W. T. Smedley.

One of the liveliest questions concerning our Western territory is that relating to the system of land tenure in the Indian Territory. Mr. R. W. McAdam, in an illustrated paper entitled **An Indian Commonwealth,** will discuss this question in all its bearings.

A novel species of recent literature in France and England, commanding the attention of thoughtful critics—represented in the writings of the Goncourt brothers, in the poetry of Verlaine and Mallarmé of Paris, and of W. E. Henley of London, and in the peculiar plays of Maeterlinck—will be considered by Mr. Arthur Symons in an interesting article entitled **The Decadent Movement in Literature,** and illustrated by portraits of the writers treated.

In connection with this article, especial interest will attach to a remarkable example of the highest order of this class of literature, not "decadent," however, in any proper sense, but rather poetically interpretative, presented in Mr. Walter Pater's new "imaginary portrait," **Apollo in Picardy.**

Col. Theodore A. Dodge, U.S.A., will contribute a striking article, beautifully illustrated, on **The Riders of Turkey.**

In fiction the Number will be peculiarly rich, including besides Mr. Pater's brilliant imaginative sketch already mentioned, the conclusion of Mr. William Black's charming novel, **The Handsome Humes;** a New York story entitled **The Frog that Played on the Trombone,** by Mr. Brander Matthews, illustrated by Mr. C. D. Gibson; **Em'ly,** a humorous Wyoming sketch by Mr. Owen Wister, illustrated by Mr. H. M. Wilder; and a society story entitled **Vorbei,** by Annie Nathan Meyer.

Mr. Frederic R. Coudert will consider the subject of **Arbitration**—its historic development and its present importance.

A beautiful poem by John Hay entitled **Love and Music** will be attractively illustrated by Mr. W. T. Smedley.

· Mr. Charles Dudley Warner, in **The Editor's Study,** will consider criticism in the United States; and **The Editor's Drawer,** with Mr. Thomas Nelson Page's humorous introductory story and other entertaining features, will conclude a very brilliant and attractive Number.

Subscription price, $4 oo a Year.

Figure 6.2 Trailer from *Harper's New Monthly Magazine,* 1893. Decadence amid family reading.

that Ziff generates the notion 'staid' to characterise the older journals. Yet Perkins argues that *Harper's Magazine* 'reached its high point in the 1890s' (Perkins: 168), and the self-estimate of *Harper's NMM* in a promotion pamphlet of 1889, 'The Making of a Great Magazine,' is clearly an attempt to purvey itself as a rival to the new journalism as a source of information about current affairs:

> If the department of editorial comment in our daily journals be for the moment ignored, and their character as purveyors of current news alone considered, HARPER'S MAGAZINE is journalistic. It supplements the newspapers; not in the sense of being subsidiary to them, but of working along the same lines with different aims and equipment. The daily gives the skeleton of an occurrence; the Magazine, its flesh and blood. The daily gives the *incident*, the Magazine the *movement*....
>
> What relation does HARPER'S MAGAZINE bear to newspapers, considered from the stand-point of their editorial pages? How does it deal with 'questions of the day'? ... the tariff; but upon subjects of this nature HARPER'S MAGAZINE professes to have no editorial opinion. How, then, can it treat of them....Both sides of the question were presented [in two separate articles]...with equal force....Their articles, taken together, furnished material from which any intelligent person could form an opinion founded upon the merits of the question, and free from partisan bias. (Anon.: 30)

Harper & Bros. were in all probability at this time prompted to make this bid for *HNMM*'s share of the journalism market by financial difficulties which in the following year obliged them to sell their textbook division. This appeal to the mass readership of daily newspapers in 1889 gives credence to Ziff's contention that the older journals were experiencing pressure from other forms of print journalism, but it does not prove that their response is nil, staid, or ineffectual. A second claim of the publicity pamphlet is 'state of the art' technology, in the high artistic and technical quality of the illustrations. *HNMM* may be construed as fighting to hold its place in the marketplace as early as 1889, and by November 1893, the attempt to maintain circulation through a reputation for topicality and news stretched to the publication of two works of British decadence in one number.

Richard Ohmann's argument that in the 1890s in the US, monopoly capitalism began to deploy advertising 'to add the control of *sales* to the control of production' (Ohmann 1984: 16) has direct consequences for *Harper's NMM* whose small if wealthy readership, along with the *Atlantic's*, resulted in 'small and decorous' advertising sections. For their rivals, magazines such as *McClure's, Munsey's*, and *Cosmopolitan*, Ohmann contends that the 'main customers were advertisers rather than readers, and [the main] product was the *attention of the audience*, more than the physical magazine itself' (Ohmann 1984: 17). These titles, which led a price war of 1893, could afford, unlike *Harper's*, to drop their cover prices dramatically, as they made their money primarily from advertising rather than from readers. At the same time, they had to attract sufficient reader/consumers to command the advertising, and beside increasing sales through low prices, they introduced different kinds of copy – such as the *Ladies' Home Journal* admixture of household hints with middle-brow culture (Ohmann 1984: 17). Exman argues that a temporary decline was detectable:

By 1895 a frost was on the leaves of the *Magazine*, with circulation down and advertising gross falling off badly. Along with the *Atlantic* and the *Century* it was losing out to the new *McClure's* magazine, which could be bought at newsstands for fifteen cents a copy compared to their thirty-five cents. S.S. McClure was not only competing for their best authors, many of whom were won over by his big newspaper syndicate, but was also ambitious to turn serials into books. (Exman: 180)

If we examine the Archives there is evidence in a contract with Sampson Low (Reel 2, A5 378) to show that as early as 1887 the parent company was conscious of the need to increase the circulation of the *Magazine*; by January 1893 Harper lower the cost to McIlvaine per copy from 7d to $6\frac{1}{2}$d, with the aim of increasing circulation. McIlvaine is to raise the discount to the trade who may then buy more. Harper also instructs McIlvaine to permit for the first time the *return* by traders of up to 5 per cent of the *Magazine* in exchange for new supplies of subsequent issues (Reel 2, Vol. 6, 520–2). If an increase in sales does not result within a reasonable time, Harper plans to decrease the size of the *Magazine* by a signature of 16 pages. In September 1893 one of its new rivals, *Munsey's*, in a bid to increase its circulation, lowers its price drastically, from 25¢ an issue to 10¢, or from $3 annually to $1.50. Two years later, in December 1894, we see evidence of the promotion methods for the *Magazine* (Reel 2, Vol. 6, 575–6) in a mild disagreement between Harper and McIlvaine about the number of copies – 500 or 1000 – to be sent on the day of publication 'to a carefully selected list of names ... considered as used for advertising purposes' and 'charged to advertising account'.

I want briefly to construe three aspects of the unexpected efflorescence of European decadence in an American family monthly magazine: how and why it might have happened; who is responsible for commissioning it; and how it contributes to a biographical crux.

Perhaps the preliminary move must be to indicate the nature of Pater's and Symons' contributions. Pater's story is a sensuous and suggestive narrative about the foredoomed return or 'resurrection' of a Greek god in the form of a beautiful male youth, and his fatal impact on an all-male Christian community of France in the Middle Ages. It is one of Pater's most undiluted reveries on homosexual motifs such as male youth and beauty, male bonding, and male communities since 'Winckelmann' was published anonymously in the *Westminster Review* in 1867, and subsequently as successive editions of *The Renaissance* appeared. Symons' 'The Decadent Movement in Literature' is an annotated catalogue of the main writers in the French and English decadent tradition which Symons does not refrain from defining. It is likely that without knowledge of the work (and perhaps lives) in question, readers would not be offended by the presence of a text probably negotiated between Symons and the editor of *HNMM*. Yet Verlaine and Huysmans are named by Symons, and figure in his definition of typical Decadence: 'To fix the last fine shade, the quintessence of things; to fix it fleetingly, to be a disembodied voice, and yet the voice of human soul: that is the ideal of Decadence, and it is what Paul Verlaine has achieved' (Symons: 862) and '*A Rebours* is the history of a typical Decadent – a study, indeed, after a real man, but a study which seizes the type rather than the personality. In the sensations and ideas of Des Esseintes we see the sensations and ideas of the effeminate, over-civilized, deliberately abnormal creature who is the last product of our society: partly the father, partly the offspring, of the perverse art that he adores' (Symons: 866). This is hardly staid, and might well be objected to by a traditional reader of *HNMM*. However, there is an unmistakable effort to domesticate and gentrify this material by way of illustrations; this can be seen in the Symons article which includes drawings of the Decadents in reassuring and familiar surroundings. An illustration for a poem by Verlaine himself, translated by John Gray in *McClure's* in December 1893, exemplifies this ploy in another magazine of the day. 'Mon Dieu m'a dit' had appeared earlier in the year in Gray's *Silverpoints*, an exquisite and decadent volume published by John Lane and Elkin Matthews.[6] Although the author and translator of this poem are named for advertisement purposes in earlier numbers, and included in the Contents of the number in which the poem appears, no names appear on the page of the poem itself, only a sentimental illustration – familial and religious – which occupies three-quarters of the page (Figure 6.3).

Indeed, the inclusion of such material in *Harper's* may be an index to the degree to which the new forms of print journalism were threatening the old cultural formation to which HNMM belonged, and the attempt by the firm to meet the challenge to its circulation, future, and cultural authority. It is of interest that decadence is precisely the topic Ziff singles out (Ziff: 134) as an index of difference between new little magazines such as the *Chap Book* (May 1894 – July 1898) and HNMM. But six months before the *Chap Book* appeared, with its introduction of foreign decadent art and literature, HNMM anticipated the nature of the opposition. Quite apart from any personal patronage or links between Pater, Symons, and the commissioning editor of *Harper's*, the explanation of why this material appeared in the November 1893 issue seems clear: decadence, distasteful to both Howells and Lang, part of the cadre of 'old gentlemen' associated by Ziff with this period of HNMM, was nevertheless deemed topical and commercially necessary to continue to attract readers by the redoubtable Alden, in his fourth decade as editor.

Although the identity of the person who commissioned Symons and Pater to contribute to HNMM remains unknown, it is most likely that the two commissions are related, as Pater and Symons were friends. However, my hypothesis when I began work, that Andrew Lang secured the articles, now is problematic (if still possible) in that Lang's role as editor of the English edition, frustrating and ineffectual as it was, apparently ended in 1889. Moreover, R.L. Green suggests that Lang was opposed to the 90s poets and Decadents (Green: 165). Against that might be set Lang's likely friendship with Pater (there are no extant letters), Lang's notorious distaste for realism and his militant defence of the romance genre into which Pater's 'Apollo in Picardy' falls, and the appearance of Lang's friend

Figure 6.3 Verlaine illustrated. *McClure's Magazine*, December 1893.

Henley in Symons' catalogue of English Decadent writers. Demoor denies the suggestion of Howells' biographer E. Wagenknecht that Lang resumed his position as editor of the British *HNMM* after W.D. Howells left its payroll at the end of 1891. Exman implies that Wagenknecht is correct: 'Paradoxically the London edition of *Harper's*, under Andrew Lang, was at this time [1900] enjoying its greatest acceptance. It led all competitors with a circulation of 100 000, and most of its readers considered it as originating in Britain' (Exman: 250–1). The appearance of these two pieces in November 1893 indicates that this question may be kept open, in the absence of evidence to the contrary, or knowledge of the identity of the editor of the English edition after 1889.

Symons' piece has a further interest. Since Lawrence Evans published his edition of Pater's letters in 1971, scholars have believed that the cordial relationship between Pater and Symons had cooled after 1890 for unknown reasons. It is altogether possible that Symons' inclusion of Pater in the catalogue of English decadents, and his unmistakable association of Pater's work with that of the French Decadents kindled Pater's fear of homophobia, and anger at Symons for construing his work as part of this dangerous cultural formation. Symons' enthusiastic praise of Pater's work nevertheless exposes it as firmly situated in the tradition of Decandence:

> But those qualities which we find in the work of Goncourt, Verlaine, Huysmans...are not wanting in the recent literature of other countries....The prose of Mr. Walter Pater, the verse of Mr. W.E. Henley – to take two prominent examples – are attempts to do with the English language something of what Goncourt and Verlaine have done with the French. Mr. Pater's prose is the most beautiful English prose which is now being written; and, unlike the prose of Goncourt, it has done no violence to language, it has sought after no vivid effects; it has found a large part of mastery in reticence, in knowing what to omit. But how far away from the classic ideals of style is this style in which words have their color, their music, their perfume, in which there is 'some strangeness in the proportion' of every beauty! The *Studies in the Renaissance* have made of criticism a new art – have raised criticism almost to the act of creation. And *Marius the Epicurean*, in its study of 'sensation and ideas' (the conjuction was Goncourt's before it was Mr. Pater's), and the *Imaginary Portraits*, in

their evocations of the Middle Ages, the age of Watteau – have they not that morbid subtlety of analysis, that morbid curiosity of forms that we have found in the works of the French Decadents? A fastidiousness equal to that of Flaubert has limited Mr Pater's work to six volumes, but... there is not a page that is not perfectly finished...(Symons: 866–7)

This unmasking of Pater's reticence is both generous in its praise and unwavering in its construction of Pater as a Decadent author. Readers of *HNMM* have the privilege of reading as praise from the pen of a friend of Pater's what he might have expected as denunciation from an enemy in the pages of the *Quarterly* or the *Contemporary*.[7] It is unlikely that Pater, who guarded his reputation jealously, welcomed this piece from the rash Symons, and Symons' piece may have been the occasion of or evidence of the coolness between the two. For the purposes of comparison of periodicals of the period, on the basis of the November *Harper's*, a juxtaposition between *HNMM* and periodicals such as the old *Quarterly* and the remnant of the *Contemporary*, suggests *Harper's* is by far the more progressive, open and welcoming to new developments in literature.

I conclude that Harper & Bros.'s attempt to keep abreast of their market in the 1890s was concerted. It seems to me altogether possible that the circulation figures quoted by Perkins are a measure of their momentary success; while Ziff's comparators are useful indications of the nature of the opposition, the existence of the new journalism does not *per se* dispatch its predecessors. Nor do the details of censorship indicate a moribund institution. That Harper & Bros. published Hardy at all in the late nineteenth century is, as we have seen, what numerous other publishers and editors refused to do. Moreover, the appearance of these pieces by Symons and Pater in the pages of an established family magazine such as *HNMM* indicates the elasticity of this cultural formation, and the parameters if not the absence of American censorship.

Notes

1.	See the letter of termination between Harper and Sampson Low, 3 May 1890 in Archives, Reel 2, A5, 429.

2. By 16 October 1889 Harper writes to W.D. Howells of the 'English' market; see Reel 3, 227b.
3. While Andrew Lang acted as the British editor of *HNMM* for five years, neither his office nor his duties are mentioned in the standard biographies such as R.L. Green's, Eleanor de Selms Langstaff's, or the *DNB's*; J.H. Harper gives Lang's editorship two lines. This silence is in marked contrast with his famed leaders in the *Daily News*, his reviews in the *Saturday*, and his long stint on *Longman's* as the author of 'At the Sign of the Ship'.
4. The initial agreement with Sampson Low provides for Harper to '"deliver" the Magazine ready for publication, with the imprint of Sampson Low & Co., at least three days before "Magazine Day"' (*Archive*, Reel 1, A3 462).
5. Both James Osgood, who had been Harper's representative in Britain since 1886, and Charles McIlvaine who had worked for Harper in their literary department since 1885 were American. When Osgood died in 1892, McIlvaine continued as Harper representative, and publisher of *HNMM*. A letter in the Archives (Reel 2, Vol. 6, 570) suggests that McIlvaine, in the absence of any formally designated English editor after Lang was dismissed, may have acted as administrative coordinator and editorial channel to Alden for *HNMM*.
6. For more on Gray's translations in *Silverpoints*, see McCormack, 124–41.
7. Symons removed Pater and Henley from his catalogue of Decadence when a revised form of this article appeared in 1912.

Works Cited

Alden, H.M. (1880). Letter to W. Pennypacker. (26 May). Letterbook 1869–92. 'Harper's Magazine' Archive, Library of Congress.
Anon. (1889). 'The Making of a Great Magazine. Being an inquiry into the past and the future of HARPER'S MAGAZINE', London and New York.
The Archives of Harper & Brothers 1817–1914. (1980). London.
Burlingame, Roger. (1946). *Of Making Many Books*. New York.
Demoor, M. (1989). *Friends Over the Ocean. Andrew Lang's American Correspondents. 1881–1912*. Gent.
Demoor, M. (1987). 'Andrew Lang versus W.D. Howells: A Late Victorian Literary Duel', *Journal of American Studies*, 21: 416–22.
Douglas, G. (1892). 'Tess of the D'Urbervilles', *The Albemarle* I(Feb.): 71–2.
Exman, E. (1967) *The House of Harper. One Hundred and Fifty Years of Publishing*. New York, Evanston and London.
Ford, James L. (1899). *The Literary Shop and Other Tales*. New York.
Gatrell, Simon. (1988) *Hardy the Creator. A Textual Biography*. Oxford.
Green, R.L. (1946). *Andrew Lang. A Critical Biography*. Leicester.
Harper, J. Henry. (1912). *The House of Harper*. New York and London.
Howells, William Dean. (1980). *Selected Letters*, ed. by George Arms, et al. Vol. 3, *1882–1891*, ed. by Robert C. Leitz III et al. Boston.
Lang, Andrew. (1887). 'Realism and Romance', *Contemporary Review*, (Nov.), 683–93.

Langstaff, Eleanor de Selms. (1978). *Andrew Lang*. Boston.

Locker, William. (1889). Letter to Thomas Hardy. 25 June. Quoted by Gatrell, p. 81.

Macmillan, F. (1904). Letter to H.G. Wells. 11 July. Macmillan Archive 55477/1, f. 80. British Library.

McCormack, J.H. (1991). *John Gray*. Hanover and London.

Ohmann, Richard. (1984). 'The New Discourse of Mass Culture: Magazines in the 1890s', *University of Hartford Studies in Literature* 16. 16–35.

Ohmann, Richard. (1981). 'Where did Mass Culture Come From? The Case of Magazines', *Berkshire Review* 16. 85–101.

Pater, W. (1893). 'Apollo in Picardy', *Harper's New Monthly Magazine* (Nov.) 949–56.

Perkins, Barbara M. (1986). '*Harper's Monthly Magazine*' in Chielens, Edwards, ed., *American Literary Magazines*, Westport, Conn. pp. 166–71.

Symons, A. (1893). 'The Decadent Movement in Literature', *Harper's New Monthly Magazine* (Nov.) 858–68.

Verlaine, Paul. (1893). 'Mon Dieu m'a dit', *McClure's Magazine* 2(Dec.) 67.

Wagenknecht, Edward. (1969). *William Dean Howells: The Friendly Eye*. New York.

[Warner, C.D.]. (1894). 'Editor's Study', *Harper's New Monthly Magazine* (August) 476–7.

[Warner, C.D.]. (1892). 'Editor's Study', *Harper's New Monthly Magazine* (June) 152–3.

West, J.L., III. (1990). 'Book Publishing 1835–1900. The Anglo-American Connection', *Papers of the Bibliographical Society of America* 84. 357–75.

Ziff, Larzer. (1979). *The American 1890s*. Lincoln, Nebraska and London.

II

Gendered Space

7

Oscar Wilde and
The Woman's World

The Woman's World is a nineteenth-century woman's magazine edited by a male editor whose editorial project included not only the construction of the cultivated new woman but the introduction of male homosexual discourse into female space. The negotiation of gender in *The Woman's World* is perhaps atypical of women's magazines of the period, but it alerts us to the element of gender in the Victorian press. I shall be approaching *The Woman's World* principally as a serial production which exists over time in the market and as a 'class' periodical with a readership and discourse determined by shared characteristics, primarily gender, education and wealth.

Gender in periodicals is a subject which has received some attention. Relations between the periodical press and women have been considered in some breadth in recent work by Cynthia White, Janice Winship, Judith Williamson, Ros Ballaster *et al.* and Kathryn Shevelow. At least one book for the Victorian period (by Margaret Beetham) is under way and Gaye Tuchman's *Edging Women Out* (1989), which looks at women novelists and the Victorian publishing world, approaches the territory. The explicitly male dimension of gender studies on Victorian literature (not periodicals) has a long history which pertains to work on marginalised men's writing such as Steven Marcus's *The Other Victorians* or Brian Reade's *Sexual Heretics*. Books in this category, after the flourish of their publication, themselves became part of coterie reading, even exotica, and outside of the mainstream of criticism and the dominant interpretative community. It is only very recently that Eve Sedgwick's pioneering *Between Men: English Literature and Male Homosocial Desire* (1985) and now Richard Dellamora's *Masculine Desire* (1990) have entered the discourse of gender studies as such.

Like many of those who study periodicals I came from a
discipline which marginalised them, and my (authorial) path to
The Woman's World, through Oscar Wilde, who is also its editor, is
characteristic of 'English'. I have tried to resist approaching *The
Woman's World* primarily from these directions, authorially or top
down (from the position of the editor). These approaches often
serve to obscure the periodical format, such as the collective nature
of periodical publication, the shape of individual numbers, the
grouping and order of text(s), the role of the readership, the
element of time in serial publication, and the multiplicity of discourses. The categories of author and editor can make the periodical invisible, and transform its texts into forms valorised by the
discourse of literature – parts of books, oeuvres, arguments. The
flourishing research and writing on Victorian periodicals since the
founding of *Victorian Periodicals Review* in 1968 and work on
culture and media by Raymond Williams and many others have
alerted us to the implications of exclusively *literature*-based critical
practice.

*   *   *

In October 1887 Cassell & Co. announced dramatic changes of
editor and title for *The Lady's World*. From November, its first
birthday, it was to appear as *The Woman's World*, edited by Oscar
Wilde. The change of name, suggested to Wilde by Dinah Craik,
implied a significant move from the world of the 'lady' to that of
'woman', a word associated at the time with 'commonness',
suffrage and higher education, and a move between two kinds of
gendered discourse. Wilde glossed this as a distinction between
'feminine' and 'womanly' (Nowell-Smith: 253). However, except
insofar as these discourses predominantly addressed women
readers, they cannot accurately be termed female because of the
anonymity of the authors of the articles in *The Lady's World* (who
may well be men) and because both editors were male. There is
yet another distinction between the two titles to be made: rather
than 'male' editors existing as a unified subject, it can be seen that
Wilde's notions of masculinity and the feminine or womanly
differ markedly from those of Wemyss Reid, thought to be the
previous editor. In the late 1880s and the 1890s homosexual male
discourse can be seen to be moving tentatively into the public
sphere in magazines. The contrast made by the anonymous
reviewer of *The Picture of Dorian Gray* in the Tory weekly the

St. James Gazette in June 1890 (Anon. (1890): 3), between the 'garbage of the French Decadents' found in Wilde's novel and his implicitly benign stint as editor of a magazine for ladies will not survive a reading of the documents in question. It is perhaps a function of the gendering of Victorian periodical discourse that the indignant critic from the *St. James Gazette* never read *The Woman's World*.

The 'other side' of the gender-designated women's magazines in the nineteenth century is the great bulk of the press, male but so dominant that its gender requires no adjective or explicit sign, and the family press, for both male and female readership such as the *Cornhill Magazine* and the hugely successful *Cassell's Family Magazine*. This latter category does normally signal its suitability for women readers by the presence of fiction, or, like the *Cornhill* which prohibited articles on religion, politics, and philosophy, by the public exclusion of material regarded as potentially controversial and inappropriate for women. While illustrations were rare in the intellectual monthlies of the 70s and 80s aimed at male readers only, visual material was more likely to play an important part in family and women's magazines.

In the gender spectrum of magazines for women, men, and families there was a fourth element. By 1887 homosexual discourse had begun to appear intermittently in periodicals largely read by men, and to be denounced as well; an early example of the discourse is Walter Pater's 'Winckelmann' which appeared in 1867 in the *Westminster Review* edited by John Morley, and of a denunciation, Revd St. John Tyrwhitt's 'The Greek Spirit in Modern Literature' in the first number of the born again *Contemporary Review* in March 1877. But by the mid 1880s periodicals in which homosexual discourse and subjects were characteristic if not entirely dominant began to develop, and in the decade between 1885, the year of the Labouchère amendment outlawing homosexuality, and the Wilde trials in the spring of 1895, magazines such as *The Artist and Journal of Home Culture* (under Kains-Jackson 1888–94), *The Pagan Review* (1892), *The Spirit Lamp* (1892–3), and *Chamelon* (1894) provided homosexual writers and readers with the same means afforded to other 'class' groups in Victorian Britain for circulation of their ideas and discourse, and consolidation of their cause through the press. At the same time this public visibility rendered the editors, contributors and periodicals vulnerable to the slightest disapproval; two of these titles only survived for one issue with the *Chamelon* stopped by *To-day* (29 December 1894), and Kains-Jackson resigning in fear earlier the same year. In this respect, more covert, masked publication of homosexual discourse, in among other kinds of periodical material but coded for the coterie reader,[1] had its attractions. Walter Pater, for example, continued to take this path throughout his writing career, avoiding entirely the homosexual press, even writing for the high Anglican weekly, *The Guardian*, while Wilde in the 90s contributed signed articles to *The Spirit Lamp* and anonymously to *The Chamelon*. In the period of *The Woman's World* however, Wilde is writing elsewhere, for the straight press, articles which he is to anthologise in *Intentions* to make his name as a critic, and trying to earn a living by editing in order to help support a wife and children. In both the critical writing and editing of the late 1880s Wilde can be seen to be covertly transgressive, stretching the limits of the periodicals to which he is attached. Comparison of his work in the two discourses, that of (male) higher criticism and that in *The Woman's World*, shows that Wilde's work is significantly implicated in the respective discourse of which it is part.

While *The Woman's World* remains a magazine for women readers, distinct from these for men, the coding of its contents and the attraction of its space to Wilde are clarified by the contents of the gay press and other alternative journals such as *The Yellow Book*. For example, the undergraduate Max Beerbohm's contributions on fashion and cosmetics to *The Spirit Lamp* IV (June 1893) and *The Yellow Book* I (16 April 1894) represent subjects normally available to male authors in the nineteenth century only in connection with the theatre, visual art or fiction. Beerbohm's provocative titles, 'The Incomparable Beauty of Modern Dress' and 'A Defence of Cosmetics' inscribe this status of the taboo and gendered subject. By 1893 in *The Spirit Lamp* (which as an Oxford undergraduate magazine was addressed to male readers) Beerbohm was able to celebrate male dress:

> I doubt if there has ever been a time when dress amongst men reached so high an artistic level as in England at this moment, when the fashion was so reasonable and beautiful or the desire to conform to it so widespread...
> At all events, the spread of foppery from the upper to the middle classes is a cause for great aesthetic gladness (Beerbohm 1893: 92).

and to trail its androgynous character, explicitly linking male and female characteristics to construct an eroticised hybrid to engage his coterie readers:

> In one of the minor Colleges of Oxford, a mimic court was lately held to try the case of an undergraduate, against whom an indictment for excessive foppery had been lodged by one of his friends... The defendant, one of those who try to realize the ideal man by combining in themselves whatever seems best in either sex, was rather rich and not ill looking; he could paint very nicely in water-colour, spoke French with an accent that was the envy of all Paris, and though not exactly clever, had a considerable fund of woman's wit. (Beerbohm 1893: 90)

This opening paragraph of Beerbohm's also encodes the marginalisation of the type and its endangered position within the law, self-conscious signs in narrative which both warn and titillate.

Beerbohm's pieces of the 90s echo moves by Wilde in the 80s. Wilde used other, non-verbal strategies to put male dress on the agenda. An anonymous author of 'Local Art Notes: Leeds' in *The Artist* in 1884 discusses male dress by way of commenting on Wilde's lecturing persona:

> Great exception has been taken to his dress both in our daily papers and among people one meets, but it is difficult to see what that has got to do with the substance of the lecture.
> Artistically his dress was good: a short black velvet coat and vest, trousers of a light warm grey tint, cuffs turned over the coat-sleeves (a vast improvement, by the way, in wearing those "shams"), turned down linen collar and a couple of spots of delightful colour in the form of a tie, and a handkerchief of Indian silk of a delicate and well chosen red tint; no jewellery except perhaps a ring; certainly nothing *outré* in his costume, but such a dress as would be an excellent example to copy if ever the much needed dress reform for gentlemen gained ground. (Anon. 1884: 78)

Wilde's articles in 1885 included 'The Relation of Dress to Art. A Note in Black and White on Mr. Whistler's Lecture' in the *Pall Mall Gazette* (28 February) and 'Shakespeare and Stage Costume' in the *Nineteenth Century* in May. Appearing in straight magazines, they

Figure 7.1 (*above*) and 7.2 (*opposite*) Male actor displaces female fashions.
The Woman's World, November 1887.

conform more closely to the expected (and permitted) contexts for
these constructions of the gendered subject, and ostensibly
foreground *other* (authorial, artistic/theatrical) subjects, while
Beerbohm in the alternative periodical press feels free to make male
dress his principal concern.

In *The Woman's World* however, a gendered periodical where
fashion for women is valorised, Wilde is seen to value fashion for
women less than that of men, and he imposes this view on the
magazine. He associates it with frivolity in women, vulgar
commodification, and rival publications in the market, and
juxtaposes it with more spiritual elements of women, their intellect
and emotion. 'No one,' he writes to Wemyss Reid in 1887 'appre-
ciates more fully than I do the value and importance of Dress, in its
relations to good taste and good health...but the field of mere
millinery and trimmings, is to some extent occupied already by such
papers as the *Queen* and the *Lady's Pictorial*, and ... we should take a
wider range, as well as a higher standpoint, and deal not merely
with what women wear, but with what they think, and what they
feel' (Nowell-Smith: 253). In the first issue he removes the monthly
fashion slot from the prominence it gained as one of the first

articles in *The Lady's World*, and changes it to the last article of *The Woman's World*. In its place in the first number is a piece on a theatrical subject, 'The Woodland Gods', heavily illustrated with plates of comely young men in costume. The languorous Orlando (Figure 7.1) which greets the reader of the revamped and renamed magazine is to be contrasted with the fashion plate of women's dress which formerly appeared here; at the same time Orlando is able to function as an image (akin to a pin-up) which cultured women and aesthetic or gay men consume. Wilde objected to the consumer element of the fashion in *The Lady's World*:

Figure 7.2

It seems to me also that just at present there is too much money spent on illustrations, particularly on illustrations of dress. They are also extremely unequal, many are charming such as that on page 224 of the current number, but many look like advertisements, and give an air to the magazine that one wants to avoid, the air of directly puffing some firm or *modiste*. (Nowell-Smith: 255)

This reads tellingly beside the commodification of the illustrations of the male figures which displace it. The male readers of *Woman's World* must have been confined to those who knew Wilde personally or through repute. They were not a readership that was ever articulated between Wilde and Cassell if Max Pemberton's[2] account of the later studied innocence of the firm is credited:

You were not permitted to mention a chambermaid in my day at Cassell's. I remember once merely hinting that all women were not virtuous, and being summoned before a board of the white-whiskered gentlemen...they declared emphatically that they had never met any of the ladies to whom I referred. (Pemberton: 8)

It is clear that Wilde's project of the male homosexual sub-text was private, available only to those who could read the discourse. Unshared with his publisher or the public, it is to be contrasted with Alfred Douglas's statement in his prospectus in 1893 for *The Spirit Lamp* (Vol. 4) which 'should be read by all who are interested in modern life and the new culture', the latter phrase referring to homosexual life.[3] In his letter of acceptance of the post of editor Wilde did, however, moot the possibility of male readers and contributors: 'The *Lady's World* should be made the recognized organ for the expression of women's opinions on all subjects of literature, art, and modern life, and yet it should be a magazine that men could read with pleasure, and consider it a privilege to contribute to' (Nowell-Smith: 253). In the event Wilde employed men on the magazine mainly as illustrators.

In the absence of an available prospectus for *Woman's World* or the Cassell archives, Wilde's letters of 1887 remain to suggest his conception of how this gendered space was to be filled, and the type of woman contributor, subject and reader he was constructing. In a letter to solicit copy Wilde specifies the socially and intellectually élite readership and authors he seeks, and compares the new enterprise to the most intellectually liberal and demanding of the general monthlies, the *Nineteenth Century*.

Madam,
Will you allow me to add your name to the list of contributors to a magazine I have been asked to edit? The magazine in question is published by Messrs Cassell + Co, and I am anxious to make it the recognised organ Through which women of culture and position will express Their views. Lady Dorothy Nevill, Lady Archibald Campbell, Lady Pollock, Mrs. Francis Jeune, Mrs. Henry Fawcett, Lady Ferguson, Miss Thackeray, and others, have promised to write for it, and I would be very pleased if you would do something: either an article or a short story.
I should prefer an article...The honorarium for writers is a pound a page, and the page something longer than a page of the 'Nineteenth Century'. The magazine will appear in October. (Wilde: 1887a: $1^{r/v}$, $2^{r/v}$)

In another letter he specifies the cultural and social positions of contributors: 'Tomorrow I start for Oxford to arrange about the Lady Margaret [Hall] article, and to meet some women of ability. We must have the Universities on our side....June, as you know, will be for the aristocracy a very busy month, so I want to complete our arrangements now' (Nowell-Smith: 256).

To George Macmillan, publisher, he writes in October 1887:

> I am going to make literary criticism one of the features of the *Woman's World*, and to give special prominence to books written by women. Should you care to send me any books of the kind I will see that they are duly noticed (Hart-Davis 1985: 70–1).

In the event, Wilde's *Woman's World* offers a number of competing discourses which include parody and self-parody; as editor he appropriates the gendered discourse of women's magazines to take in what the discourse formerly excluded and to overstep the limitations of the gendered discourse of the men's magazines. He is a male editor with a difference.

I am going to use *The Lady's World* as a comparator to its successor, in part to facilitate reading *The Woman's World*, and in part to identify Wilde's policies as editor.

Both titles are shilling monthlies at the outset, but where *The Lady's World* carries on the cover the description *A Magazine of Fashion and Society*, *The Woman's World* announces prominently the names of its editor and select contributors. To this day it is only conjecture that Wemyss Reid himself acted as editor of *The Lady's World*. The personalising of journalism and the trailing of names associated with the slow disappearance of anonymity and the advent of the new journalism are far more pronounced in *The Woman's World*; these new features credit the reader with more knowledge of authorship in general and also make more explicit the commodity identity of the periodical (it is commercial and for sale) and the consumer position of the reader whose discretion in purchasing the article is wooed through the renown of named contributors. Whereas signature in the contents list of the bound volume of *The Lady's World* is relatively infrequent, with the number of unsigned pieces far outnumbering them, in *The Woman's World* contents list, and in the periodical itself, signature is the rule. Few of the infrequent signatures in the earlier title belong to well-known authors and more than a quarter seem to be male, whereas

in the later title a preponderance of the contributors are recog-
nisable and almost all are women. What the prospectus and
contents page of *The Lady's World* emphasise are the range and
subjects of articles: fashion, household management, cookery of an
exalted kind, needlework, artistic occupations for ladies, gossip
(which is the first article of each number), and articles on aspects of
culture associated with women, such as music, visual art and,
minimally, books. Each number contains at least one fashion plate,
but unlike working-class women's magazines there is no correspondence or advice column. There is one story a month, seven
poems which are all illustrated, and a notable number of pieces in
serial on lady role-models such as 'society types' and 'ladies of
note'. Perhaps less expected is the steady supply of articles on
sport, including tricycling, fly-fishing and yachting as well as
skating, hunting and sleighing.

A few articles in *The Lady's World* on higher education for women
link it closely with its successor, one describing a day in a
Cambridge women's college, and another by Mary Alford called
'What will Become of the Girls?'. This last plaintive essay represents higher education for women as life training for unmarried
or widowed life, precisely the utilitarian view that Elizabeth
Wordsworth, Principal of Lady Margaret Hall – the college
featured in *The Woman's World* – was anxious to dispel, lest
aristocrats be unwilling to associate their daughters with such
vulgarity as paid work. There is another article in *The Lady's World*
which suggests that its readers were not all 'high class' and society
ladies as the prospectus projects, and that is on 'Music as a
Livelihood' by a male contributor. These articles are atypical of *The
Lady's World* which is characterised by 'A Run Through the Gallery'
and 'A Chat about Books', and the Girton piece, penultimate in its
issue, is followed by 'The Art of Giving Dinners'. While the
discourses in *The Lady's World* are diverse, the construction of
women as leisured, domesticated, interested in society gossip,
seemly accomplishments, sport, clothes, and a modicum of culture
predominates. Women as consumers are invoked, as Wilde
suggests, in the plates but also in the 16 pages of 'The Lady's World
Advertising Sheet' hidden from view inside the green wrapper
with its idealised if decolleté goddess/woman (Figure 7.3) holding
an unregarded book in one hand and a mirror into which she gazes
in the other. These advertising supplements accompanied most
periodicals, although many of the library copies either excluded

them when they were bound or constitute contemporary printings of annual volumes which also discarded them at the time. Their absence induces later readers such as ourselves to forget the commodity and temporal qualities of periodicals and to accord them the status of the book. The cover of the periodical conspires to perpetuate the high culture's values as well.

Meanwhile, the Advertising Sheet purveys the virtues of products such as cosmetics, interior design, domestic machines, and various articles of clothes (dresses, corsets, gloves, waterproofs, hats, mourning) all of which figure in the text of the periodical. But by far the biggest single category of advertisements, dispro-portionate to the place these products occupy in *The Lady's World*, pertain to books and magazines in the main published by Cassell, the publisher of the magazine. So, not only does the periodical itself sell, but it reaps income from those who advertise in the sheet and it serves to advertise the other publications of the publishers. In an important respect, the Cassell woman's magazine is a vehicle for advertising as well as letterpress and illustrations, much as women's magazines function today. But the Victorian format rigidly separates the two elements, one overtly commercial and cheaply printed, designed and produced which may be disre-garded and discarded, and the other ostensibly 'literary' and non-commercial. It was the presence of commerce in the arguably literary to which Wilde objected in his letter to Wemyss Reid.

This division between commerce and text purveys the illusion that magazine journalism is tantamount to literature through identity of the print format of periodical and book texts at a time when the separation of journalism from the general inclusive notion of literature contributes to the élitist definition now in common usage. Numerous expressions of contempt for journalism survive from this period: Mark Pattison, Rector of Lincoln College, writes in his diary 'This article writing is detestable – when this is done, never will I write again upon a thesis set by an editor' (Pattison (1877): f.164) and in 1878 Frank Harris, editor and journalist, distinguishes British journalism from that on the Continent by virtue of its close links with commerce:

In France, Italy, and Germany journalism is a career in which an eloquent and cultured youth may honourably win his spurs. In many countries this way of earning one's bread can still be turned into an art by the gifted and high-minded; but in England

thanks in the main to the anonymity of the press cunningly
contrived by the capitalist, the journalist or modern preacher is
turned into a venal voice, a soulless Cheapjack paid to puff his
master's wares. (Harris: I, 59–60)

After Wilde finishes his stint as a magazine editor in 1889, and
after the carping reviews of *Dorian Gray*, he makes particularly
vituperative comments on journalists and journalism in 'The Soul
of Man Under Socialism' in the February 1891 number of *The
Fortnightly Review* edited by Frank Harris.

How is *The Lady's World* rethought and reconstituted in *The
Woman's World*? The new number is larger, 48 pages instead of 36,
an expansion which may have been paid for by the disappearance
of the coloured plates. The cover has changed remarkably (Figure
7.4); instead of an idealised goddess/woman on green paper it
consists of a William Morris-type spray of leaves on a vine ground
above a circular medallion holding a box in which appear the
names of well-known contributors. On either side are profiles of
mermaids or serpentine women with sensuous chests and powerful
torsos which suggest the serpent coil. The sensuous design,
detailed and large, is enhanced by colour: red ink on dusky pink
paper. Many of the illustrations in the magazine echo the style of
the cover, and it seems clear that Wilde took the opportunity to
include work from artists such as Walter Crane, Dante Gabriel
Rossetti, and Charles Ricketts. Illustrated initial letters, some
elaborate, are a feature of the new design. The magazine's
appearance justifies Valerie Steele's epithet 'vaguely Aesthetic'
(Steele: 152).

One of the numerous discourses of the contents and narrative is
that of aestheticism: there are articles on 'Japanese art wares' and
'Pictures of Sappho' and Beatrice Crane's 'Legend of the Blush
Roses'. But *The Woman's World* lives up to the compendium element
of the magazine format, and offers a variety of discourses to entice
a varied readership – from among new women, intelligent society
ladies, middle-class working women or young girls who may have
to work in future, and cultivated intellectual women of the middle
and upper classes who, already readers of male and family magazines, turn to *The Women's World* for its dissemination of women's
writing and its attention to a spectrum of the woman's 'sphere'.

One peculiar manifestation of parallel and incompatible
discourses is the way authors' names are deployed: within the text

of individual numbers, signature is mainly in the form of forenames and surnames such as Annie Thackeray and Constance Wilde, a form which invokes the convention of the professional (male) writer. However, the suppressed detail indicative of marital status or class ('Mrs' or 'Lady'), or the marital form of the name (Mrs Richmond Ritchie), or the name of renown (Violet Fane) or with a connection (Mrs St. Loe Strachey) is exploited in the contents page of the annual bound volume; both forms (and others) appear on the medallion on the cover of each issue. These varied forms arise from different discourses and appeal to a wide range of women readers, with the 'new woman' addressed by the forename/surname form, the older or simply more conventional woman by the married women's forms of the name, and readers of various categories drawn to the trailing of famous or society names. It is also interesting that what appears on the cover is authorial names, rather than the topics of articles; the appeal is only guardedly intellectual.

The contents page, however, does contain subject entries. The *subjects* of the 1887/8 volume are similarly diverse; they show a breadth of appeal, and a far greater range than those in *The Lady's World*. If anything, the reiterated subjects indicate that *The Woman's World* aims at a readership downmarket in economic terms and upmarket intellectually. Subjects treated by more than one article stand out in serial publication: although unmarked by a common title or by chapter designations, they are a covert serial form as they reappear month after month and raise expectations and reinforce readers' interest. In *The Woman's World* 1887/8 these subjects include higher education for women, the status of women and the 'woman question', prospective professions for women, working women, women abroad, fashion and its history, needlework, drama and Ireland. None of the topics relating to Ireland – crafts, education and architecture – is directly political, and apart from the politics of the 'woman question' *The Woman's World*, like *Cornhill*, avoids 'masculine' subjects such as politics/economics, philosophy (which includes science) and religion.

Another subject firmly within the experience of many cultivated women readers is denied them; music was banned by Wilde early on ('Music in a magazine is somewhat dull; no one wants it' (Nowell-Smith: 255)), perhaps in reaction because it was such a favoured subject in *The Lady's World*. For women, gossip too was to go; the gossip section which opened *The Lady's World* is replaced by the

Figure 7.3 Cover, 1886.

Figure 7.4 Cover, 1887.

Editor's 'Literary and Other Notes' which appears in the back of the magazine just before the last article, on women's fashion. So, in effect, the new Editor reverses the values of the periodical he supplants, putting last what was formerly first. He retains the form of gossip but elevates it by transferring its subject from social to literary tit-bits. Wilde's treatment of music and gossip in *The Woman's World* may be compared to his treatment of fashion for women. These subjects are presented as trivial and demeaning to women. Instead, women are constructed as serious readers who want (and need) education and accculturation. It is just these qualities rejected as unsuitable for women – a taste for triviality, dress, gossip and pleasures such as music – which are valorised in Wilde's own writing. In this value structure, men are free to be trivial; women are not; men may be useless, and women must be useful.

This palpable divergence of view between the male editor of a woman's magazine and the male writer about men is in part a function of the social constructions of gender in the period but also one determined by the site of literary production, in this case a woman's magazine which as a form had long been associated with moral conduct and instruction. In two obituaries which the Editor includes in his first 'Literary and Other Notes' two women authors are praised for their useful accomplishments in terms which, for twentieth-century readers familiar with Wilde's later work, suggest irony and self-parody. Of Dinah Craik, author of the morally exemplary novel *John Halifax, Gentlemen*, Wilde writes:

> Mrs Craik was one of the finest of our women-writers, and though her art had always what Keats called "a palpable intention upon one", still its imaginative qualities were of no mean order. There is hardly one of her books that has not some distinction of style; there is certainly not one of them that does not show an ardent love of all that is beautiful and good in life. The good she perhaps loved somewhat more than the beautiful, but her heart had room for both. (Wilde 1887b: 40)

With Lady Brassey he was more blatantly satiric, at her expense:

> In all modern movements Lady Brassey took a keen interest. She gained a first-class certificate in the South Kensington School of Cookery, scullery department and all; was one of the most energetic members of the St. John's Ambulance Association, many branches of which she succeeded in founding; and, whether at Normanhurst or in Park Lane, always managed to devote some portion of her day to useful and practical work. (Wilde 1887b: 40)

That Oscar Wilde wrote this is indicative of the combined sway of the site of the writing, the occasion (of death) and its elegaic form, his editorial role, and the social construction of gender. To the male coterie readers of *The Woman's World* the ironies would be clear. The view of useful and practical work valorised in other texts by Wilde involving male worlds and primarily addressed to men tended to be languid, if open, disdain.

The first number of the new magazine contained, in order: 'The Woodland Gods', signed Janey Sevilla Campbell (Lady Archibald Campbell in the Contents); 'The Position of Woman', signed Eveline Portsmouth (Countess of Portsmouth in the Contents); 'Madame de Sévigné's Grandmother' by Annie Thackeray, 'Hazely Heath' (sonnet) by Violet Fane; 'The Truth about Clement Ker' (serial fiction attributed to George Fleming[4] in the Contents); 'Above the Cloud-line', signed Marie E. Bancroft; 'The Children of a Great City. I', signed Mary Jeune; 'The Recent Telegraphic Occurrence at the British Museum', signed Amy Levy; 'The Oxford Ladies' Colleges. By a member of one of them'; 'Literary and other Notes. By the Editor'; and 'November Fashions', by Mrs. Johnstone. The phenomenon of multiple discourses and breadth of appeal characteristic of the annual volume as a whole may be construed from this outline of a single number. Particular communities of women – in society, in and associated with the universities (as students, mothers and sisters of actual and potential women and men students, teachers and lecturers in the new institutions, wives of male university teachers, higher education activists, and feminists), and literary women are all addressed. The two articles which deal most blatantly with the 'woman question' straddle discourses. The one on women's position is written by a Countess in a matter-of-fact tone, rather than stridently or by a middle-class radical, and the one on higher education surprisingly appears anonymously. Is this due to modesty, or fear? In any case, this is not a woman student who is prepared for exposure in the public sphere or to answer for her convictions. This compares with a signed article in *The Lady's World*, 'A Day at Girton College' by M.F. Donaldson who was, however, a reporter visitor rather than a student.

'The Woodland Gods' with which the first number opens is an intervention in the art vs. nature debate which exercised Wilde and almost all Victorian authors and critics concerned with realism and its attendant issues. The context here is the historical productions of portions of Elizabethan and Victorian plays produced outdoors in

1884 and 1885 under the aegis of E.W. Godwin, and the argument, in light of what is taken retrospectively to be Wilde's unmistakable defence of art in this debate, seems astounding: it is a spirited consideration of how acting and dramatic productions may be made infinitely more natural and realistic by performance outdoors. It is clear from the text that the author, Janey (Lady) Campbell has insider knowledge of Godwin and the production, and the egregious case is competently put, but why has Wilde given so much space and prominence to a position so at odds with his own? Explanations abound: the author is female, a Lady, and knowledgeable; the subject is defined as literature, criticism, drama, and Shakespeare, all aspects of culture within women's province; the critical position is the hegemonic one which the laywoman would hold and assent to.

However, another factor, pertaining to the editor as critic, figures here. This position is one which Wilde is in the course of abandoning. Certainly, by the time of 'The Decay of Lying', which appeared in the *Nineteenth Century* in January 1889, it was resolutely reversed, though as late as December 1888 in a review of 'Poems by Henley and Sharp' in *Woman's World* Wilde singles out drama from other forms of literature as a form that is 'imitative' and claims 'to mirror life'. This position is one in which Wilde is deeply implicated: he had actually helped Lady Campbell with the 1885 production of *As You Like It* and reviewed it himself enthusiastically at the time. His 1885 essay 'Shakespeare and Stage Costume', in the *Nineteenth Century* in May (along with earlier essays of the 1870s) also argues for realism and historical accuracy in productions of Shakespeare, and these arguments were masked by emendation[5] when the essay reappeared as 'The Truth of Masks' in *Intentions* in 1891. So, Wilde's publication of this article does signal his tolerance as editor at a relatively late date of this surprising view of the art–nature debate: 'Nature is the test, the touchstone; she shows up what is false, what is exaggerated, what is theatrical. She is the ever-present standard' (Campbell: 2). The other editorial point attaching to this essay is its part in the covert homosexual discourse to be found in *Woman's World*. The numerous illustrations in the article alert readers to this, but the letterpress also contains comments on boy actors and cross-dressing which may be read as part of this discourse:

It seems remarkable that whilst Hamlet, Romeo, even Shylock, and many other male Shakespearean characters have been played by women, we do not hear that Orlando has ever been included in the number; yet, on reading the part, one can feel that it might have been written for one of those youths who in Shakespeare's time played female characters.... A youth who had probably played the parts of Rosalind, Imogen, and Viola, played amongst his latest the part of this romantic lover (Campbell: 5–6).

It has to be said that the piece by Eveline Portsmouth on 'The Position of Women' seems calculated not to offend; while it does firmly list the considerable recent improvements in the law regarding women, its vision of the future of improvements in opportunities and rights of women is entirely in terms of propping up men. It concludes: 'May not the time be come when the strength of women is imperative to make men stronger? – when it is necessary for him that she should be his fitting companion – loyal but not servile? May not the hour have struck when her own elevation is absolutely necessary to prevent his deterioration?' (Portsmouth: 10). While anger may have been the response of the new women reading this, other groups of readers (including the male editor, publisher, and ordinary readers envisaged by the editor) might be relieved and reassured.

The new women would have been a lot happier with the piece on 'The Oxford Ladies Colleges'. It is significant that it pertains to the more conservative of the two strains of women's halls in Oxford in 1887, that is the Anglican institutions represented here by Lady Margaret Hall rather than the non-denominational represented by Somerville. The piece should be seen as a follow-up to the article on Girton in *The Lady's World* but was also almost *de rigeur* for a new woman's magazine that wished to attract the new class of educated women readers; both the *Universal Review* (in December 1888) and *The Lady's Pictorial* in 1891–2 followed suit. If unsigned, Wilde's anonymous author is strident and critical in places:

I should like to inquire why it is that every one when speaking in public thinks it necessary to assume an appearance of such excessive modesty and self-depreciation....two out of every three seem invariably to preface their remarks with the sometimes wholly unnecessary assurance that they have really nothing to say worth hearing, and do not in the least understand the motion before the House (Anon. 1887: 35).

That the discourses of the two articles on the position of women differ so greatly is a function of the broad spectrum of women (authors and readers) to which *The Woman's World* at its price and level of literacy and cultivation had to appeal to survive. Whereas today different groups of women read *The Lady, Cosmopolitan* and *Women*, in 1888 they might all have read *The Woman's World*. Gay readers today still have a limited choice of 'class' periodicals, but changes in the construction of gender have resulted in the acknowledgement of a greater breadth in the spectrum of each sex. Men now openly read women's magazines such as *Cosmopolitan* or *Vogue*, and magazines with a predominantly male readership (*The Face*) take on subjects formerly gendered as female.

Notes

1. These are diverse, varying in explicitness and nature according to the gender of the space in which they are produced and circulated. Allusions to a range of symbols of current homosexual codes can alert the gay reader: in the late nineteenth century these included St Sebastian, a number of classical male and female figures with erotic associations, and coterie terms or phrases such as 'the new culture'. Subjects such as male dress, Greek studies generally, and male beauty, and narrative structures of male friendship, particularly those between an older and a younger man, are also appropriated by gay discourse in the period.
2. Max Pemberton joined Cassell's in 1892.
3. See Gagnier: 147. In a letter of 1893 Alfred Douglas writes to Kains-Jackson: 'Perhaps nobody knows as I do what he [Oscar Wilde] has done for the "new culture"' (Douglas 1893).
4. George Fleming is the pseudonym of Julia Constance Fletcher.
5. See Kohl: 106ff.

Works Cited

Alford, Mary. (1887) 'What Will Become of the Girls?', *Lady's World*, 386–7.

Anon. (1890). 'A Study in Puppydom', *St. James Gazette* (24 June), 3.

Anon. (1887). 'The Oxford Ladies' Colleges, by a member of one of them', *Women's World* 1 (Nov), 32–5.

Anon. (1884). 'Local Art Notes. Leeds', *The Artist* 5 (March), 77–8.

Ballaster, R.; Beetham, M.; Frazer, E.; and Hebron, S. (1991). *Women's Worlds: Ideology, Femininity, and Women's Magazines*. London.

Beerbohm, M. (1894). 'A Defence of Cosmetics', *Yellow Book* 1 (April), 65–82.

Beerbohm, M. (1893). 'The Incomparable Beauty of Modern Dress', *Spirit Lamp* 4.(June), 90–80.

Campbell, Lady J.S. (1887). 'The Woodland Gods', *Woman's World* 1 (Nov.), 1–7.

Dellamora, R. (1990). *Masculine Desire. The Sexual Politics of Victorian Aestheticism.* Chapel Hill and London.

Donaldson, M.F. (1887). 'A Day at Girton College', *Lady's World*, 142–3.

Douglas, Lord Alfred. (1893). [Prospectus] for *The Spirit Lamp* (May).

Gagnier, R. (1987). *Idylls of the Marketplace. Oscar Wilde and the Victorian Public.* London.

Harris, Frank. (1916). *Oscar Wilde: His Life and Confessions.* 2 vols. New York.

Hart-Davis, R., ed. (1985). *More Letters of Oscar Wilde.* London.

Kohl, Norbert. (1989). *Oscar Wilde.* Cambridge.

Marcus, Steven. (1977). *The Other Victorians: A Study of Sexuality and Pornography in Mid Nineteenth-Century England.* New York.

Nowell-Smith, S. (1958). *The House of Cassell 1848–1958.* London.

Pattison, Mark. (1877). MS. Pattison 130, fol. 164r [19 Jan.]. Bodleian Library, Oxford.

Pater, W. (1867). 'Winckelmann', *Westminster Review* n.s. 31 (Jan.), 80–110.

Pemberton, Max. (1920). ' "The Yard". Memories of the House of Cassell,' *Sunday Times* (19 Sept.), 8.

Portsmouth, E. (1887). 'The Position of Women', *Woman's World* I (Nov.), 7–10.

Reade, Brian, ed. (1970). *Sexual Heretics: Male Homosexuality in English Literature from 1850 to 1900.* London.

Shevelow, K. (1989). *Women and Print Culture.* London and New York.

Sedgwick, Eve. (1985). *Between Men: English Literature and Male Homosocial Desire.* New York.

Steele, Valerie. (1985). *Fashion and Eroticism.* New York.

Tuchman, Gaye (1989). *Edging Women Out.* London.

Tyrwhitt, R. (1877). 'The Greek Spirit in Modern Literature', *Contemporary Review* 29 (March), 552–66.

White, Cynthia. (1970). *Women's Magazines 1693–1968.* London.

Winship, J. (1987). *Inside Women's Magazines.* London and New York.

Wilde, O. (1891). 'The Soul of Man Under Socialism', *Fortnightly Review* 55 o.s. (Feb.), 292–319.

Wilde, O. (1887a). A.L.S. to Madam [London, Summer]. Henry W. and Albert A. Berg Collection. The New York Public Library, Astor, Lenox and Tilden Foundations.

Wilde, O. (1887b). 'Literary and other Notes', *Womans World* I (Nov.), 40.

Wilde, O. (1885a). 'Shakespeare and Stage Costume', *Nineteenth Century* 17 (May), 800–18.

Wilde, O. (1885b). 'The Relation of Art to Dress', *Pall Mall Gazette* (28 Feb.), 4.

8

The Savoy: 1896.
Gender in Crisis?

The eight numbers of *The Savoy* which span 1896 not only postdate the Wilde trials; the magazine is doubly their descendant, in the aggressive heterosexuality with which it registers the prohibition on homosexual discourse which the trials effected, and in its birth from the ruin of *The Yellow Book*, that manifestation of decadence condemned by association during the trials, attacked by the mob, and finally disempowered by a censorious act of self-purification. I want to consider the dominance of male discourse in *The Savoy*, the male gaze and the construction of women, the relation of the magazine to the new journalism, and the curious but unmistakable efforts of twentieth-century scholarship to detoxify *The Savoy*'s defiant provocations and eroticism.

When *The Savoy* appeared in January 1896, its relation to *The Yellow Book* was that of a rebellious and rejected offspring whose project, tacitly, was to surpass and displace its parent. Perceived by the press in this light, the *Savoy* team of Arthur Symons and Aubrey Beardsley, literary and art editor respectively, had provoked vociferous criticism precisely two years before when Symons' poem 'Stella Maris' (in which the memory of intercourse with a prostitute – 'the Juliet of a night' – is compared with the star of the Virgin or Stella Maris) and Beardsley's accompanying drawing, 'A Night Piece' had appeared in the first number of *The Yellow Book* in April 1894. In a painstaking task of erasure, Beardsley's sizeable contribution to the fifth issue of *The Yellow Book* in April 1895 was extracted *after the type was set* in response to pressure on its publisher John Lane from the public and from fellow contributors such as Alice and Wilfrid Meynell and William Watson. So Beardsley was licking his wounds from the outset of *The Savoy*, and by the time it ceased publication in December 1896, 14 out of the 38 letterpress contributors were *Yellow Book* authors. *The Yellow Book* itself collapsed one issue later in April 1897.

While initially both publications were quarterlies and illustrated, describing themselves as 'An Illustrated Quarterly' on their title pages, and while both highlighted their visual content by publishing separate contents lists for letterpress and pictures, the quarto format, cloth binding, considerable expense (5s.), length and bulk of *The Yellow Book* made it appear booklike,[1] while the folio format, paper boards, price (2s. 6d.), and relative slimness of *The Savoy* made it look more like a periodical; this identity was confirmed when its boards lapsed to paper covers in July, and it became a two-shilling monthly after this third number. So while the link between the two periodicals was very strong, involving frequency, division of contents, and contributors, *The Savoy* sought to compete with its famous predecessor initially by undercutting its price by half, and eventually by entering the monthly periodical market.

These strategies of cheap pricing and greater frequency may be related to the pulsations of the new journalism, named by Matthew Arnold in 1887 (Arnold: 629), which led to the creation in 1896 of the first mass-market newspaper in Britain, the *Daily Mail*.[2] The ubiquity of the newspaper in late Victorian culture, and its inroads into daily life in this momentous year of British press history are registered, even featured, in the first number of *The Savoy*, as an adjunct of the naturalism which constitutes, along with symbolism and impressionism, one of the characteristic discourses of its entire run.

Under my window in the foggy, dripping street, those little imps, the newspaper-boys, are making the hour horrisonant with their yells. What voices the urchins develop, at what tender years! You and I, Mr Editor, we could not advertise our wares so penetratingly, though we strove till our throats cracked over it. I hear there is a movement on foot for the suppression, or at least, the discipline, of these too-raucous vendors of our news; and with all one's jealousy of the law's interference, it would be difficult reasonably, perhaps, to oppose this exercise of it. Yet, after all, how much are these rude and hideous cries of a piece with the thoroughfares they resound in, or, for the matter of that, with how much of our manners at large! (Image: 141)

Other characteristics of *The Savoy* chime with developments in the press associated with the new journalism, such as sensationalism, giveaway gifts, signature, the use of 'star' contributors to increase readership, and a topicality akin to gossip which, even in a monthly, supplied a news element. Two aspects of *The Savoy* illustrate this topicality: the multivalence of its title invokes, perhaps first, the fashionable, elegant and cultural world of the luxury hotel in the Strand[3] (built by Richard D'Oyly Carte who had privately commissioned Whistler to design his personal library and billiard room). Before the hotel opened in August 1889, it was described in an advertisement in *The Times* as 'The perfection of luxury and comfort. Artistic furniture throughout. Electric light only everywhere' (Jackson: 293; Anon. 1889: 1). With an *haute cuisine* restaurant intended for the theatre-goers, the Savoy was frequented by decadents and the famous. However, there is also in the title of *The Savoy* a range of references, cheeky and daring in the circumstances, to Wilde and the recent trials, insofar as Wilde was associated with the theatre which had opened in 1881 with *Patience*, and subsequently housed productions of Wilde's own plays. Moreover, some of Wilde's assignations with boys were alleged during the trial to have taken place at the hotel. If the referent of the title of *The Yellow Book* was to risqué French yellowback novels, then the allusions of the title of *The Savoy* were parallel and similarly provocative.

The second, topical invocation of gossip is equally oblique if unmistakable: Symons's long article in the first number, 'Dieppe: 1895', would entice potential readers, for at the time of the trials in the spring and summer of 1895 when fear was widespread, Dieppe was one of the principal destinations of Wilde's friends, associates, and likeminded men. That *The Savoy* was planned in Dieppe during that summer is itself testimony to the widespread sense in sexually avant-garde circles that England was not safe, as is the implicit, coded suggestion of a link between the new publication and the events of the previous spring by the publication of such a title as 'Dieppe: 1895' in its first number. In the event, however, neither those in flight nor the germination of *The Savoy* occupy Symons's provocative and erotic article, the title of which, like the burgeoning use of the headline in the new journalism of the period, is designed to stimulate purchase and to set the tone for the new magazine.

Like the cries of the news-vendors described by Selwyn Image, *The Savoy* itself could be construed in its time as 'rude' and 'hideous'. Most nineteenth-century women readers would have found the contents of Symons', Smithers', and Beardsley's venture offensive, and at the very least unrespectable. One significant difference between *The Yellow Book* and *The Savoy* lies in the latter's exclusion of women, not merely from its readership, but from its founding coterie, from its contributors, and from its editorial staff. Where women are conspicuous as authors of fiction, essays and poems in *The Yellow Book* and Ella D'Arcy acted in an editorial capacity, women appear in *The Savoy* exclusively as authors of poems, with the single exception of Olivia Shakespear, writer of a two-part prose 'Phantasy' entitled 'Beauty's Hour', and one of Yeats's circle at the time. *The Savoy* is an aggressively male and heterosexual magazine, full of male discourse, masculine constructions of women, and misogyny, bristling (if that is the word) with erotic drawings, and clearly (and exclusively) aimed at male readers.

If many and varied, the codes of exclusion were easily readable by contemporaries. First, the publisher and editors had eloquent track records: Leonard Smithers, personally a paedophile, and professionally the publisher of Richard Burton's salacious edition in 1890 of *Priapeia, or The Sportive Epigrams of divers poets on Priapus* and a dealer in and publisher of pornography;[4] Beardsley had recently illustrated Wilde's *Salome* with exquisite if sexually explicit drawings; and Symons's volume of poems, *London Nights*, published by Smithers in June 1895, elicited the charge from the *Pall Mall Gazette* (Anon. 1895: 4) that Symons was 'a dirty-minded man.... his life's more like a pig-sty.... Every woman he pays to meet him, he tells us, is desirous to kiss his lips; our boots too are desirous, but of quite another part of him, for quite another purpose'. Symons, Beardsley, and Smithers were, by any contemporary perception, an unholy if talented trinity. Then too, the first version of the prospectus, which Beardsley had designed and 80 000 of which Smithers had circulated, consisted of a drawing of a sexually aroused John Bull. Before it ever appeared, *The Savoy* was coded as an 'advanced' magazine, unsuitable for respectable women and the drawing-room, to be read by a male readership in the safety of the club and the privacy of the study. Its prospective readership knew that.

In the event of its publication, both its contributors and distributors affirm its masculinity and its marginality. I want to illustrate these identities of masculinity and marginality through examples of four kinds of cultural discourse in and about *The Savoy*. The first example relates to the discourse of secularism, the anti-religious nature of the content of the magazine, and to the pervasive discourse of misogyny; the second to the conceptualisation of its audience by two of its contributors; and the third to the discourse of commerce used by W.H. Smith when it refused to distribute *The Savoy* in September 1896, an event which contributed substantially to its demise in December of that year.

The first article in the first number of *The Savoy* is a heavily ironic, even sardonic piece by Shaw ('On Going to Church') in which church buildings are viewed as sources of spiritual restoration and aesthetic pleasure along with alcohol, tobacco and public houses. On the whole preferring church architecture to its alternatives, the author laments 'There is still one serious obstacle to the use of churches on the very day when most people are best able and most disposed to visit them – I mean, of course, the services' (Shaw: 23). The attack on religion, the adumbration of a range of bodily pleasures largely confined to men – stimulants and drugs, most of which involve smoking – and the recommendation that it is preferable to visit the parish church (as described) than the village inn all construct a male readership, one accustomed to agnosticism, smoking, drinking and the freedom to choose between the church and the public house. Other essays which involve an irreverent and radical attack on religion include Havelock Ellis on 'Zola' (in which he claims 'If some of the stories of the Old Testament were presented to us under some trifling disguise on week-days we should declare that they were filthier than the filthiest things in Zola' (Ellis 1896c: 77), and on Nietzsche 'the modern incarnation of that image of intellectual pride which Marlowe created in Faustus' (Ellis 1896b: 79). Yeats's story, 'Rosa Alchemica', which is also Faustian and explicitly secular, aesthetic and pagan, similarly constructs the knowing reader of *The Savoy* as male and 'advanced'.

It was probably the *Savoy's* impressionist prose, short stories and artwork which, on balance, elicited Lenore Casford's superlative claim in 1929 that *The Savoy* is 'the high watermark in achievement of English periodicals' (Casford: 21), and I want to look at this material for a moment, in connection with its construction of female subjectivity and of the male spectator and his gaze. In particular I will comment on two essays by Symons, 'Dieppe' (No. 1) and 'At the Alhambra' (No. 5); two stories by Frederick Wedmore, 'To Nancy' (No. 1) and 'The Deterioration of Nancy' (No. 2), another called 'Mutability' by Theodore Wratislaw (No. 5), and 'A Mere Man', one of two anonymous tales by one author in a magazine which is characterised by a policy of signature. Certain material is excluded, such as Beardsley's two instalments of *Under the Hill* and Conrad's brutal and determinist tale, *The Idiots*, which is both better known and less germane to the misogynist strain than the work selected.

The two pieces of Symons, Editor of *The Savoy*, signal preoccupations which are taken up elsewhere in the magazine by others: the pre-pubescent and nubile female body as seen by the male spectator, in particular in states of exposure such as at the beach (Dieppe),[5] in rehearsal, and at the music hall performance. None of this material is exclusive to *The Savoy*, and John Stokes' *In the Nineties* provides particularities of the range of attention to the music hall and the beach, but it is nevertheless important to say that *The Savoy*, taking up the allusion of its title to the theatre, *is* characterised by numerous examples of short stories, drawings, poems which treat performing women or women as the object of the gaze of males, in the theatre particularly, but also at the fair, on the beach, or on the street. Usually these women are in a subordinate power-relation to the male spectator, through class and/or age, education, experience or self-control. Naturalism, impressionism and symbolism can be revelatory modes for the decadent male author, providing a discourse which authorises the (male) gaze upon the detail of corrupt flesh and its inscription in the name of scientific observation, at the same time as allowing the scientific 'distance' to slip into a preference for the symbolic or artifice proclaimed by the decadent. It is a style which trails both prurience and misogyny, as may be seen in Beardsley's illustration (Figure 8.1). For Symons and Beardsley, as for other contributors to *The Savoy*, characteristically, detailed attention to clothes takes over and substitutes for discourse of the body; Finch argues more generally that in 'late nineteenth-century England ... a new sartorial iconology [emerges] that collapses the age-old dialectic between the body and its clothes' (Finch: 339). Here is the male spectator on female bathers at Dieppe:

> white *peignoirs*, bright and dark bathing costumes, the white and rose of bare and streaming flesh, passing to and fro, hurriedly, between the bathing machines and the sea. The men, if they have good figures, look well; they have at least the chance of looking well. But the women! Rare, indeed, is the women who can look pretty, in her toilette or herself, as she comes out of the sea, wraps herself in a sort of white nightgown, and staggers up the

Figure 8.1 Female bather under male gaze. Aubrey Beardsley in *The Savoy*.

beach, the water running down her legs. Even at the more elegant moment when she drops her *peignoir* at the sea's edge, before stepping in, it is hard for her, with the best intentions on her part and the best of wishes on ours, to look desirable. She is often wise enough to wear corsets; without them, even an excellent figure may appear a little extreme, in one direction or another. It is with a finer taste, after all, that in England the women are not allowed to bathe with the men, are kept out of sight as much as possible. A sentimental sensualist should avoid the French seaside. He will be pained at seeing how ridiculous a beautiful woman may look when she has very few clothes on. The lines of the body are lost or deformed; there is none of the suggestion of ordinary costume, only a grotesque and shapeless image, all in pits and protuberances, for which Nature should be ashamed to accept responsibility. Complete nudity, there is no doubt, has its charm, though of a somewhat primitive kind; but this state of being undressed and yet covered, in this makeshift, unmilliner-like way, it is too barbarous, Mesdames, for the tolerance of any gentleman of taste. (Symons 1896b: 86–8)

This positioning of the figures of women as the objects of the censorious and appetitive male gaze of the 'sentimental sensualist' and 'the gentleman of taste' is transferred to the theatre, a setting which legitimises it, in Symons' other divagationary piece, 'At the Alhambra':

The front row of the stalls, on a first night, has a character of its own. It is entirely filled by men, and the men who fill it have not come simply from an abstract aesthetic interest in the ballet. They have friends on the other side of the footlights, and their friends on the other side of the footlights will look down, the moment they come on the stage, to see who are in the front row, and who are standing by the bar on either side. (Symons: 1896a: 81)

Both pieces also position the male spectator as an outsider privy to prohibited or even female space; the 'Dieppe' piece ends with an account of the male narrator watching Jane Hading:

in that absurd little dressing room, where I had to squeeze myself into a corner, while the actress stood, hot and impatient, in front of the long glass, in which from time to time I caught the charm of a somewhat pre-occupied smile, as the dresser stitched and pinned the separate fragments of a bodice which was to be so magnificently torn off, with so considerable a view of such superb shoulders, in the fine, exciting scene of the second act. (Symons 1896b: 102)

This titillating and salacious scene which produces and circulates male sexual fantasy in the male triangle of dramatised spectator, the writer and the reader of the text is reproduced in an aroused and arousing passage on another glimpse of female undress, in 'At the Alhambra':

> Rehearsal costume, to the casual outside spectator, is rather curious. There is a bodice, which may be of any kind; there is a short petticoat, generally of white, with discreet linen drawers to match; the stockings are for the most part black. But a practising dress leaves room, in its many exceptions, for every variety of individual taste. A lively fancy sometimes expends itself on something wonderful in stockings, wonderful coloured things, clocked and patterned. Then there are petticoats plain and ornamented, limp and starched, setting tightly and flapping loosely; petticoats with frillings and edgings, petticoats of blue, of pink, of salmon colour, of bright red. But it is the bodice that gives most scope for the decorative instinct (Symons 1896a: 79)

If Symons as *The Savoy's* editor gives the lead to the potential of the world of the theatre for the 'sentimental sensualist', Frederick Wedmore's two stories about Nancy offer a prurient view of the inevitable 'progress' of corruption which the theatre world imposes in the careering 'development' of a working-class 'child' (pre-pubescent) actress to an adult woman performer. The construction of the male spectator here is also individualised and detailed; he is an experienced, upper-class portrait painter, accredited and author-ised to gaze 'scientifically' at the female body and study the female mind by thirty years as an RA, so that the trope of spectatorship is both theatrical – the actor and the audience – and that of visual art, the artist and his model. Wedmore includes visual stills ('But you want an Ingres to do you justice. The slimness of the girl, and what a fineness, as of race; and then, the agility of infinite practice, and sixteen young years!' (Wedmore 1896a: 35)) as well as breathless descriptions of her dance performance:

A third turn – then it was that you were agile most of all. The flying feet went skyward. Black shoes rushed, comet-like, so far above your head, and clattered on the floor again; while against the sober crimson of the background curtain – a dull, thin stuff, stretched straightly – gleamed the white of moving skirts, and blazed the boss of brightest scarlet that nestled somewhere in the brown gold of your head. Then, flushed and panting, it was over. (Wedmore 1896a: 35)

The preoccupation of the nineties more generally with dance is discussed by John Stokes (Stokes 1989) and memorialised by Yeats's later, and still haunting question from 'Among School Children' which interrogates the distinctions between physicality and spirituality, the sexual and the aesthetic, 'How can we know the dancer from the dance?' For Wedmore the interplay between the immediate sexual frisson of spectatorship ('the boss of brightest scarlet that nestled somewhere' (Wedmore 1896a: 35) and the inevitable corruption that follows in the overdetermined narrative of naturalism ('it was over' (Wedmore 1896a: 35)) is made explicit in the form of the story (warning letters 'To Nancy'), in the narrator's melodramatic fears and anticipations on the occasion of her sixteenth birthday ('Would she be like the rest? – at least, too many. Besmirched, too?' (Wedmore 1896a: 40)), and in his fantasies in the theatre in which he neatly exempts himself from any part in the destructive process by identifying the (exciting) perpetrators of her sexual corruption as 'other', *'false* friends'.

Last night, it seemed to me, the dark was peopled with your enemies; with your false friends, who were coming – always coming – the unavoidable crowd of the egotistic destroyers of youth. Their dark hearts, I thought, look upon her as a prey. (Wedmore 1896a: 40)

Set five months later, the follow-up story in the second number of *The Savoy,* 'The Deterioration of Nancy', continues the determinist narrative process; we are vouchsafed short letters from Nancy herself whose 'innocent' texts are deconstructed in the long letters of experience from Clement Ashton: 'all that it really comes to is that you will be "spoilt". "Spoilt" or "ruined".' (Wedmore 1896b: 103) Nancy's narrative is mediated by Ashton's, and the curve of her life is determined by the plot of naturalism. *The Savoy's* use here of two linked short stories by the same author in successive numbers represents an interesting variant on the use of serial fiction in other periodicals to ensure readers from number to number. The failure of the plot of 'To Nancy' to develop arresting turns and directions, though attributable to the deterioration plot of naturalism, certainly vitiates the force of the 'serial' appeal to readers. There was no third instalment.

But other, single, stories in *The Savoy* have similar determinist plots for women outside of the theatrical and artistic worlds. These involve middle- and upper-class women who also, pregnant, addicted to drink, or merely sexual, 'fall' in sight of the male spectator and author. The anonymous 'A Mere Man' by 'A New Writer' (No. 2) and 'Mutability' (No. 5) by Theodore Wratislaw both 'show' marriageable women in society to be equally as corruptible as actresses and models; in 'Mutability' the story is told from the point of view of the culpable, consciously corrupting male who nevertheless takes second place in the guilt stakes at the denouement of the tale in which the respectable society woman, knowing his past, wittingly encourages his advances. The story represents a distinct shift from Hardy's constructions of the femme/homme moyen sensual in *Tess* where the heroine is 'pure' and in *Jude* where both Jude and Sue act in good faith. In 'Mutability' neither party does.

More than half way through the run of *The Savoy*, in October, Havelock Ellis's review essay on *Jude* raises the question of female readership of such explicitly sexual material as *Jude* – and implicitly *The Savoy* – within the magazine itself. Ellis spends a good deal of energy and space arguing that both working-class men (e.g. the compositor) and the 'Young Person' (girls and women) should have free access to *Jude* which 'is an artistic picture of a dilemma such as the Young Person, in some form or another, may one day have to face. Surely, on moral grounds, she should understand and realize this beforehand' (Ellis 1896a: 47). In the first number Ellis had already alluded bitterly to the period restrictions on language usage:

We have almost lost the indispensable words "belly" and "bowels", both used so often and with such admirable effect in the Psalms; we talk of the "stomach", a word which is not only an incorrect equivalent, but at best totally inapt for serious or poetic uses ... In modern literary language, indeed, man scarcely exists save in his extremities. For we take the pubes as a centre, and we thence describe a circle with a radius of some eighteen inches – in America the radius is rather longer – and we forbid any reference to any organ within that circle, save that maid-of-all-work the "stomach"; in other words, we make it impossible to say anything to the point concerning the central functions of life. It is a question how far any real vital literature can be produced under such conditions. (Ellis 1896c: 78)

but, perhaps strategically, at the launch of *The Savoy*, Ellis does not explicitly attribute these restrictions to the sensibilities of the female reader to whom George Moore points in his pamphlet *Literature at Nurse* (1885). Clearly the issue of the female reader, and the tendency to lay the prevailing censorship of fiction at her door, are contributary to the phenomenon of the male gendering of *The Savoy*.

One reason why *The Savoy* failed was that its aggressively sexual discourse, its predominantly male contributors, and its reiterated misogyny excluded the increasing market of literate middle- and upper-class female readers. When W.H. Smith refused to distribute the first monthly number in August, they stated, according to Yeats, 'We have an audience of young ladies as well as an audience of agnostics' (Yeats 1955a: 216). Smith's apparently economic objection to the exclusion of women readers from the readership of *The Savoy* has not been taken seriously by later commentators; given Smith's well-known proclivity to censorship, it is possible, as was believed at the time and more recently, that Smith was obscuring the *firm's* objection to the inclusion of a hitherto unpublished illustration of a full frontal male nude classical figure by William Blake behind the alleged offence to women readers; but it is similarly possible that having objected to Beardsley's work in past numbers, his absence through illness that the three linked Blake articles by Yeats addressed, became the object of Smith's displaced ire.

Nevertheless, it should be recognised that the publication of Yeats's articles, but particularly the drawings by Blake, *was* daring, provocative, and even sensational on the part of *The Savoy*, and Smith was quite correct in surmising that these articles and illustrations excluded women readers, as the rest of the letterpress and artwork did. It is all of a piece. Ellis's article on *Jude the Obscure* and female readers *was*, in respect to salvaging *The Savoy*, late in the day – after the explanation and ban by Smith and simultaneous with the announcement of the demise of the magazine. However, Ellis can be seen to address the issue of female readers raised by Smith. Likewise, it is tempting to see Beardsley's title-page design for the next number, 7, as a response to the question of the missing female readership. In what might be dubbed Beardsley's plain style it depicts a spectacled, censorious female Elderly Person reading, and in possession of a book coveted by her pained youthful companion – a Pierrot figure of indeterminate sex but more probably a male Compositor figure rather than a female Young Person.

Edgar Jepson, one of the new author contributors to *The Savoy* notes in his *Memories* (1933) that '*The Savoy* was the last effort of the nineties that I knew. It has been said that the conviction of Wilde was the end of the nineties. It was not. No one, equipped to judge, in those days reckoned his work of the importance his imprisonment has given it' (Jepson: 287), and Jepson goes on to argue 'The truth is the nineties came to an end because the poets and the artists were tired' (Jepson: 288). I want to suggest, unlike Jepson and unlike Stanley Weintraub who also yokes *The Savoy* (which he dubs *The Beardsley)* to the fortunes of its most renowned individual contributor(s), that the short life and ultimate failure of *The Savoy* had its basis in discourses of literary naturalism, impressionism, symbolism and visual decadence, with a targeted readership which was exclusive, male, connoisseur, while its low price, monthly publication, topicality and sensationalism seemed to align it with the larger readership imagined and courted by the new journalism. Its demise seems to me to be due to its economic and cultural straddling of the formations of the male avant-garde/erotica market which excluded the female educated reader, Ellis's gesture at the market for family reading which the *Cornhill* and *Macmillan's Magazine* and later the illustrated *Strand Magazine* represent, and the mass market which the *Daily Mail* captured in the lifetime of *The Savoy* in 1896.

Given the place that gender occupies in *The Savoy*, it is particularly interesting that a number of late twentieth-century critics are at pains either to take no account of its aggressive heterosexuality and its male discourse or insistently to deny its decadence and to detoxify it that way. Ian Fletcher is the distinguished and notable exception in his contribution on 'Decadence and the Little Magazines' in his own anthology *Decadence and the 1890s*. However,

'Innocent Decadence: The Poetry of the *Savoy*', an article by
Wendell Harris in *PMLA*, quoted recently with approval in Karl
Beckson's biography of Symons and Alvin Sullivan's *English
Literary Magazines*, is a fascinating example of a desperate and
apparently widespread wish to exonerate the magazine from the
charge of Decadence. I don't wish to make a detailed argument
about the contestable conclusions of this article; I am principally
interested in the methodology which leads to them.

Historically, Harris is contributing to a debate on the definitions
of decadence and the usefulness of the term, but the form of
cultural production is ignored, as if it were transparent: the poetry
is separated out from the contents of a journal in which illustration
plays an equally important role as the letterpress. This is a critical
act of denial which stems from logocentrism, and from an insens-
itivity to a mode of cultural production, the press, which lies
outside the boundaries of high culture. In the case of *The Savoy* the
illustrations as a group, all else aside for a moment, would clinch
the argument for decadence. So would the prose – the essays and
short fiction – if we were going to isolate genres (in the mode of the
new criticism).

There are two aspects of the choice of poetry I want to remark on;
it is the principal genre in the magazine in which women are
represented as contributors, and it is largely poems by women
(such as Mathilde Blind and Lelia Macdonald) that Harris is able to
dismiss in one-liners as 'innocent'. Mostly, Harris is interested in
particular and renowned male writers, arguably the '(male) major
authors' published in *The Savoy*, namely Yeats, Symons, and
Dowson. Now, it is interesting to note that *The Savoy* had a tendency (and perhaps a policy) of publication of work in more than
one genre by its individual contributors, so that Symons publishes
poetry, essays and fiction, Yeats the same, Dowson and Wratislaw
poetry and fiction, and Beardsley art work, poetry and fiction. Both
Yeats and Dowson published prose in *The Savoy* which is virtually
ignored by Harris. My point is that even if, as is the case, the focus
in Harris is drearily authorial, it is exclusive in its excision of the
totality of the contributions of the authors in question.

But there is a more profound problem with Harris's selection of
text, and it is this. The periodical text, the format in which these
poems appeared, is completely ignored; by this sleight of hand
alone, is it possible to read the poetry in *The Savoy* as 'innocent
decadence'. One example will have to suffice; on the basis of many

examples I am certain that scrutiny of most of the poems discussed
by Harris, as part of periodical texts rather than as autonomous
texts, shows how meanings are generated by an intertextuality
which emanates in part from the structure of the individual
periodical issue. For Harris the sexual explicitness of

Beloved, let your eyes half close, and your heart beat
Over my heart, and your hair fall about my breast
Drowning Love's lonely hour in deep twilight of rest;

in Yeats's 'The Shadowy Horses' (Yeats 1896c: 83) is unexception-
able and remains innocent. Several points may be made to contest
this claim. Yeats's poem, which appears in the first issue of *The
Savoy*, is placed between an article by Havelock Ellis on Zola, and
Symons's piece on Dieppe. Zola's work was still controversial eight
years after Henry Vizetelly had been imprisoned in Britain in 1887
for publishing *La Terre*, and in 1892 Hubert Crackanthorpe's then
anonymous article, 'Realism in France and England' in the *Albemarle
Magazine* had renewed controversy over Zola. *The Savoy's* 'Zola: the
Man and His Work' begins, as it goes on, sensationally and
provocatively: 'Zola's name – a barbarous, explosive name, like an
anarchist's bomb – has been tossed about amid hoots and yells for a
quarter of a century' (Ellis 1896c: 67). Symons's 'Dieppe: 1895'
begins with the unusually sexually explicit description of women
bathers, and interspersed between the Ellis article and the Yeats
poem is a full-page illustration of a fetching 'Parisienne' demi-
monde, set against a background of peacock feathers and with a
border including an ironic bouquet of fresh flowers, champagne and
a death's head. Lastly, the most incriminating silence on Harris's
part is that he fails to mention that Yeats's poem is one of 'Two Love
Poems' by Yeats on that page, the second being 'The Travail of
Passion': deploying the figure of the transfer of Christ's passion to
mortal love, it inscribes bondage and sadism, as well as blasphemy:
'The knotted scourge, the nail-pierced hands, the wounded side'. A
context for this religious imagery is provided by the first article in
the number, Shaw's irreverent 'On Going to Church'.

This example is not atypical of the methodology of the rest of
Harris's article, and a question arises which might be phrased, Why
go to these lengths to deny the decadence of *The Savoy*, a decadence
which is claimed by Symons (1896a: 75) and Yeats (1896b: 118). This
question is posed in terms of individual authorial intention, and an

answer may be put in those terms: a desire by the critic to deny decadence as 'other', and to absorb *The Savoy* into the hygienic 'objectivity' of the dominant hegemony of high literary culture in the 1960s. Another framing of the question – What does that methodology [Harris's] disallow? – implies that the individual critic is written by language, and that the language system and episteme in which that critical text was produced determined and overdetermined the outcome. Perhaps a last point should be made about our present, yours as reader and mine as author: thanks to the gestation of feminism and women's studies in the last forty years, we have seen the appearance of theories of masculinity outside sociology, the institutional incidence of gender studies, and perhaps most recently the visibility and audibility of gay and lesbian discourse. Our own period, almost a century after that of *The Savoy*, might itself be viewed as one of gender in crisis, a moment in history in which gender constitutes a conscious factor in conceptualising the problematics of historical writing,[6] as in this scrutiny of *The Savoy* and its readings.

Notes

1. In its prospectus, the editors of *The Yellow Book* were explicit in their wish to distinguish their new venture from 'bad old...periodical literature' on the one hand and to associate it with book publication on the other:

    The aim...of *The Yellow Book* is to depart as far as may be from the bad old traditions of periodical literature, and to provide an Illustrated Magazine which shall be beautiful as a piece of bookmaking, modern and distinguished in its letter-press and its pictures, and withal popular in the better sense of the word. It is felt that such a Magazine, at present, is conspicuous by its absence...
       In many ways its contributors will employ a freer hand than the limitations of the old-fashioned periodical can permit....(Quoted in Harrison: 4–5).
       It will be charming, it will be daring, it will be distinguished. It will be a *book* – a book to be read, and placed upon one's shelves, and read again; a book in form, and a book in substance; a book beautiful to see and convenient to handle; a book with style, a book with finish; a book that every book-lover will love at first sight; a book that will make book-lovers of many who are now indifferent to books.

The Yellow Book will contain no advertisements other than publishers' lists. (Quoted in Harrison: 5–6)

2. See Elliott who connects Beardsley's work in the *Yellow Book* and elsewhere with the New Journalism.
3. See Jackson.
4. For Smithers, see Jepson, Sims, and Weintraub.
5. See Stokes (1990).
6. See Showalter on sexual anarchy in the *fin de siècle*, and the link of the 1890s with the 1990s.

Works Cited

Anon. (1896). 'A Mere Man', *Savoy* 1(April), 26–52.

Anon. (1895). 'Pah!' [review of *London Nights*], *Pall Mall Gazette* (2 Sept.), 4.

Anon. (1889). Advertisement for *The Savoy; The Times* (2 Aug.), 1.

Arnold, M. (1887). 'Up to Easter', *Nineteenth Century* 21(May), 629–43.

Beckson, K. (1987). *Arthur Symons. A Life*. Oxford.

Benkowitz, M. (1981). *Aubrey Beardsley*. London.

[Burton, R.] Outidanos, transl. (1890). *Priapeia or The Sportive Epigrams of Divers Poets on Priapus*. Cosmopoli.

Casford, E.L. (1929). 'The Magazines of the 1890s'. Oregon.

[Crackanthorpe, H.]. (1892). 'Realism in France and England', *The Albemarle Review* 1(Feb.), 39–43.

Dowling, L. (1986). 'Letterpress and Picture in the 1890s', *Yearbook of English Studies* 16, 7–31.

Elliott, Bridget. (1989). 'Sights of Pleasure. Beardsley's Images of Actresses and the New Journalism of the 1890s', *Rediscovering Aubrey Beardsley*, ed. Robert Langenfeld. Ann Arbor. pp. 71–101.

Ellis, H. (1896a). 'Concerning Jude the Obscure', *Savoy* 3(Oct.) 35–49.

Ellis, H. (1896b). 'Friedrich Nietzsche. I', *Savoy* I(April), 79–94.

Ellis, H. (1896c). 'Zola. The Man and his Work', *Savoy* 1(Jan), 67–80.

Finch, C. (1991). 'Victorian Underwear and Representations of the Female Body', *Victorian Studies* 34 (Spring), 337–63.

Fletcher, I. (1979). 'Decadence and the Little Magazines', in *Decadence and the 1890s*, ed. I. Fletcher. SUAS 17. London. pp. 173–202.

Garbaty, T.J. (1960). 'The French Coteries of the *Savoy*', *PMLA* 75, 609–15.

Harris, W. (1962). 'Innocent Decadence: the Poetry of the Savoy', *PMLA* 77, 629–36.

Harrison, Fraser. (1974). 'Introduction', *The Yellow Book. An Anthology*. London.

Image, S. (1896). 'On Criticism and the Critic', *Savoy* 1(Jan.), 141–5.

Jackson, S. (1979). *The Savoy* [Hotel]. London.

Jepson, E. (1933). *Memories of a Victorian*. London.

Mix, K. (1960). *A Study in Yellow*. Lawrence, Kan. and London.

Shaw, G.B. (1896). 'On Going to Church', *Savoy* (Jan.), 13–28.

Showalter, E. (1991). *Sexual Anarchy*. London.

Sims, G. (1983). 'Leonard Smithers', *Antiquarian Book Monthly Review*, X(July, Aug.), 248–51; 294–9.

Stokes, J. (1990). 'Dieppe: 1895', *Essays and Poems*. ELT Special Series No. 4. Greensboro, NC.

Stokes, J. (1989). *In the Nineties*. Hemel Hempstead.

Symons, A. (1896a). 'At the Alhambra: Impressions and Sensations', *Savoy* 2(Sept.), 75–83.

Symons, A. (1896b). 'Dieppe: 1895', *Savoy* 1(Jan.), 84–102.

Symons, A. (1895). *London Nights*. London.

Symons, A. (1894). 'Stella Maris', *Yellow Book* 1(April), 129–31.

Wedmore, F. (1896a). 'To Nancy', *Savoy* 1(Jan.), 31–41.

Wedmore, F. (1896b). 'The Deterioration of Nancy', *Savoy* 1(April), 99–108.

Weintraub, S., ed. (1966). *The Savoy. Nineties Experiment*. University Park, Pa., and London.

Wilde, O. (1894). *Salome*, illus. A. Beardsley. London.

Yeats, W.B. (1955). *Autobiographies*. London.

Yeats, W.B. (1896a). 'Rosa Alchemica', *Savoy* 1(April), 56–70.

Yeats, W.B. (1896b), 'II. Verlaine in 1894', *Savoy* 1(April), 117–18.

Yeats, W.B. (1896c). 'Two Love Poems. "The Shadowy Horses" and "The Travail of Passion"', *Savoy*, 1(Jan.), 83.

III

Biography and the
Construction of Authorship

9

The *DNB* and the *DNB* 'Walter Pater'

The *Dictionary of National Biography* is a great achievement of nineteenth-century English scholarship, and its first two editors, Leslie Stephen and Sidney Lee, were knighted for their work. The double focus of this paper is designed to ensure that we see it not only in terms of its self-proclaimed theory but also in practice, through considering the versions, author, and adequacy of one biography.

For the twentieth-century scholar who consults it exclusively, for rapid reference, the *DNB* has several pitfalls. First is the problem of editions. The original *DNB* appeared quarterly between 1886 and 1900. To these 63 volumes three more, called the *Supplement*, were added in 1901 to admit notables who had died during the course of publication. In a 1904 volume of *Errata* Sidney Lee included the following statement of policy:

> Various volumes of the 'Dictionary' have been reprinted from the stereotyped plates in the course of the past few years, and before the reprinting was begun in each case several corrections were incorporated in the plates. Recent purchasers of the 'Dictionary' will consequently find their sets to include some reprinted volumes in which many of the corrections that are noted here have been made already. (*Errata*: v)

Then in 1908–9 the *DNB* reappeared on india paper in a compact 22-volume edition called the 'Re-Issue' edition. It included the 66 volumes of the first edition (63 original and 3 *Supplement*) and incorporated the 1904 corrections. Readers were encouraged to treat it as a reprint of the first edition by the following note: 'Errors have as far as possible been corrected, and some of the bibliographies have been revised, but otherwise the text remains unaltered' (*DNB* 1908–9: I, ii). By 1921, in the Oxford University Press reprint of the

Re-Issue edition, the editors seemed aware of the confusion which the policy of continuous correction of entries, without bibliographical acknowledgement, was creating.

> In the present reprint (1921–1922) of the twenty-two volumes of the main Dictionary it has seemed best to leave the text unaltered. The bulk of the corrections hitherto received, or collected, by the present Publishers is insignificant when compared with the magnitude of the work, and would not justify the issue of a 'new edition' purporting to supersede the editions now in the libraries and in private hands. The collection and classification of such corrections for future use is, however, being steadily carried on. (*DNB* 1921: I, v)

Nevertheless, as a result of this ambiguous explanation, readers who consulted the Re-Issue edition still tended to treat it as a reprint of the original text. And readers of subsequent impressions today remain unaware of numerous revisions of the first edition silently incorporated into the text before them.

From its inception the editors, readers, and critics of the *DNB* uneasily called attention to errors, but no satisfactory method of acknowledging errors and of incorporating them into the text of new editions has resulted. According to George Smith, accuracy was so important in the first edition of the *Dictionary* that correction charges for some volumes overtook the initial cost of setting up type (Huxley: 186). However, machinery for rectifying errors after publication was less elaborate and adequate. During the entire run of the first *DNB*, *Notes and Queries* published corrections compiled regularly by the Revd W.C. Boulter, and sporadically by others who came across errors through using the *Dictionary*. Then, in the first *Supplement*, Sidney Lee added some 200 lives, which had been omitted by mistake, to lives of those who had died too late for inclusion in the first 63 volumes; and in 1904 he made a further attempt to deal with mistakes by providing the purchasers of the *DNB* with a free volume of *Errata*. These corrections and other changes were incorporated into the Re-Issue edition in 1908–9 which J.L. Kirby thus calls the standard edition (Kirby: 189).

Errors continued to appear, unearthed by the methods and findings of twentieth-century scholarship. In 1921 Arthur Pollard, a veteran of the *DNB* editorial office, founded the Institute of Historical Research, and from 1923 *DNB* corrections were gathered and published regularly in the Institute's *Bulletin*; those appearing between 1923 and 1963 are now available bound as *Corrections and Additions to the Dictionary of National Biography*, and this compilation or its equivalent should stand in libraries beside every edition of the *DNB* with a notice calling attention to it on each volume. In 1938 Pollard published a 'Bibliographical Note' in the *Bulletin*, in which he discussed discrepancies between impressions and came to the following conclusion:

> These changes have all, except the Bangor cross-reference, been made in two out of the thirty thousand pages of the original *D.N.B.* Unless they are quite exceptional, "reissue" would obviously be a terminological inexactitude for "second edition" (London 1908–9, "reprinted" by the Oxford University Press in 1920); and readers need only consult two "editions" instead of an indefinite number of "copies". Even so, possessors of, and users of libraries which only possess, the first edition would be glad to have a list of the additional lives, and also of corrections not contained in the 'Errata' appendix to the first edition (Pollard: 47).

Then in 1949 the advisability of a revised edition of the *DNB* was reiterated. In the wake of a review of the *DNB, 1931–40*, in the *TLS* and a letter in *The Times* from the Director of the Institute of Historical Research, a meeting between publishers and scholars decided that revision or rewriting of the *Dictionary* was impossible, given the cost and time required (*TLS*: 819; Edwards: 5c). The Oxford University Press did, however, agree to include a separate list of corrections (of errors in the text of the *Concise Dictionary* only) in the new impression of that work which duly appeared in 1953 and 1961. And in 1958 the compiler and editor of these corrections published an article in which he sketched the history of the *DNB* and its editors and indicated some of its strengths and weaknesses. His underlying admiration for the work, coupled with his knowledge of its errors and the decision not to revise, prompts him, shamefacedly, to defend it as a minimal authority. It is a sad claim for the great *Dictionary*:

> [Leslie Stephen believed that] the first object of the *Dictionary* was to provide a guide to the enquirer through the vast masses of printed materials accumulating in the libraries. And there he

was, I think, right. It does still serve that purpose. The *D.N.B.* is a
starting point, and one still uses the bibliography attached to
each article, painfully aware though one is that it is now something like 70 years out of date....

Obviously its value diminishes as the years pass, but I think
that it will remain an essential work of reference, with all its
defects, not only to the ordinary enquirer, but even to the
historian and specialist for many years to come (Kirby: 184, 190).

It is precisely the 'ordinary enquirer' who should be amply warned,
and perpetuation of inaccuracies in the *DNB* caught in a *Victorian
Periodicals Newsletter* project shows that the problems of using the
Dictionary have not been sufficiently aired even to reach scholars
(Houghton: 31–2).

Over the last twenty years, a procession of critics have drawn
attention to the problems and lacunae of past and present volumes,
using the occasions of the centenary of the project (Cockshut) and
the publication of recent volumes (Carpenter) to prompt the
publishers to devise means to address them. In one of the most
cogent of these assessments Janet Adam Smith noted in 1972 that
the past and present policy of immediate publication after the
decade covered by a volume is likely to leave out more artists and
musicians than politicians and men of action; thus, Dorothy
Wordsworth, Gerard Manley Hopkins and Wilfred Owen are
missing from their respective volumes, with no mechanism of
restitution since 1901. This problem is now remedied, as OUP has
published a Supplement volume for 1086 persons omitted in past
volumes. However, as recently as 1990 Humphrey Carpenter
observed that the most recent volume (for 1981–5) is 'untouched by
new technology'; that omissions are all 'somewhat radical or
unestablishment figures'; and that the style of most of the entries is
still 'Johnsonian'. Most of all he objects to the subjection of the style
of individual contributions to the 'headmaster's style book', an
editorial process which renders the volume fit 'for the elderly lady
in Hastings with two cats'. A useful perspective on the Victorian
volumes (1885–1901) is opened by Gillian Fenwick's *Contributors'
Index*, but Carpenter notes wryly that in the 1981–5 volume the
incidence of *DNB* biographers who are eventually included as
biographees after their deaths is singularly high. While the original
problems of how to incorporate corrections in this serial
publication, and the stylistic latitude and authority given to

individual contributors continue to bedevil the twentieth-century volumes, developments in information technology (such as the perpetual updating of compact disks) may eventually solve these problems for future issues of the *DNB*. The problems of the Victorian volumes however remain with us.

The impressions of the *DNB*, after the first edition, amount to new editions. For its factual and typographical corrections the most recent edition is preferable. But other corrections make the original indispensable: in subsequent editions articles have been modified in response to criticism from friends and other readers or pressures by relatives; the original contributor's point of view is obscured. In this way one of the great strengths and sources of authority of the *DNB* for the student of the nineteenth century, the immediacy and special knowledge of contributions penned by authors who had known their subjects personally, is reduced. Even in the first edition, the attribution of articles by initials belied the extent of editorial revision by the *DNB* staff.

The *DNB* articles on Walter Pater (1839–94) specifically illustrate the problems which plague the *Dictionary* as a whole. The first entry for Pater appeared in Volume 44 published in December 1895. Written by Edmund Gosse, it was drawn from his obituary of Pater in the *Contemporary Review*, December 1894. But by 1909, for the Re-Issue edition of the *DNB*, the entry was amended, particularly with respect to Pater's acquaintance as a young man with Jowett. Where the 1895 article reads 'His interests were at the time, however, mainly philosophical. He had come from school with a tendency to value all things German. The teaching of Jowett and of T.H. Green served to strengthen this habit. Mr. Capes warned him against its excess' (Gosse 1895b: 14), the same passage in the 1909 edition omits Jowett altogether: 'His interests were at the time, however, mainly philosophical. His early visits to Germany led him to value all things German. The influence of T.H. Green served to strengthen this habit. For a time he was a confirmed Hegelian' (Gosse 1909a: 459). Another revision in the 1909 entry explicitly disengages Jowett from Pater where the 1895 entry attempts to associate them and to minimise their differences:

He was the pupil of Mr. W.W. Capes, then bursar and tutor of Queen's, and he was coached by Jowett, who was struck by his abilities, and who said to him, "I think you have a mind that will come to great eminence". Some years afterwards there was an estrangement of sympathy between Jowett and Pater, but this was removed in the last year of the life of each, and the master of Balliol was among those who congratulated Pater most cordially on his "Plato and Platonism". (Gosse 1895b: 13)

His college tutor was W.W. Capes, afterwards canon of Hereford. During Lent term 1861 he prepared a weekly essay for Benjamin Jowett, professor of Greek and later master of Balliol, but was in no other way associated with him in early days. Pater and Jowett were in after years estranged, although in the last year of the life of each, the master of Balliol congratulated Pater on his "Plato and Platonism". (Gosse 1909a: 458)

It is uncertain who made these revisions. No reference to them appears in biographies of Gosse or in his letters, and several possible sources exist. A description of the editorial practice of the *DNB* staff under Lee suggests that the revisions may well have been theirs:

Their work upon the articles of other people was not confined to the elimination of verbiage and the correction of erroneous statements; they inserted fresh biographical facts, information about portraits, and bibliographical details. Some articles were partially rewritten; a paragraph or a column was often added; once the assistant editors increased a three-page life to nine pages. To another life Lee added about ten pages, and his initials appeared at the end beside those of the original author. An article which was completely rewritten in the office became anonymous, and anonymity was also the custom when an author found the alterations more than he was willing to accept (Firth: xx).

At the same time other evidence shows that this general practice may not have been true in the Gosse biography of Pater. Gosse was not a new contributor; indeed, he had written for the *Dictionary* from the first volume in 1885, having met Leslie Stephen ten years before when Stephen edited the *Cornhill Magazine* and Gosse contributed. From their correspondence in the Brotherton Collection at Leeds it would seem that the two men were good friends, and Stephen asked Gosse for suggestions for the post of sub-editor (to which Sidney Lee was appointed) when he first organised the *Dictionary* in 1882. Stephen alone edited the *DNB* until December 1889 when the work became too onerous; then between March 1890 and March 1891 Stephen and Lee shared the editorship. Forced to do less and less by ill health, Stephen finally resigned, and Lee reigned as sole editor until his death in 1926. Gosse's contributions to the *DNB* (1886–1927) span the careers of both Stephen and Lee.

Gosse, then, wrote the Pater entry for Sidney Lee, and not for his friend Leslie Stephen. By all accounts the editing styles of the two men differed notably. Even F.W. Maitland, Stephen's biographer and editor of his letters, regards Lee as the better editor 'in some respect'; more exacting with his editors and contributors, he had a nose for inaccuracy, and happily spotted a case of plagiarism in the first volume before it went to press. However, Stephen's style of editing gave good contributors more freedom than Lee's; Maitland includes several testimonies of appreciation of 'the liberty that he allowed to real researchers' (Maitland: 370). Professor T.F. Tout, the medieval historian, describes Stephen's method in detail:

Like many Oxford men of my generation, I approached historical investigation without the least training or guidance in historical method, and felt very much at a loss how to set to work. The careful and stringent regulations which he drew up, and the brusque but kindly way in which he enforced obedience to them, constituted for many of us our first training in anything like original investigation. At first we found him critical and exacting, but as soon as we had gained his confidence he gave us absolute liberty within the limits of his scheme, and, while insisting on brevity, scholarship, punctuality and businesslike precision, he never worried his contributors by fussy insistence or trivialities, but let each of them go his own way (Maitland: 370).

Stephen's personal acerbity spiced his own *DNB* biographies, and he termed Tito Melmo one of George Eliot's 'finest feminine characters' (Stephen 1880: XIII, 220). He also tolerated the following, in the first *DNB* piece which Gosse wrote: 'It is sad to be obliged to record that even in those lax days Akenside shocked his contemporaries by his brutal roughness and cruelty to the poor. His learning and sagacity were only just sufficient, on more than one occasion, to preserve him from dismissal upon this ground.' (Gosse 1885: I, 210).

Still, available evidence implies that Stephen did not respect Gosse's powers. The infrequency of his contribution to Stephen's *DNB* is one indication of this. Gosse's work appears again only in the third volume, with a short article on the Elizabethan poet Richard Barnfield. In 1884 Stephen offered Gosse the Mrs Browning biography, but in the event it was written by Lady Ritchie, Thackeray's elder daughter (Stephen MS. 1884). Then, in 1887, in a letter in the Brotherton Collection, Stephen asks him to help with the article on Thomas Gray without relinquishing his own hold on it:

I meant to consult you upon the subject and had thoughts of asking you to write it. I am, however, the more persuaded the longer I walk on my treadmill, that no one should contribute who is not either a Dryasdust by nature; or – as in my own case – been dragged into the damnable thing by Fate like a careless workman passing moving machinery. You can employ yourself to very much better purpose: but if you preferred to do this job, I would willingly hand it over to you and be thankful. If, on the whole, you would rather not, I will do it as well as I can. So kindly consider the request made in such a way as to be accepted or rejected of your own free will. (Stephen MS. 1887b)[1]

Stephen's reservations about Gosse reappear in his offer in 1884 to help Gosse secure the Clark Lectureship in English Literature at Cambridge. Gosse had applied for the post the previous year when Stephen was successful. From the Brotherton Collection letters, it would seem that Gosse still wanted it and that Stephen resigned because the *Dictionary* required more of his attention (Stephen MS. 1884). But letters which Maitland quotes suggest that Stephen found lecturing tedious and otherwise uncongenial:

I shall have to go to Cambridge three times a week to talk twaddle about Addison and Pope to a number of young ladies from Girton and a few idle undergraduates and the youthful prince, and feel down to the soles of my shoes that I am making an ass of myself...I feel that I am out of my element in this kind of work, and, when I have made my bow and earned my wages, I shall shake off the dust off my shoes and find more congenial occupation in writing a book...It will probably come to little enough; but at least it will let me talk my own dialect and not be a-mouthing of effete criticism. It strikes me as superlatively absurd to go on talking about the reign of Queen Anne. (Maitland: 380–1)

It is likely that Stephen did not think highly of Gosse, who wanted this job, and Stephen's politeness and generosity seem to mask disregard and mild contempt.

Yet another reflection of Stephen's doubts about Gosse exists. In 1887 Stephen defended Gosse publicly (although not by name) against charges of sloppy and inaccurate scholarship made in the *Quarterly Review*. When Charles Eliot Norton showed surprise at Stephen's defence in a letter in 1900, 'Stephen admitted that Gosse was fussy and conceited and not "in a high rank among friends"; but Gosse had been kind to him and Gosse should be protected' (Annan: 302).[2] All in all, Stephen seems fully aware of Gosse's pretensions and unreliability, their correspondence, protestations of friendship, and mutual flattery notwithstanding.

If Stephen was conscious of these shortcomings it is probable that the more fastidious Lee, for whom Gosse wrote the Pater entry, edited it and even revised it. There is some evidence in the Gosse correspondence that editorial revision had proved a sensitive issue between Gosse and Lee sometime before 1913. In April of that year Gosse and his friend, T.J. Wise, were embroiled in argument with Isabel Swinburne, who alleged that Gosse's description of her brother's physique in the *DNB* entry was libellous and untrue. Ever since it had appeared in 1912, the poet's irascible sister had attacked Gosse's caricature (Gosse 1912).[3] Isabel proposed going directly to Lee with her complaint, a plan which Watts-Dunton revealed to Wise. On 28 April 1913 Wise writes to Gosse:

> He quite agrees that you could not possibly make any alterations if such were suggested via Lee, but thinks I.S. cannot appreciate this. He thinks I had better write to I. S., and ask her to definitely say what she does want, pointing out to her that via Lee is not possible for you. (I await your instructions before doing this.)

and the next day he writes that Watts-Dunton 'expressed himself as fully appreciating that you could not possibly accept instructions to alter your article from Sir Sidney Lee, he being your editor. He said in this respect "dear Isabel is wrong"' (Wise MSS. 1913). Gosse's sensitivity suggests some problem with Lee in the past, and it

might well have been the Pater entry, which was so heavily revised.
The Swinburne entry was published without change on this point
in the 1920 and 1927 editions.

If the origins of the revisions in the Pater entry are obscure the
reasons prompting them are not. A.C. Benson and Thomas Wright
published biographies of Pater in the interval between the 1895 and
1908–9 editions of the *DNB*, Benson's a decorous biography sanc-
tioned and aided by Pater's friends and relations, Wright's outspoken and somewhat sensational. Both take up issues raised by
Gosse's *Contemporary Review* and *DNB* articles. Benson quarrels first
with Gosse's version of the Roman Catholic tradition in Pater's
family: 'It is stated in biographical notices of Pater that for some
generations the sons of the family had been brought up as Catholics,
the daughters as Anglicans. But this has been too much insisted
upon; as a matter of fact the Roman Catholicism in the family was of
late date' (Benson: 2). This was not altered in the 1909 *DNB*. But
Benson disagrees with Gosse principally about the most revised
aspect of the *DNB* entry, Pater's relations with Jowett. Benson tries
to clear Pater on two counts. Contrary to the implication of Gosse's
phrasing in the *Contemporary Review* ('Having in the ordinary course
of his studies submitted some work to Jowett, that astute observer
was so much struck with his power that he very generously offered
to coach him for nothing. The offer was gratefully accepted' (Gosse
1894: 799)), Benson claims Pater had no money problems in
pursuing his studies. And Benson tries to make Jowett bear the
blame for the estrangement that existed between the two men
during the greater part of their lives at Oxford. He argues that
Jowett misunderstood Pater's ideas, and that he actively opposed
Pater's advancement in the University (Benson: 55).

Initially Gosse associated Pater with Jowett to suppress the
notoriety of their differences. But Benson, writing after the
publication of a letter from Pater to Lewis Campbell praising Jowett
(Abbott and Campbell. I, 329–30), wanted to establish Pater's
innocence and generosity in the affair at the expense of exposing
the rift and Jowett's culpability. From Benson's letters to Gosse in
the Brotherton Collection it is clear that Pater's biographers were
intimate friends, particularly in 1893 and 1894, when Benson wrote
of attacks of severe depression and of disagreeable matters at Eton,
where he was a master.[4] Their biographies of Pater reflect a tacit
agreement to protect him from Jowett's charges, but they took

different tacks. And Benson, in agreeing to write the official biography and accept the help of the Pater sisters, had committed himself overtly to others with that aim.

Thomas Wright, in *The Life of Walter Pater*, published a year later, addressed himself to Gosse's *Contemporary Review* article rather than to the *DNB* entry. On the whole he claims Gosse as an ally against Benson, whose biography of Pater he methodically attacks in a thirteen-page Preface. He alludes to Gosse's help, and to his approval of Wright's intention to explore Pater's early years; Wright even includes several anecdotes from Gosse's *Contemporary Review* portrait, and another, concerning the Shelly centenary celebration at Oxford, which he claims Gosse sent him in a helpful letter. But Wright, like Benson, reflects some of the biographical questions which Gosse's articles raised; how far back the Paters' Catholicism went, Jowett's relations with Pater, and whether Pater returned to religion as he grew older. Anxious to claim Gosse's support, Wright flatters him by using some of his material. But by suggesting that Pater was responsible for the misunderstanding with Jowett, Wright also criticises Gosse's means of protecting Pater.

Ingram Bywater (1840–1914), Pater's close and old friend, also objected (privately) to the *DNB* article. Asked for his opinion about Pater, at some time between the publications of the first and Re-Issue editions, Bywater referred Hermann Diels to the 1895 *DNB* with the following reservation:

> You will find a fairly full account of Pater's life in the *Dictionary of National Biography*, vol. 44, – a book no doubt to be found in some Berlin library.
>
> The writer of the article did not know Pater in his early days: there are several grave mistakes in his account of his intellectual development. I knew Pater very intimately at this time: we were undergraduates of the same College (Queens), we attended the same lectures, and were in every way inseparable (Jackson: 78–9).

In addition to identifying some of the issues in the *DNB* biography of Pater through a comparison of the 1895 and 1908 texts, we can look at the *DNB* entries in the light of the original Gosse obituary in the *Contemporary Review*, December 1894. In general, the shorter *DNB* articles include more details than the longer *Contemporary Review* piece. Both *DNB* entries explain Old

Mortality and Pater's participation in it, though it is not mentioned in the periodical portrait; the *DNB* essays also specify the
time and existence of Pater's connection with the Pre-Raphaelites;
and in both Gosse describes *Marius* as 'an apology for the highest
epicureanism', an observation which the periodical portrait lacks,
though Gosse singles out *Marius* there as the book by which
posterity will know Pater. However, Gosse includes much general comment and information in the *Contemporary Review* which
are notably absent in the *DNB* entries, and he retells several
endearing anecdotes exemplifying Pater's wit and humour.
Disarmingly, he admits his limited knowledge of Pater – they
became friends only in 1874 – and anticipates Bywater's objections
to the *DNB* articles. He even discusses Mallock's parody of Pater
as Mr Rose in *The New Republic* in 1876/7, and assesses its effect
on Pater and his decision to remove the 'Conclusion' in the 1877
edition of *The Renaissance.*

Perhaps fear and distaste of scandal are what prevented Gosse
or Sidney Lee from acknowledging *The New Republic*, a work which
Gosse claims Pater enjoyed and took in his stride, in the *DNB*. More
certainly, similar reasoning prompted the ban, Gosse's or the
editors', on passages in the *Contemporary Review* describing Pater's
religious beliefs and homosexuality. About these two aspects of
Pater's life, Gosse and Bywater substantially agree. They both
believe Pater had returned to religion towards the end of his life,
Bywater confiding to Diels 'I always thought there was a possibility
of his ending his days as a Catholic' and describing Pater's final
posture as 'that of a sort of lay "director" or confessor' (Jackson:
79–80), and Gosse writing. 'His talk, his habits, became more and
more theological, and it is my private conviction that, had he lived
a few years longer, he would have taken orders and a small college
living in the country', and elsewhere in the article he asserts that
Pater 'never had any serious leaning towards Rome' (Gosse 1894:
805, 798). But the *DNB* entries are remarkable for their abrupt,
staccato presentation of Pater's religious development: his childhood design to be an Anglican clergyman, his later intention
(abandoned by 1864) of entering the Unitarian ministry, and the
final stage of loss of belief in the Christian religion 'with the
accession of humanistic ideas'. They depict Pater as an unrelenting
humanist from 1866 to his death in 1894, and make no reference to
his return to religion in later life, or to any persistent religious
strain in his thought.

Pater's two friends also attest to Pater's homosexuality, and both introduce it in connection with the essay on J.J. Winckelmann. Bywater writes to Diels: 'you will notice, I think, a certain sympathy with a certain aspect of Greek life; I must tell you that that was not confined to him' (Jackson: 79).[5] Gosse makes a similar point in the *Contemporary Review* piece, where he calls Winckelmann Pater's 'true prototype' and illustrates his point with an apposite description of Pater at the time:[6]

Pater's studies in philosophy now naturally brought him to Goethe, so massive an influence in the Oxford of that day, and the teaching of Goethe laid a deep impress upon his temperament, upon his whole outlook on the intellectual life. It was natural that one so delicately sensitive to the external symbol as was Pater should be prepared by the companionship of Goethe for the influence of a man who was Goethe's master in this one direction, and it was to a spirit inflammable in the highest degree that in 1866 was laid the torch of Otto Jahn's Life of Winckelmann, the "Biographische Aufsätze". There was everything in the character and career of the great German restorer of Hellenic feeling to fascinate Pater, who seemed, through Ruskin, Goethe and Hegel, to have travelled to his true prototype, to the one personality among the dead which was completely in sympathy with his own. Pater, too, among the sand-hills of a spiritual Brandenburg, had held out arms of longing towards ideal beauty, revealed in physical or sensuous forms, yet inspired and interpenetrated with harmonious thought. The troubled feverish vision, the variegated and indeed over-decorated aesthetic of Ruskin, had become wearisome to Pater – not simple enough nor sensuous enough. Winckelmann was the master he wanted.[7]
(Gosse 1894: 800)

In both *DNB* entries this passage on Pater and Winckelmann is greatly abbreviated. The original's meaning and fervour are buried beneath a more propitiatory description of the nature of Winckelmann's influence on Pater: 'a profound impression' and a 'new enthusiasm'.

His studies in philosophy naturally brought him to Goethe, and it was only natural that one so delicately sensitive to the external symbol as Pater was, should be prepared by the companionship

of Goethe for the influence of a man who was Goethe's master
in this one direction. The publication of Otto Jahn's "Life of
Winckelmann" in 1866 made a profound impression on Pater.
His famous essay on Winckelmann was the result of this new
enthusiasm. It was published in the "Westminster Review" for
January 1867. (Gosse 1895b: 14)

Again we do not know who is responsible for this. Whoever the
censor was, he merely honoured one of the great taboos of
Victorian biography. The *DNB* editors encouraged frankness on
many subjects, but homosexuality proved an exception. Similarly it
is significant that neither Benson nor Wright chose to raise this
point directly, in response to Gosse's articles.[8]

A striking contrast between the decorum of the *DNB* entries and
the *Contemporary Review* portrait also occurs in Gosse's concluding
remarks. In both *Dictionary* and periodical he ends by summarising
Pater's temperament. The last paragraph of the periodical piece is
an effusive, impressionist, poetic evocation of Pater's talent and
presence: 'He was not all for Apollo, nor all for Christ, but each
deity swayed in him, and neither had that perfect homage that
brings peace behind it'. The *DNB* biographies terminate noticeably
lamely: 'He disliked noise and extravagance of all kinds; his
manners were of the utmost simplicity, and his sense of fun as
playful as that of a child', the real, decorous conclusion ('He
possessed all the qualities of a humanist') being appended somewhat arbitrarily to the preceding paragraph.

The last element of the *DNB* Pater to consider is the choice of
biographer. Gosse qualifies principally because he knew Pater and
he had written for the *DNB* before. Pater had closer friends, Ingram
Bywater, F.W. Bussell, and C.L. Shadwell for example, but their
silence suggests reticence to discuss him publicly. His sisters were
forced to resort to A.C. Benson, who seems to have met Pater once,
as the author of the official biography.[9] The worth of Gosse's word
has been reduced by his reputation for inaccuracy, snobbery, and
general pretentiousness but, happily, other sources show that he
and Pater were moderate, if not intimate, friends.

Their correspondence and social intercourse reflect decorous
warmth in Pater and persistence and enthusiasm in Gosse, who
initiated the friendship in a characteristic manner. After meeting
Pater for the first time in the Chelsea studio of the painter William
Bell Scott, Gosse sent his new acquaintance a copy of his recent book.

Pater duly wrote a letter of thanks, and the contact became a relationship. But the record of the letters and visits shows that a friendship began only with the onset of 1877, when Pater saw Gosse at his home twice in January and invited him to stay with him and his sisters in Oxford the following month.[10] Through the late seventies Pater visited Gosse once a year in January, and twice Gosse sent copies of his work which Pater acknowledged with thanks. After a gap Pater visited Gosse in London, four times in 1886 (the first year Pater spent in the city), once in 1890, once in 1892, and three times in 1893, making thirteen visits altogether. Their correspondence reflects a similar dearth of contact between the two men in the early eighties while Pater was writing *Marius*, but even afterwards the initiative in the friendship seemed to remain with Gosse; Pater's letters to him abound with thank-yous for kind reviews and for copies of others' books and of Gosse's own work. Eighteen ninety-three, the third period in which the friendship became intense, includes the other two recorded invitations from Pater to Gosse, sandwiched between the now customary acknowledgements, thanks, and rejections of Gosse's invitations and propositions. But the posture of reticence Pater assumed in this relationship was as characteristic as Gosse's ambitious persistence. Sporadic, formal, and apparently thin, this friendship was more than professional, if less than intimate. Of Pater's relationships with his closer friends, such as Bywater, Bussell, and Shadwell, we know little, with only one letter and spotty biographical accounts to go on. In the absence of such information, the friendship with Gosse is valued by Pater's biographers, but they should also bear in mind how small a part of his life and attention it occupied. Only one among Pater's kindly responses to Gosse's solicitations of approval of his work stands out as consciously supportive, feeling, and sincere: it was occasioned by the same attack on Gosse's scholarship that Leslie Stephen responded to with mixed feelings. In answer to the reply Gosse circulated among his friends, Pater writes 'Many thanks for the copy of your letter to the Athenaeum. It gave me sincere pleasure to see your ponderous antagonist so lightly, gracefully, promptly, overturned. With best wishes for the continued prosperity of your admirable book and your work generally' (Evans: 67; Gosse 1886: 534–5).[11] Gosse is not the one among Pater's friends whom students of Pater, and perhaps even Pater himself, would have chosen as biographer; nevertheless he remains the only person who knew Pater at all well to have written a sustained biography.

Pater enjoyed the *DNB*, and read through its volumes as soon as they appeared. No doubt he often applied his personal knowledge and critical intelligence to the biographies of contemporaries written by contemporaries in the way we do when faced with a review of a twentieth-century book by a critic whose strengths, tastes, and limits are familiar to us. Unhappily the *DNB* encouraged later readers, often not in possession of sufficient knowledge to read it critically, to treat it as a neutral compendium of definitive biographies. This it is not, and never was; its very value for us lies in its peculiar combination of accuracy and individual perspectives. The degree of both of these elements in the *DNB* is obscured by its failure to acknowledge properly the editions it went through, and the policy of combining signature with heavy editing by staff. Moreover, the biographers, in so far as they were responsible for their entries, should not be regarded as neutral either, and their identities and relations to their subjects should be taken into account by the *DNB* reader. These are considerations which make the *DNB* inappropriate for rapid reference; it should always be used in conjunction with other sources.

The Pater entries also contribute to our knowledge of Victorian biographical conventions in general as well as in the *DNB*. Although outspoken about many personal idiosyncrasies and qualities they rigorously exclude any mention of sexual deviance from the strictest norm. In this respect the *DNB* entries are radically truncated versions of the *Contemporary Review* article; they belie its overall spirit, and the Pater emerging from the pages of the *Dictionary* bears only the slightest resemblance to his namesake in Gosse's periodical portrait. At best, the *DNB* provides a controversial account of Pater's life and work; at worst, a misleading and incomplete one.

Notes

1.   In a later letter to Gosse, Stephen admits 'I have had to follow your Gray so closely that I feel like a thief' (19/3/88; Gosse [9], Letter 12, Brotherton). Sadly, this entry was cited as evidence for a thorough revision of the nineteenth-century *DNB* by a *TLS* reviewer: 'the late Leonard Whibley used to say that the life of Gray was not susceptible of correction; every sentence in it was incorrect, or inadequate, or misleading' (Anon. 1949: 819). All in all, Gosse made only six contributions to Lee's *Dictionary*: Pater (1895); R. Browning

(1901); Swinburne (1912); Mary Pit (1896); Eliza Brightwen (1912), naturalist; and Algernon Freeman-Mitford (1927), diplomat and author of *Tales of Old Japan*.

2. Annan quotes from a letter (27 April 1900) of Stephen to C.E. Norton who had published a review of Gosse's *Life of Donne* in which he accused Gosse of inaccuracy, wild guessing, and gross misinterpretation of Donne's poetry. In 'The Study of English Literature' in 1887, Stephen had defended Gosse in an article which was part of a general debate on the desirable qualities of Professors of Literature which grew out of Churton Collins's attack on Gosse in the *Quarterly Review*. Letters and articles on the subject filled the journals and newspapers from autumn to spring in 1886–7, with the *Athenaeum* and the *Pall Mall Gazette* the principal forums. In his article Stephen argued that, for a teacher of English Literature, taste and sensitivity take priority over formal academic qualifications and a command of facts. Stephen's position pertains directly to Gosse, who was a Lecturer in English Literature though he had never attended university, and enthusiastic about literature in the lecture hall though inaccurate. For more on Gosse, see Thwaite, and on Collins, see Kearney.

3. See also Gosse's similar vision of Swinburne in Gosse 1909b. In a letter to Watts-Dunton in the Brotherton Collection dated 17 June 1909, Isabel Swinburne objects privately to Gosse's 'disgusting description'.

4. Over twenty-seven letters from Benson to Gosse are in the Brotherton Collection, from 1893 to 1924. Benson, twelve years younger than Gosse, was 31 when the correspondence began; nevertheless, in an early letter (4 July 1893) Benson writes a poem lavishly praising Gosse, in the posture of a young protegé to his mentor (Gosse [9]). The letters of 1893–4 are characterised by pledges and acknowledgements of affection. See Newsome on Benson and Gosse.

5. Gosse corroborates Bywater's ironic self-incrimination in a letter to Robert Ross concerning Simeon Solomon's 'public disaster' in 1873. Gosse writes, 'On hearing of the scandal, Swinburne abruptly left London and went to Oxford, where he consulted with Pater and with Bywater: the latter, oddly enough, being Junior Proctor at the moment' (Ross: 315).

6. By his own admission, Gosse did not know Pater at this time; however, his sense of the affinity between Winckelmann and Pater may well be a product of his subsequent but first-hand experience of Pater.

7. See Inman.

8. It is interesting to note that where Gosse openly indicates Pater's homosexuality in his *Contemporary Review* article in December 1894, in January 1895, in a review of Horatio F. Brown's biography of J.A. Symonds, he corroborates the author's painstaking exclusion of homosexuality from his account of Symonds' life and character. This is before the Wilde trials of that year. Various factors figure in this nexus of biographer, biographee, friend, reviewer, periodical; Brown, gay himself, and a close and longstanding friend of Symonds, wrote from the authorial position of the censoring Widow, and Gosse, writing in a conservative weekly did not choose to

expose his friends, Symonds or Brown. When Gosse inherited the Symonds papers, after Brown's death, he burnt most of them. For Brown and Symonds see Grosskurth 1964: 319–20 and 1984: 27; for Gosse and Symonds see Thwaite: 320–4.

9. They both attended a luncheon given by Gosse in 1893 (See Evans: 140n). But Percy Lubbock makes it fairly clear that Benson never *knew* Pater or other subjects of his biographies: 'He cultivated the society of Carlyle, Ruskin, Rossetti, Pater, whoever it might be, with the zest which he brought to a party of friends at dinner...But then indeed there was this other trouble, that Carlyle and Rossetti and the rest were of the past, and that in life he had never known them' (Lubbock: 136–7). Benson's diary shows that he conferred with Gosse about Pater when he was writing his biography. See 'Judas and the Widow' in this volume.

10. Gosse kept a record of all his visitors after 1875 in a notebook he called 'The Book of Gosse', now in Cambridge University Library. His yearly diaries and correspondence are part of the Brotherton Collection, University of Leeds.

11. It is pertinent that in a letter to the *Pall Mall Gazette*, dated three days after his letter to Gosse, Pater expressed reservations about the establishment of a School of English Literature at Oxford. Collins's ardent support of English Literature as an academic is believed to have prompted his attack on the inaccuracy of Gosse, who held the Clark Lectureship in English Literature at Cambridge. See Kearney.

Works Cited

Abbot, E. and L. Campbell. (1897). *The Life and Letters of Benjamin Jowett, M.A.* 2 vols. London.

Annan, Noel. (1951). *Leslie Stephen*. London.

Anon. (1949). 'Worthies of Empire', *TLS* (16 Dec.), 819.

Bell, A. (1981). 'A Portable Valhalla', *Times Literary Supplement* (2 Oct.), 1115–17.

Benson, A.C. (1906). *Walter Pater*. London.

Carpenter, H. (1990). 'The Dictionary of National Biography 1981-85', *Sunday Times* (25 March), H 3.

Cockshut, A.O.J. (1985). 'The Century of the DNB', *Times Literary Supplement* (26 April), 466.

Corrections and Addenda to the Dictionary of National Biography, 1923–63. (1966). Boston, Mass.

The Dictionary of National Biography. Missing Persons. ed. C.S. Nicholls. (1993).

Edwards, J.G. (1949). 'Dictionary of National Biography' [Letter to the Editor], *The Times* (1 Dec.), 5e.

Evans, L. (1970). *Letters of Walter Pater*. Oxford.

Fenwick, G. (1989). *The Contributors' Index to the "Dictionary of National Biography" 1895–1901*. Winchester, Hants.

Firth, C.H. (1927). 'Memoir of Sir Sidney Lee', *DNB, 1912–21*. London.

G.E. [Edmund Gosse]. (1885). 'Mark Akenside', *DNB*, ed. Leslie Stephen. I: 208–11.

G.E. [Edmund Gosse]. (1912). 'Algernon Swinburne', *DNB* Second Supplement, 3: 456–65.

Gosse, E. (1909a). 'Walter Pater', *DNB*, ed. Sidney Lee. 15: 458–9.

Gosse, E. (1909b). 'Swinburne: Personal Recollections', *Fortnightly Review* 85 (June), 1013–39.

Gosse, E. (1895a). 'John Addington Symonds', *St. James Gazette* (1 Jan.), 5–6.

Gosse, E. (1895b). 'Walter Pater', *DNB*, ed. Sidney Lee. 44 (Dec), 13–14.

Gosse, E. (1894). 'Walter Pater', *Contemporary Review* 66 (Dec.), 795–810.

Gosse, E. (1886). Letter to Editor. *Athenaeum* (23 Oct.), 534–5.

Grosskurth, P., ed. (1984). *The Memoirs of John Addington Symonds*. London.

Grosskurth, P. (1964). *John Addington Symonds*. London.

Houghton, W. (1971). 'A Note on the *DNB* Project', *Victorian Periodicals Newsletter* 14 (Dec.), 31–2.

Huxley, L. (1923). *The House of Smith Elder*. London.

Inman, B.A. (1991). 'Estrangement and Connection: Walter Pater, Benjamin Jowett, and William M. Hardinge', *Pater in the 1990s*, ed. L. Brake and I. Small. Greensboro, NC. pp. 1–20.

Jackson, W.W. (1917). *Ingram Bywater, the Memoir of an Oxford Scholar: 1840–1914*. Oxford.

Kearney, A. (1987). *The Louse on the Locks of Literature: John Churton Collins*. Edinburgh.

Kirby, J.L. (1958). 'The Dictionary of National Biography', *Library Association Record* 60 (June), 181–91.

Lubbock, P. (1925). 'The Author of His Books', *Arthur Christopher Benson: As seen by Some Friends* [ed. E.H. Ryle]. London. pp. 125–40.

Lyttleton. E. (1925). 'Training and Temperament', *Arthur Christopher Benson: As seen by Some Friends* [ed. E.H. Ryle]. London. pp. 141–58.

Maitland, F.W. (1906). *The Life and Letters of Leslie Stephen*. London.

Newsome, David. (1980). *On the Edge of Paradise: A. C. Benson, Diarist*. London.

Norton, C.E. (1900). 'Gosse's Life of Donne', *Nation* 70 (8, 15 Feb.), 111–13; 133–5.

P., A.F. [Arthur Pollard]. (1939). 'Bibliographical Note', *Bulletin of the Institute of Historical Research* 16: 47.

Ross, M. (1952). *Robert Ross, Friend of Friends*. London.

Smith, J.A. (1972). 'Viewpoint', *Times Literary Supplement* (3 Nov.), 1314.

S., L. [Leslie Stephen]. (1888). 'Mary Ann Cross', *DNB* 13: 216–22.

Stephen, L. (1887a). 'The Study of English Literature', *Cornhill Magazine* 8 (May), 486–508.

Stephen, L. (1887b). MS Letter (24 Oct.). Gosse [9], Letter 11. Brotherton Collection, Leeds University.

Stephen, L. (1884). MS Letter (Summer). Gosse [9], Letter 8, Brotherton Collection, Leeds University.

Thwaite, Ann. (1984). *Edmund Gosse. A Literary Landscape*. London.

Wise, T.J. (1913). MSS. Letters from T.J. Wise to E. Gosse, 23 and 29 April. Brotherton Collection. [Bound in *Swinburneiana*, Vol. 4]

Wright, T. (1907). *The Life of Walter Pater*. 2 vols. London.

10
Judas and the Widow

It is usually Judas who writes the biography.

Wilde 1887: 378

The Widow does not always boldly appear on the title-page: she often lurks behind the apparently unprejudiced name of some docile author.

Gosse 1901: 206

Walter Pater's death in July 1894 took place towards the end of a century in which biography had great commercial success, and became one of the dominant literary modes. Accompanying its success was a protracted public debate about the nature of biography that revived on the publication of J.A. Froude's *Thomas Carlyle* (1882–4). Lytton Strachey's *Eminent Victorians* (1918) and *Queen Victoria* (1921) ended this phase of the debate resoundingly. Throughout the period two monuments of biography were built: the *Dictionary of National Biography* between 1885 and 1904, edited by Leslie Stephen and Sidney Lee, and Macmillan's English Men of Letters series, edited by John Morley, between 1878 and 1892. In the midst of this activity and fracas, in 1906 and 1907, two lives of Pater were published, by A.C. Benson (EML, Macmillan) and Thomas Wright (Everett & Co.) respectively. These are interactive texts.[1] Although Benson's appeared first, it seems to have been occasioned by Wright's project, and when Wright's two-volume life appeared, it began with a critique of Benson's volume. As the relative status of the two publishers suggests, Benson (1862–1925) was the better connected of the two, and indeed part of the Establishment culture: son of the Archbishop of Canterbury, his school was Eton, his university Cambridge, he became an Eton Master (1885–1903), took residence as a Fellow at Magdalene (1904–15), eventually serving as its Master. By contrast, Thomas Wright (1859–1936), a local schoolmaster, attended Buxton College, Forest Gate, as an articled pupil and founded his own Cowper School at Olney, where he lived for the whole of his adult life.[2] If Benson was an insider with respect to the biography of Pater, by way of family, class, education, discourse, university resources and status, Wright was the clear outsider, a position he acknowledges, even exploits in his book. If Benson is pinched by his insider status into writing a 'widow' biography, Wright is liberated to write investigatively as Judas.

Scrutiny of these two Lives, however, suggests that the discourses are not unitary. Benson's positions as author/biographer are multiple, uneasily situated between these oppositional categories of Judas and Widow. I want to consider problems of biography raised by the methods and discourses of these two Lives in terms of the ongoing contemporary debate, in particular with relation to what Edmund Gosse called in 'The Ethics of Biography' 'the duty of the biographer to the two hostile interests of the public and the family' (Gosse 1903: 322). In an earlier article in 1901, Gosse had called for skilled professional authors and characterised the worst of the untrained as the 'Widow' biographers:

> This may be taken as a generic term for the class of life-writers whose only claim is that they are 'on the spot' [commissioned], that arrogate to themselves the duty of biography merely because they are in possession of the documents....Her object is to present to the world an image of the deceased, which shall be deliberately although unconsciously false....She desires to show that he was perfect...Above all, she carefully suppresses all evidence of his being unlike other men.... For, it must be remarked, the Widow does not always boldly appear on the title-page: she often lurks behind the apparently unprejudiced name of some docile author. Her function, however, always is to stultify and misrepresent the life and character of the deceased; and the more devotion she thinks she is paying to his memory, the more completely she carries this out. (Gosse 1901: 205–6)

Gosse presents his type flamboyantly, with overstatement, but with interesting modifications it describes Benson, who wrote his relatively slim volume with the cooperation and possibly the sponsorship of Pater's friends and relations. Thomas Wright, by contrast, saw himself as an investigatory biographer, in both his life of Charles Dickens which was published in 1935 but written between 1900 and 1904, and in his two-volume, lavishly illustrated and documented life of Pater. For the life of Dickens he found and documented the Ellen Ternan connection for the first time publicly,[3] and in the Pater volumes Richard Jackson and J.R. McQueen. A *Daily Mail* reviewer commented wryly on Wright's tendency to uncover energetically the unexpected and Benson's constrastingly easeful devotion:

> After Mr. Benson, who strolled along alone to drop a rose on Pater's grave, comes Mr. Wright in his motor-omnibus, which he has crammed with extraordinary beings of whom none ever heard before, persons who, it appears, were intimately known to Pater. (Anon. 1907: II)

By many of his readers, particularly the interested ones – the Dickensians pre-eminently, but also the Pater circles – Wright was regarded as the indiscreet 'Judas' biographer.

Very soon after Pater's death in July 1894, within months, the affair and trials of Oscar Wilde commenced; male homosexuality became an open scandal, and was condemned publicly in unmistakable terms.[4] Also, in 1895 appeared Edmund Purcell's *Life of Cardinal Manning*, which revealed Manning's suppressed early marriage, his despotic temper, his love of power, and his attacks on Newman; this was followed by W.E. Henley's revelatory life of Burns in 1897. These Lives occasioned vigorous public debate on questions of religious and sexual impropriety, and the discretion of biography. Purcell saw his own life of Manning as a test-case in 1896, and published his views in the *Nineteenth Century*, a journal noted for tolerance.[5]

> The question has been taken up on both sides of the Atlantic: Is it a virtue to suppress historic truth or no? The broad issues once raised cannot now be evaded. The advocates of the art of suppression, in great histories or biographies, of historical facts, or of documents on which such facts are based, are now trembling in their shoes. They cannot lay the Frankenstein's monster they have raised.
>
> By force of circumstances, by its candour and outspokenness, and, perhaps, still more by the blunderings of its Catholic critics, the *Life of Cardinal Manning* is become a test-book, as it were: a criterion of the rival methods in the art of writing history or

biography. In all the lands where the English tongue is spoken, the question of the hour is asked: Is the publication of historical facts based on authentic documents "almost a crime" or a virtue? (Purcell: 534–5)

Like Purcell, W.E. Henley, having written an indiscreet biography (in 1897), re-entered the debate by turning critic in 1901. Henley used an opportunity to review a life, by Graham Balfour of his friend Robert Louis Stevenson as the occasion for a testy denunciation of both tame biographies and the character of Stevenson, with whom he had quarrelled:

'Tis as that of an angel clean from heaven, and I for my part flatly refuse to recognise it. Not, if I can help it, shall this faultless, or very nearly faultless, monster go down to after years as the Lewis I knew, and I loved, and laboured with and for, with all my heart and strength and understanding. In days to come I may write as much as can be told of him. Till those days come, this protest must suffice. If it convey the impression that I take a view of Stevenson which is my own, and which declines to be concerned with this Seraph in Chocolate, this barley-sugar effigy of a real man; that the best and the most interesting part of Stevenson's life will never get written – even by me....suffice it will (Henley 1901: 508)[6]

Resistance to candour was plentiful. An anonymous critic in the *Academy* in 1901 defends suppression and, hinting at an element of sensationalism in the 'new' biography, links it with the 'new journalism' by noting its similar 'journalising of a literary art' (Anon. 1901: 167). He looks backward for models and advocates discretion in a topical illustration:

From Dr. Johnson's *Lives of the Poets* the biographer may learn the dignity of his art, and the enduring value of a reverent and sagacious handling of delicate subjects: as for instance where, in discussing Dryden's suspiciously timely conversion to Roman Catholicism, he puts the matter by. (Anon. 1901: 168)

This critic refers approvingly to Gosse's 'The Custom of Biography' which had just appeared in a sumptuous quarterly,[7] and in which Gosse had contented himself with describing the English tradition of biography and attacking devotional overlong

Lives: 'We in England bury our dead under the monstrous
catafalque of two volumes (crown octavo)' (Gosse 1901: 195). The
Academy writer voices criticisms of biography which underlie
Gosse's 1901 comments and those of many others in periodicals of
the day:

> The truth is, that of the biographies published, nearly all are
> written too soon, many ought not to be written at all, and the
> majority of the remainder could be of value only if they were half
> as long and twice as well done....And who, nowadays, would not
> be glad if biographies were many and small and good? It is the
> insatiate curiosity of the age which will neither wait patiently nor
> taste nicely... the journalising of a literary art. (Anon: 1901: 167)

These complaints about size are specifically related by Gosse to the
desirable compactness of the English Men of Letters biographies.[8]
By 1903 in 'The Ethics of Biography' in *Cosmopolitan* Gosse was more
extreme: he did not content himself with attacking 'devotional' and
lengthy Lives but openly defended indiscretion in biography:

> Certain fashionable biographies of the present day deserve no
> other comment than the words 'A Lie' printed in bold letters
> across their title-pages. (Gosse 1903: 323)

It is 'more and more difficult to learn the truth about an eminent
person, if that truth can be considered in any sense undignified', he
complains (Gosse 1903: 322). Consequently, he argues that the
biographer's 'anxiety should be, not how to avoid all indiscretion,
but how to be as indiscreet as possible within the boundaries of
good taste and kind feeling' (Gosse 1903: 317). Where these boundaries lay was still being assessed in 1918 and later, when Lytton
Strachey attempted to obliterate them entirely in *Eminent Victorians*
and his life of Queen Victoria. In the case of Pater, the judgements
of three men on the issue of discretion are illuminating: Benson the
biographer; Gosse the critic and Pater's close friend; and Robert
Ross, Wilde's friend and a gay critic who knew Benson, Gosse and
Pater. But their degree of engagement with this problem and their
positions are part of the public debate which may be seen in two
contrasting reviews of Benson's EML biography of Rossetti which
appeared in 1904, two years before Benson's Pater volume. The
anonymous critic in the *Spectator* calls Benson 'a new biographer of

exceptional gifts of sympathy and judgement,' but s/he does audibly regret and ponder the absence of an element of Rossetti's personality:

> The only side of Rossetti's nature at which Mr Benson does not even hint is his scornful yet Rabelaisian humour....Echoes of certain rhymed irreverences, caustic and vigorous, float through our mind as we write these words; but whether there was any call for Mr. Benson to record them in a book in this series is a question which he has perhaps answered rightly by silence. And yet one or two, among the prose passages from the letters at the end, might have added another lamp with which to light this curious character. (Anon. 1904b: 225)

The *Athenaeum* reviewer is less favourably impressed by Benson's biography: 'A good superficial view of the subject is conveyed; but the reader knows no more of the man as he lays down the book than he did as he opened it'. He too objects, though more strongly than the critic in the *Spectator*, to Benson's handling of these boundaries:

> As regards the most tragic episode of Rossetti's life, and that which may be supposed to have clouded its close, the information supplied is inadequate and in a sense misleading. There are two manners in which that painful subject, exact knowledge concerning which is in a few hands, may be treated. The truth may be told, or the subject may be, as it has hitherto been, ignored. What is said, however, on p. 49 as to speculation regarding the state of mind of the victim being "worse than useless", is itself "worse than useless", there being no room for speculation to arise. (Anon. 1904a: 197)

The reviewer goes on to consider Benson's treatment of two other delicate matters – Rossetti's 'violating of the secrecy of the grave' and the poet's 'indulgence in chloral hydrate' (Anon 1904a: 197). The intensity of the interest in this matter of what is included and how, and what suppressed, is unmistakable.

The use of letters figures importantly in this notion of 'indiscretion' or honesty. William Mason's memoir and letters of Gray (1775) is an early example of the modern use of letters in biography. Purcell printed very revealing correspondence between Manning and Newman, and the ethics of the use of private letters and papers is often discussed. Gosse demands that the biographer 'open letters' and 'unclasp diaries'. Leslie Stephen declares

> The question of whether a really satisfactory life can be written is essentially the question of whether letters have been preserved....It should therefore be regarded as a duty...to keep all letters written by a possible biographee. (Stephen 1893: 178–9)

Purcell, Gosse and Stephen all manifest a consciousness of the method of biography and exude a desire for rigour and professionalism, but Stephen (previously editor of the *Dictionary of National Biography*) believes accuracy to lie primarily in the former intimacy of the biographer with his subject, and Gosse in the professionalism and skill of the biographer. Where Stephen writes in 1893:

> Nothing is more striking to the biographer than the rapidity with which all possibility of satisfactory portraiture vanishes. Nobody, as Johnson somewhere says, could write a satisfactory life of a man who had not lived in habits of intimacy with him. (Stephen 1893: 175)

Gosse implies in 1901 that he would prefer a professional who never knew the biographee to an inexpert interested 'Widow'. By 1894, then, and in the decade following Pater's death, the parameters of biography were debated in some detail.

*   *   *

Apart from the *DNB* entry in 1895 by Gosse, no official biography of Pater appeared during the decade, and the impulse towards a memoir was also vitiated. It has been suggested that the Wilde trials may account for this (Levey: 20–1).[9] Fears in Pater's sisters may also have been created by the religious controversies fanned by biographies. Moreover, Gosse, who had written a fairly full obituary for the *Contemporary Review* in 1894 and the *DNB* entry the following year was, by 1901, decidedly against the standard ritual of a two-volume tribute or 'magnified epitaph' and may well have advised the sisters against such a project earlier. Similarly, from accounts in A.C. Benson's diary and Thomas Wright's autobiography, it seems unlikely that Pater's Oxford colleagues, such as F.W. Bussell, Ingram Bywater, Lancelot Shadwell, and Benjamin

Jowett, would welcome any scrutiny of their own or Pater's personal affairs.

How A.C. Benson who did not know Pater (although he had *seen* him) came to write the English Men of Letters Pater is instructive. John Morley, the advisory editor of the second series for Macmillan, it may be supposed was favourably inclined toward Pater: he published Pater's first signed article in the *Fortnightly* in 1869 and subsequent *Fortnightly Review* essays, and wrote a tolerant review of *The Renaissance* in 1873.[10] Benson had been a friend of Gosse from 1893, and Benson's biographer David Newsome, suggests that it was as Gosse's protegé that Benson had been introduced into the London literary world (Newsome: 88). Benson had his first EML commission in 1903 for *Rossetti* (1904); a life of Edward Fitzgerald (1905) and the Pater volume (1906) followed. However, from correspondence in the Macmillan archive in the British Library, it appears that the arrangement between Benson and Macmillan for the Pater volume bypassed Morley, the 'adviser' of the series entirely, having been initiated by the *author* (Benson) and agreed, directly, by the publisher (George Macmillan).

In some respects Gosse seems a more suitable candidate for the biographer of Pater: he knew Pater well, and a respectable time had elapsed since the author's death. However, Gosse's antipathy to 'the monstrous catafalque of two volumes (crown octavo)' (Gosse 1901: 195) was public knowledge and in the event of Benson's biography of Pater, we see Gosse in Benson's diary as unwilling at worst and ambivalent at best to serve the interests of the public and follow his own defence of the professional biographer's duty to truth. Negative factors may have put George Macmillan and Morley off Gosse, whose contributions to the second series of the EML had been volumes on Jeremy Taylor (1903) and Sir Thomas Browne (1905), authors from an early period. Moreover, in 1886, Gosse's accuracy and degree of knowledge of literature had been scathingly attacked by J.C. Collins in a review of Gosse's *From Shakespeare to Pope* in the *Quarterly*; in 1900 Charles Eliot Norton censured Gosse's *Life of Donne* for similar faults, and a *TLS* reviewer reported that 'the late Leonard Whibley used to say that the life of Gray [written for the *DNB* by Leslie Stephen who followed Gosse's biography of Gray so closely he felt like a thief] was not susceptible of correction; every sentence in it was incorrect, or inadequate, or misleading' (Anon. 1949: 819). By contrast, George Macmillan regarded Benson as a well-connected and tried professional ('If you do not know him I can assure you that he is a very charming fellow, and a true lover of good literature....You are no doubt aware that he is the late Archbishop's eldest son' (Macmillan 1904b: f.1931) who had recently contributed two Lives of near contemporaries. Benson, either having been approached first by a representative of the Pater group, or perhaps out of rivalry with Thomas Wright, evinced interest to Macmillan in doing the Pater volume, and it was simply agreed.

Versions of how Pater's EML biographer emerged articulate an array of historical and cultural models which were coexistent and available: if Gosse as a Macmillan author who knew Pater well was asked at any point, and demurred because his first-hand knowledge was incriminating and his 'Widow' loyalty overcame his sense of professional, authorial responsibility; if Benson was regarded as the more professional of the two; if Benson was recruited by the family and friends, among whom Macmillan themselves may be counted; or if Benson proposed himself to a publisher for whom he had already written two EML volumes in rapid succession. It may well be that by 1904 there was no explicit competition between Gosse and Benson for the Pater volume, because Gosse's opportunity over the decade since Pater's death had long lain fallow. As far as the two EML biographies by Benson of this period, on Edward FitzGerald and Pater, the subjects do not stem from the publisher or their representative *but from the author*, suggesting that the character of the EML series in its second phase is determined far less by the publisher than might otherwise have been thought. George Macmillan's reply to Benson's offer to write the Pater volume reveals the decision-making process:

> Your letter of September 22 reached me at Danby, but as you kindly allowed me to answer it at my leisure I thought it best to wait until I could consult my partners....having now discussed the matter here I write to say that we shall be very glad to have a volume from you on Walter Pater in our Series of English Men of Letters. (G. Macmillan (1904a): f.1545)

Moreover, insofar as John Morley, adviser to the series, is nowhere in evidence in this assignment which stems directly from correspondence between the author and the publisher, the stamp of the 'editor' of the series on its character in its second phase appears to be negligible. It is unclear from the Macmillan archive whether

Benson had communicated with Pater's sisters or executor before he wrote to Macmillan proposing the volume in 1904 but he did have contact with them ('Shadwell & the Misses Pater have been most kind & have given me a benediction' (Benson 1905b: 1^r)) and the diary yields nothing more than this May 1905 visit.

What is clear from the Archive is Benson's involvement with Thomas Wright: from the summer of 1904, when Benson wrote the FitzGerald life that immediately preceded his Pater book, Benson as a biographer had a vexed and dependent relation with Thomas Wright; also clear is Benson's awareness in July 1904 that Wright's book on Pater was in progress. From the Archive, it may be speculated that Wright's work on Pater prompted Benson, the *author* himself, independently of Macmillan, the executor, or the sisters to undertake a parallel and rival life; Benson pays Wright, against Macmillan's advice, to quote from Wright's already published life of FitzGerald. Its achievement and centrality are fully acknowledged by Benson, and contested by Macmillan, with Benson explaining 'He has discovered & put together so many biographical facts about FitzGerald that it would be very hard to write without making use of his book' (Benson (1904d): I.1^r). In the next letter to Macmillan, Benson shows that he is aware of the investigative mode of biography in which Wright worked, *and its value.* Interestingly, the repugnance to Wright's revelations and the undisguised disdain for the 'new' biography by an 'outsider' comes not from Benson, but from *the publisher*, which raises the interesting possibility that pressure on Benson to write a discreet life of Pater came not only from the widow faction of Pater's family and friends, but from the gentility of the particular publisher and of the series: precisely the origin of the censorship of fiction that antagonised George Moore and Thomas Hardy in the 1880s and 1890s, it is here transferred to biography. Here is George Macmillan's frank expression of disdain for Thomas Wright's class (a 'bookmaker' rather than a gentleman author) and fear of what Wright will include in his life of Pater. It is marked 'Private and Confidential':

Mr Thomas Wright is a man of a very different order [than Aldis Wright] – a bookmaker rather than a man of letters – and I think it is rather a pity that you communicated with him at all. Mr. Aldis Wright I know did his best to keep him at arm's length, and had a very poor opinion of the book when it came out. The same man is now trying to get his hands on to Walter Pater, and all his best friends dread the consequences. We have ourselves warned Pater's sisters to have as little to do with him as possible. T. W. had no proper access to new material for FitzGerald except such as he was able to scrape up in all sorts of corners and back alleys. It is of course for you to judge whether you should pay him a fee of five guineas for the right to pick about in his dust heap, but personally I should greatly doubt if it is worth your while. I have spoken somewhat freely as I feel bound to do, but these remarks are of course intended only for your own eye. I return Mr. Thomas Wright's letter. (Macmillan 1904c: ff.1934–5)

Benson, to his credit, defends Wright's life of Rossetti, and correctly surmises that George Macmillan had not read it:

As to Thomas Wright's book, no one can possibly think it a worse book than I do. The style is deplorable, and the general result of the picture is very unattractive.

But, though I am aware there are many mistakes of fact in it, it is a book that no biography of FitzGerald can afford to neglect. He has followed F's movements; he has persistently questioned everyone that could have known anything of F. The result is a Boswellian collection of material most of which is important from a biographical point of view however much one may question the taste of the production.

I don't think, from your letter that you can have read the book. I don't think that it was wanted – at least not all of it. But if one has a right to the lives of great men at all, one is in a perfectly different position to judge what kind of man F. was after reading this book, which it is not quite fair to call a dustheap, though there is a good deal of dust there.

I think I shall pay him £5.5.0 & then I shall feel free to do as I like...

I believe that the wretched man has nearly finished the Pater. (Benson 1904c: I1$^{r/v}$, 2$^{r/v}$, II1$^{r/v}$, 2^r)

The Archive also shows that while writing and cutting his first EML life, of D.G. Rossetti, Benson was conscious of the necessity for discretion in the handling of 'delicate' topics; in his next two letters to Macmillan, first mooting and then accepting the life of Pater, Benson uses the word 'entrust' in both contexts, signalling his acknowledgement of the element of discretion, and his acceptance of the necessity for it in the EML life of Pater that he is to write: 'you might be inclined to entrust it to me' (Benson (1904b): 1^r) he writes in his initial offer, and 'It is a great pleasure to be entrusted with the "Pater"' (Benson (1904a): 1^r) he reiterates in his letter of acceptance. In the course of writing it, and making his visits to Pater's friends, Benson observes that 'he was a mysterious fellow!' (Benson (1905b): 1$^{r/v}$) and concludes evasively 'But the books are the life, in the case of a man like Pater – & yet it is hard to see where fact ends & dream begins!' (Benson (1905b): 2^r). Having finished the manuscript, Benson is cautious and apprehensive about just such issues: having requested four copies of the FitzGerald proofs, he requires *seven* copies of the Pater proof for friends to read: 'It is a delicate job, & I should like to submit the proofs to several of my friends....It would be a comfort to me to have it put into proof as soon as possible, so that I might have plenty of time to consider possible modifications' (Benson (1905a): 2^r,2^v). To what extent Benson's biography of Pater is professional and to what extent protective remains to be seen.

That Benson secured the contract is possibly the cause of what he refers to in his diary as Gosse's self-confessed jealousy in November 1904:

> [G] Thought I was doing too much; ought to be silent for a bit [He] Praised the Rossetti, + said it had made me a real position. I pointed out that I did my best, that my work was not hurried or particularly slipshod. That one must follow one's bent in the fruitful years; that he wrote much more than I did...I don't think I converted him; but he said smiling "Perhaps it is only jealousy, after all" – + we went in to lunch. (Diary 62: 4)

This paragraph is then immediately followed by the second mention of Pater in the diary, in November 1904, a date which follows Benson's letter of confirmation to Macmillan of 12 October. From this entry until 4 March 1907, when Gosse shows Benson Thomas Wright's biography, Pater figures regularly in the diary. In January 1905 Benson had talked with Oscar Browning about Pater; in May and in June he visits Oxford; on 30 May he visits Pater's sisters in London, plainly for the first time; he records that he began writing 31 May, and that he finished 25 August. He corrects proof in December, and the volume appears in May 1906. The diary shows the process by which Benson created the EML life; it appears that he relied almost entirely on hearsay, on long discussions with those of Pater's intimates who would see him, and who were easily accessible in Oxford, Cambridge or London; for example, it appears from the diary that he never conferred with Ingram Bywater, a close friend of Pater's, who retired from Oxford as Regius Professor of Greek only in 1908. He appears to have seen only a few letters (Hester Pater writes in 1905 'Walter's letters are so rare – only a stray one here and there to be found' (Evans: 157)), and to have confined his other research to a rapid survey of Pater's Oxford environment. His mains sources were Gosse; Herbert Warren, President of Magdalen; Rev. F.W. Bussell, Vice-Principal and Tutor at BNC; Basil Champneys, architect and author; Douglas Ainslie, diplomat and writer; Clara and Hester Pater; Shadwell, Pater's friend and Literary Executor; Oscar Browning. The Pater sisters and Shadwell were reticent and told him little of use, and Oscar Browning, apart from leering 'I was very intimate with him – he was very attached to me', could tell Benson nothing. After talking with two sources – Champneys and Bussell – Benson records that he immediately wrote up sections of the book. But Gosse, on the occasion of the jealousy in 1904, provides him with basic information with which he can understand the reticence, the hints and innuendos, and the franker talk of his other sources. Gosse tells Benson, at the beginning, 'two things I didn't know':

> (1) that Pater's character was a good deal blown upon – that Jowett was said to have some mysterious letters, which he vowed he would produce if P. ever thought of standing for any University office. Probably some indiscreet devotion, Pateresquely expressed – for that Pater was ever anything but frigidly Platonic in his affections I decline to believe. (Diary 62: 5^r–5^v)

and second, that Pater was 'the most secluded of men, the most averse to *action* – just desirous of garnering impressions, + filling the space of life, between the dark + and the dark with colour + sweetness'. Benson goes on to describe Pater, dejected, asking Gosse to write an article about him. After Oscar Browning and Gosse, Benson saw Dr Daniel, Provost of Worcester College and head of the Daniel Press, and Shadwell; the Daniels

> both talked of Pater, but saying much conveyed very little idea, except that he was humble, simple, easy to get on with. The

Provost hinted at the dark chapter but I know all about that, + it will want great care. (Diary 69: 52^r)

Herbert Warren of Magdalen, Oxford, talked of 'the aesthetic movement, Symonds, Pater, Jowett + others. Rather a dark place, I am afraid' (Diary 69: 48^v–49^r). Benson makes explicit the connection between aestheticism, Hellenism and homosexuality, and between Pater and Symonds, but he also distinguishes between the two men:

But if we give boys Greek books to read + hold up the Greek spirit + the Greek life as a marvel, it is very difficult to slice out one portion, which was a perfectly normal part of Greek life, and to say that it is abominable etc etc. A strongly sensuous nature – such as Pater or Symonds – with a strong instinct for beauty, + brought up at an English public school, will almost certainly go wrong, in thought if not in act. But Warren revealed to me a depth of corruption in Symonds of which I had not dreamed. When he was well + strong he remained free from the shadow. (Diary 69: 49^r)

Also at Oxford, Shadwell 'walked up + down discoursing of Pater for an hour, till I was giddy, + telling me nothing. But I got a faint impression' (Diary 69: 52^r). From Pater's by then eccentric sisters Benson seems to have had little about Pater except their blessing on the project: 'There is no one in whose hands we would rather see this. You will treat it justly + sympathetically' (Diary 70: 7^v). But Benson notes: 'I felt an even greater interest in my peep at this odd interior than even in Pater himself... the thought of the dim half-lit light, the faded + dreary atmosphere in which these two refined ladies sit, waiting for the end struck me as horribly pathetic and futile' (Diary 70: 8^r–8^v). Likewise, when Benson visits Bussell in late June he echoes this greater interest in his source than in his object:

I must say this. Though I came in search of Pater, + though I found much that I wanted + desired, yet the discovery of Bussell has amused + interested me much more! Like a man who goes out to catch a rare + shy moth, + catches instead a rare + effusive butterfly. (Diary 71: 27^v)

Benson's attitude to Pater might be described as mere mild interest. His searching is not very vigorous nor is his desire, and he is easily distracted. The very qualifications Benson seems to bring to the task are those which disabled him, and rendered him ambivalent rather than disinterested. His knowledge of Oxbridge is vitiated by his participation in its culture and a loyalty to his fellows; he is unwilling to expose an insider to outsiders. In this respect Benson participates in the reticence to speak found in those closer to Pater. Another important factor is Benson's own participation in gay discourse and culture in his fantasy and emotional life, which his diary corroborates with its reiterated exempla of male objects of desire. A third factor in Benson's ambivalence, and perhaps what contributed to his decision to undertake the book, was a lurking sense of rectitude deriving from his high Anglican childhood as the son of an important Churchman. It should be noted that Benson had access during Pater's lifetime to contemporaries of Pater and his sisters in Oxford, notably the children of the Bishop of Lincoln, John and Elizabeth Wordsworth, with whom Benson had played as a child. The conservative religious views of John, a Fellow at BNC at the time of the publication of the first edition of *The Renaissance*, and of Elizabeth, the first Principal of Lady Margaret Hall, pitted John Wordsworth against Walter Pater in male Oxford, and Elizabeth Wordsworth against Clara Pater, a residential tutor at the rival, non-sectarian Somerville in the fledgling world of the women's colleges.

When Benson's biography of Pater appeared, Benson's response is repugnance:

> Gosse + Warren wrote in warm praise of the book – which appeared yesterday [i.e. 11 May]. But the truth is that when a book comes out, so long has elapsed since one had anything to do with it, that it is like cold-pie-crust. I open Pater, + the caked fat seems to stand on the gravy (Diary 81: 69^r).

This reveals something of Benson's depression and bouts of despair during the writing of the Pater life; he expresses it more explicitly in the entry for 25 June 1905.

> I had mildly melancholy thoughts. Why do I achieve so little? Why do I give up practical life from a sincere diffidence + a sense of incompetence? and having done so why can I not write anything to my mind? I *can* write, but I have nothing to say, + when I say it sincerely, Cornish [Francis Warre, Vice-Provost of Eton] says it is rancid, + the Guardian that a character is revealed

which one cannot sympathise with, or even respect!... Some deep
rooted weakness of will, no doubt – but I did not make my will!
Who made it weak, + why?

But I don't despair – I repent, I repent! I will try to do better,
+ I hope + believe I shall. It is useless to say "Why are you so
self-absorbed, with so narrow a view?" One may as well say to
a lame man, "Why is your leg crooked?" or to an ugly man
"Why is your face displeasing?" (Diary 71: 30^r)[12]

Benson's 'sincere diffidence', his 'weakness of will' is everywhere
apparent in the diary, with respect to Pater. Benson seems to lack
commitment to his task and strong interest in his subject. Only once
in the diary can he be said to enter imaginatively and feelingly into
Pater's situation, in his last discussion with Gosse, after the manuscript had been finished.

Bussell emerges as markedly less serious and austere, and more
colourful than his memorial sermon on Pater suggests. He was, it
seems, particularly good at imitating Pater, and this he did for
Benson, who graphically describes his first sight of Bussell:

He looked like a man dressed for a garden party, as indeed he
was. This was Bussell. Add to this an elaborately civil, slightly
simpering, slightly giggling, infectious, humorous, ironical, *petting*,
caressing kind of manner – (like Gosse in the mood I do not think
his best) – as a smooth + engaging – but not wholly trustworthy –
cat might play + bound about you, + and you have this singular
man. He is very able, very accomplished (Diary 71: 19^v–20^r)

The rest of the long diary entry on Bussell reveals nothing about
Pater directly – only implicitly through its portraits of Bussell and
Shadwell. After Benson's visits to Bussell and the sisters, Benson
indicates that he made notes. On 10 June he talked with Basil
Champneys who was 'highly illuminating' about Pater because he
didn't 'shirk the unpleasant side' (Diary 70: 33^r). Champneys
pleased Benson 'by saying that he was deeply thankful that the
truth was in discreet hands'. What is noteworthy here is the
mutuality of belief in loyalty to the group, and knowledge between
men coupled with discretion in the face of the public and outsiders.
The discourse reproduces the conditions of male bonding among
university men; in its access to these inside sources lies the
explanation of the nature of the biography – its crucial reticences;

its use of language codes to obscure meaning; its failure of will and thoroughness; its constitutional ambivalences; its uneasy sexual politics; and its admixture of ideologies.

In July Benson visited Douglas Ainslie for an hour. Curiously, this entry shows Benson's limitations as well as Ainslie's: a kind of aesthetic snobbery; a taste for 'good + wholesome work' and a tendency to indulge in self-contradiction, without examining what lies behind the paradoxes:

> Sunday 11 July The heat was awful. Arrived in town I went straight to Mount Street + had an hour's interview with Douglas Ainslie, aged about 35, dramatic critic, poet, + ex diplomatist, about Pater. How I hate the sort of room he lived in – many books + evidently well-read, but semi-artistic things about – the whole thing dusty + a little pretentious – no *grace* – + then the noise + stench of London pouring in at the window. How can good + wholesome work be done under these conditions. He told me some interesting things about P. But seemed to me too anxious to get himself mentioned. I thought him a clever man, of much aesthetic perception; but all in the outer rooms + corridors of art. I should not trust his judgment for an instant. He would easily mistake secondrate for firstrate...I thought him *very* kind, rather clever, rather graceful, not impressive. (Diary 71: 77^v–78^r)

The first mention of Pater in the diary shows Benson, in 1902, to be offended by Pater's taste for ritual in *Marius*:

> Today I actually had but 3 letters; so I read Marius the Epicurean + tasted its luscious sentences deliberately – but Pater's taste for *ritual* offends me – there is something radically silly I think in the assembling dressed-up for solemn ceremonial. It is rather impressive when you drop in upon it, + don't know the people, but to do it with people one knows, over + over again seems to me truly absurd. (Diary 17: 42^r)

It reveals a temperamental intolerance of a persistent element of Pater's prose and life. Elsewhere in the Diary Benson contrasts Pater (among others) with a precious visitor, J.C. Squire, who was translating Baudelaire:

> The strange Squire of John's to lunch – in pumps! – the day being wet; hair in curled masses, + with a gold chain round his waist.

He is a confirmed *poseur*, I fear. He said he had been applying for a tutorship to prepare a little boy for school, his real object being to get leisure to finish a translation of *Baudelaire!* How good for the little boy to be under this influence.

I am very sorry for him – I think he has many pretty thoughts – but he is morbid; corrupt, hysterical. We talked of Pater; + I read S a concealed lecture on the absurdity of *personal* eccentricity, + how the masters, like Pater, Pusey, Ruskin abhorred all formal preciousness in life etc. (Diary 82: 24^r – 24^v)

Such a wrenched reading of Pater who wore an apple green tie and whose eccentricity, if quiet, appears highly personal, indicates the lacunae in Benson's concept of Pater; they are reflected at one point in the biography where Benson characterises Pater's ideal of life as 'sober and strenuous' (Benson 1906: 54). On 28 August, three days after he finished writing, Benson rejects. H.E. Luxmoore's 'ugly Puritanism' about Pater; to his friend's contention 'that Pater was a dangerous man, corrupt + vile when he was at Oxford', Benson 'interposed, + said that he was reckless at first but became different, very different in later life' (Diary 73: 57^r): this is one expression of Benson's beliefs about Pater at the point of his finishing the narrative – that Pater *had* been 'reckless' early on but that he changed. If it marks Benson's aversion to harsh judgement of Pater from a superior position of high moral ground which he characterises here as 'ugly Puritanism', it also shows Benson's limits, his incapacity to entertain the notion of Pater as a lifelong practising homosexual. This view of Benson is borne out by Edward Lyttelton who notes his friend's incapacity to comprehend 'the deep motives of human action' (Lyttelton: 154).

Finally, on 1 September, having 'FINISHED PATER' on 25 August, Benson records that Gosse revealed that 'it was *Mallock* who took the terrible letters to Jowett, which gave Jowett such power'. Benson here affords us more of his final estimate of Pater; and a rare sign of empathy with his subject.

What a donkey P. must have been to *write* them – It is a mistake one makes to feel that writing is somehow more impersonal than speech – It is: but it is also imperishable!

Pater's whole nature changed under the strain, after the dreadful interview with Jowett. He became old, crushed, despairing – + this dreadful weight lasted for years; it was years before he realised that J. would not use them. And then came the time when Jowett, finding P. famous, called, when Pater was ill to enquire. J. was a little hypocrite, I fear; or at all events a vile little opportunist. (Diary 73: 66^r)

It seems clear that, even after Benson had finished his research, and written and sent off the manuscript on 31 August 1905, he had not known who supplied Jowett with the letters until Gosse told him in September. His research seems precariously thin, and when he was accused of inaccuracy by Thomas Wright, he blames his informants, without any self-consciousness, it seems, about his research methods or the concomitant debates about biography:

There is a very severe + nasty attack on my book. This only moved me with a faint discomfort. All my facts were got from the nearest friends and relations, + I am not responsible for my errors. But I expect I shall have to answer him. (Diary 90: 44^r)

Even in the light of what Benson did know about Pater, his 'speculations' about Pater and Jowett in the EML volume appear positively disingenuous:

Although Pater had been a pupil of Jowett's, and although there was a *rapprochement* in later life, when Jowett took occasion warmly to congratulate Pater on his *Plato and Platonism*, there was a misunderstanding of some kind which resulted in a dissidence between them in the middle years. It has even been said that Jowett took up a line of definite opposition to Pater, and used his influence to prevent his obtaining University work and appointments. It is not impossible that this was the case. Jowett, in spite of his genius, in spite of his liberality of view and his deliberate tolerance, was undoubtedly an opportunist. He was not exactly guided by the trend of public opinion, but he took care not to back men or measures unless he would be likely to have the support of a strong section of the community, or at least conceived it probable that his line would eventually be endorsed by public opinion....

Probably Jowett either identified Pater with the advanced aesthetic school, or supposed that at all events his teaching was adapted to strengthen a species of Hedonism, or modern Paganism, which was alien to the spirit of the age. Or possibly he was alarmed at the mental and moral attitude with which Pater was publicly credited, owing in considerable measure to the appearance of the *New Republic* – in which he himself was pilloried as the representative of advanced religious liberalism – and thought that on public grounds he must combat the accredited leaders of a movement which was certainly unfashionable, and which was regarded with suspicion by men of practical minds. Whatever his motives were, he certainly meant to make it plain that he did not desire to see the supposed exponents of the aesthetic philosophy holding office in the University.

One feels that Jowett, with his talent for frank remonstrance, had better have employed direct rather than indirect methods; but the fact remains that he not only disliked the tendency of Pater's thought, but endeavoured, by means that are invariably ineffectual, to subvert his influence. (Benson 1906: 54–5)

Benson misleads his readers in that he implies the principal responsibility for the rift lay with Jowett; he implies the direct involvement of Mallock but displaces it; he obscures the cause of Jowett's disapproval and confuses the date by linking it with the appearance of the *New Republic*. His tentativeness and multiple speculations are careful structures of deceit.

It is important to acknowledge, however, that Benson's allegedly 'widow' biography is more revelatory than any previous publication. Wright's volumes with their alternative, investigative methods associated with the 'new' biography only appeared in the following year, and at least one of Benson's inside informants was pleased and relieved. In November 1906 Benson notes G.T. Lapsley's account of Basil Champneys' praise:

"I took my courage in my hands, thinking it the only thing to do, + told Benson a mass of impossible things about Pater, hoping he wd be discreet. But he was more discreet than I cd have hoped – he discovered the man behind it all, he committed no indicretions, + yet one who knows the whole story can see that B[enson] knows it too". This was high praise + pleased me very much. (Diary 87: 1)

Champneys' view no doubt reflects relief from guilt, but it also indicates the full *extent* of Benson's 'discretion'. Benson's satisfaction with the notion of two audiences is notable: one élite in the know, and the other vulgarly public, excluded from the fuller private life. But does the EML Life merit such praise?

Robert Ross, a courageous gay man, offers a view of Benson's strategies in a review of the volume in the *Academy* in November 1906 (Ross: 61–2). Because this journal had close links with Oxbridge, being written by and for dons, this review was crucial in the circulation of judgement about Benson's book; its readership was the insiders. Ross had been a close friend of Oscar Wilde, and had remained openly loyal to him during the trials and his imprisonment; Ross had published *De Profundis*. He was also a close friend of Gosse, and clearly knew the details of Pater's life to which Gosse and Benson were privy.[13] At the beginning of the review Ross pays tribute to the author's 'sympathy and critical acumen', but towards the end he considers critically Benson's method of deriving the life from the self-revelatory works – which he prefers to Benson's use of empty personal anecdotes. But in both of these, Ross detects concealment, and he indicates Mallock ('some horrid undergraduate') as analogous to Henley on Stevenson and Burns, and Purcell on Manning, ready to ink the statue. Ross also suggests Benson is guilty of deliberately misleading:

> Anticipating something of the kind, Mr. Benson is careful to insist on the divergence between Rossetti and Pater, and on page 86 says something which is ludicrously untrue. (Ross: 62)

What Benson writes there is 'the innermost world of mystical passion in which Rossetti lived was as a locked and darkened chamber to Pater'. Ross defends what Purcell had called 'the publication of historical facts'. Gosse writes somewhat ambiguously and pompously to Ross about the review on 11 August 1906, perhaps on Benson's behalf:

> My dear Robbie...
> What is peculiar to your own mind and nature comes out most agreeably here and there, and I hope you will cultivate it. The article on Pater is excellently written, and with the greater part of it I agree. I do not know that I mind the end. That is a sound expression of opinion, and I do not feel that it goes too far.[14] (Ross, M.: 132)

Gosse, the vociferous defender of indiscreet biography, supplies Benson with the material for such a biography, but ambivalently –

in stages, and late; he then patronises its reviewer and only reluctantly tolerates his detection of Benson's discretion.[15]

Benson's life of Pater fails even to *mention* Pater's close friend-ships with three gay men, Simeon Solomon, Oscar Browning, and Wilde, and with the eccentric and aesthetic churchman/collector Richard Jackson. Thomas Wright was to acknowledge all four in his two volumes only nine months later. I have suggested at least two frameworks for Benson's biography, that of the debate about method in biography, and Benson's position as an Establishment figure and troubled gay man. Edward Lyttelton, Benson's friend, offers a third. What appears to be Benson's aversion of gaze is analysed by Lyttelton not only as temperamental, but as an intellec-tual incapacity:

> [his] want of interest in questions of principle; the effect of which is to enfeeble the grip on fact, or at least – if the memory is strong – to prevent the mind from seeing facts in their true proportion. Arthur's memory was good enough; but the deep motives of human action, the interplay of the forces which stir the mass-movements of mankind, no less than the mighty drama of human souls in their period of probation, remained outside his horizon. So the facts which, to some minds, speak of these and great kindred matters presented themselves to him without colour or any rich significance. (Lyttelton: 154)

This is a view put by the *Athenaeum* reviewer of Benson's *Rossetti* who noted that work's superficiality; and it seems a good descrip-tion of what Benson's diffidence, and his fear of depths, of dark-ness, engendered. Later in life, Benson acknowledges the 'company manners' which he assumes as an author of books (Newsome: 10), but it seems possible from the only known letter between Benson and Ross that Benson, accepting his limitations, did not begrudge Ross the review by 1910. The author thanks the critic for a favourable review of his latest book, noting the 'finely discrimin-ating hand', 'sympathetic praise', and the 'urbanity' in the review; he also acknowledges that though they have never met, they have 'many common friends' (Ross, M.: 187).

Benson, Gosse and Ross, then, all had access to information in 1906 which could have obviated the considerable efforts by twentieth-century critics to probe critical and biographical problems relating to Pater:[16] the withdrawal of the Conclusion from the 1877 edition of *The Renaissance*, the necessity for the apparent disjunction between the life and the work; the apparently repressed character and life; the outbreaks of vivid and vehement expression in the work; and the paucity of letters, other biographical material and biographies. These three critics all sympathised with Pater's predicament, but they had differing notions of responsible biography: Gosse preached indiscretion but remained silent, contenting himself with half-informing Benson. Ross was less mealy-mouthed: he exposed Benson's evasive methods, but only indicated where truth lay. Benson, professional and widow at once, is openly torn: his tendency to research superficially and his failure to value sufficiently 'the deep motives of human action' combine to produce a misleading, widow biography; at the same time Benson's experience with homoeroticism in his emotional life does enable him to indicate in the writing his appreciation of Pater's dilemma with Jowett and in the world more generally. Benson, in his combination of an author employed as both widow and professional, conflates the terms that Gosse juxtaposed. To the extent that Benson accepted the task knowing that access to the insiders, and their imprimatur, limited what he could write and impinged on his professionalism as a biographer, Benson writes as a widow. To the extent that, unlike any member of the Pater circle, he took it on at all, with a reputation as an author to maintain, he was writing as a professional, but *not* the discourse of the 'new biography'. To Gosse, by the turn of the century, professionalism in biography meant the 'new' investigative methods, but it was not so to Benson.

Henry James, in an article on George Sand (James 1897: 23) in the post-Wilde *Yellow Book*, foresees a future in which 'the pale forewarned victim' of biography will be a match for 'the cunning of the inquirer', 'with every track covered, every paper burnt and every letter unanswered'. In 1906 on the occasion of Benson's book James wrote of Pater as a 'figure':

> You have done in especial *this* delightful and interesting thing – that you have ministered to that strange touching edifying (to me quite thrilling) operation of the whispering of time, through which Pater has already in these few years, little as he seemed marked out for it – become in our literature that very rare + sovereign thing, a *figure*; a figure in the sense in which there are to[o] few! It is a matter altogether independent of the mere possession, of genius or achievement, even of "success", I think.

It's a matter almost of tragic or ironic (or even comic) felicity –
but it comes here + there to the individual – unawares; + it leaves
hundreds of the eminent alone. Well I feel that it has come to
dear, queer, deeply individual + homogeneous W.H.P. crowning
his strong + painful identity. (Diary 82: 40^r)[17]

In the difference between James's brief and suggestive evocation
and Benson's fissured and reticent narrative, we can see something
of what Benson has denied us. In 1926 Benson published a piece on
'The Art of the Biographer' in which he described his notion of the
biographer's 'business'. It articulates aspects of the method implicit
in the Pater biography, and also points to its dearth of 'patience,
energy and research'. He provides an 'apologia' redolent with
tensions and value-judgements:

> he must have a relentless and microscopic faculty of
> observation; he must have patience, energy and research; he
> must have a power of omission and selection; and lastly he must
> have an extreme veraciousness, which does not pay any
> particular heed to decorum or sentiment or romance. He need
> not violate privacy or sacredness, any more than a portrait
> painter need insist on always painting from the nude; but he
> must have no deference for the kind of hero-worship which
> requires that a man should be exhibited in flawless, stainless and
> radiant perfection, while his sympathy and reverence will save
> him from mere caricature and from undue emphasis on what
> was merely occasional, exaggerated or sensational. Proportion is
> the true difficulty; how to balance what is lofty, noble and awe-
> inspiring with what is minute, whimsical, humorous. Even what,
> as Rossetti beautifully said, 'is secret and unknown, below the
> earth, above the skies,' must, if not told, at least be able to be
> inferred....the best biographer must know by a kind of inspired
> tact what is essential. (Benson 1926: 163–4)

Benson knew that books 'always make me put on my company
manners' (Newsome: 10), and beyond them he could not, and did not
go. He reveals his overwhelming consciousness of the necessity for
discretion and of pleasing Pater's circle in the throes of his satisfaction
with his writing skills: 'Was in by five + and wrote a chapter of Pater
on Champneys notes. It is good work, I think; *but will Shadwell
approve*' Diary 70; 34^r).[18] There is the posture envisaged by Gosse in

1901: the professional with the widow lurking 'behind the apparently unprejudiced name of some docile author' (Gosse 1901: 206)

It remained for Thomas Wright in 1907 to apply investigative methods to the problematic of a biography of Pater, and to produce the discourse of the 'new biography'. It should be understood, notwithstanding Benson's methods, that most Pater scholars today still prefer Benson's book, while Wright's is characterised as unmethodical, inaccurate, and eccentric in its reliance on Richard C. Jackson. Thomas Wright cannot be said to have suffered from concern about approval from Shadwell; in certain respects – the vigour of his information-gathering and his use of letters – he is the more professional of the two biographers, and if definitely not a widow, not Judas either.

Notes

1. The relation between these biographies is discussed by Thomas Wright in Vol. I of *The Life of Walter Pater* as one of rivalry, and this is echoed by the press. In Brasenose College Library is a frigid letter from Lancelot Shadwell, Provost of Oriel, denying Wright information from himself and Pater's sisters. This letter is dated 26 July 1903, and dates of a letter in the Macmillan Archive from Benson to Macmillan *proposing* a biography of Pater (22.9.04) and an entry in Benson's diary (12.11.04) indicate a later commencement of his professional interest in Pater than Wright. Moreover, in an earlier letter in the Archive (5.7.04) Benson includes as an afterthought, 'I believe that the wretched man has nearly finished the Pater' (Macmillan Archive). As yet a precise link between Pater's friends, Benson's firsthand knowledge of the progress of Wright's biography from Wright himself, and Benson's proposal to Macmillan ten weeks later, is uncertain. It seems clear however, that *somehow* the threat of Wright's biography resulted in a safe 'widow' Life, possibly through efforts by Pater's family, friends and publishers, or by Benson, already a rival of Wright's in his EML volume on FitzGerald. See also Wright's explanation in his auto-biography, *Thomas Wright of Olney*, of his experiences with Pater's friends and relations, and also with Benson, who in May 1905 is alleged by Wright to have offered payment to see Wright's Pater material and the manuscript of his biography. Benson's Life appeared in May 1906 and Wright's in February 1907.

2. For more on Benson and Thomas Wright, see Newsome, and Samuel Wright (1975): 149–50.

3. For the first biography of Ellen Ternan, see Tomalin.

4. For the effect of the Wilde trials and verdict on the periodical press, see '*The Savoy:* 1896: Gender in Crisis?', Chapter 8 in this volume.

5. See 'Theories of Formation: the *Nineteenth Century*', Chapter 3 in this volume.
6. For the Stevenson-Henley quarrel see Cohen.
7. *The Anglo-Saxon Review. A Quarterly Miscellany* (1898–1901) in which Gosse's article appeared, was edited by a society figure, Mrs. George Cornwallis-West (= Lady Randolph Spencer Churchill), illustrated, and sumptuously bound as a drawing-table book in red leather with gold tooling. In that wives and widows of famous men may have been among the readership of *The Anglo-Saxon Review*, the periodical is an appropriate site to attack 'widow' biographers.
8. See Kijinski, Howarth (185), and Van Arsdel on the English Men of Letter series.
9. Recent research has shown conclusively that Pater's homosexuality had resulted at least once in threats of exposure – from Benjamin Jowett. See Inman.
10. I say 'tolerant' because in 1866 Morley published anonymously in the *Saturday Review* such a vituperative review of Swinburne's poems that the publishers withdrew the book from circulation. Morley's review of Pater in 1873, by which time he had clearly changed his mind about aestheticism, appeared in the more liberal periodical, the *Fortnightly Review*. However, F. W. Hirst quotes a portion of a letter from Morley to Frederic Harrison which shows Morley to be well disposed towards Pater and his 'transgressions' in particular:

> I think it very desirable to call attention to any book like Pater's, which is likely to quicken public interest in the higher sorts of literature. And, moreover, a young and unknown writer like him ought to be formally introduced to the company by the hired master of the ceremonies, myself, or another to wit. So pray pardon my light dealing with his transgressions. (Hirst I: 240)

11. Gosse *had* already written one EML volume for Morley on Gray in 1882 in the first series, but only one, and was to do the *DNB* and EML Swinburnes in 1912 and 1917.
12. Although dated 24 June in the Diary, the entry appears, from the designation 'Sunday', to have been written on the 25th.
13. See Letter from Gosse to Ross in M. Ross, 132–3.
14. Gosse's pomposity regarding Ross and homosexuality is nowhere more apparent than in his letter to Ross during the Wilde trials; cf. M. Ross, 36–7.
15. In this connection Harold Nicolson's judgement of the nature of Gosse's biographies, other than *Father and Son*, is pertinent:

> Sir Edmund Gosse has relieved the pressure of facts, the explosive force of the scientific element, by the safety-valve of innuendo....while not denying truth, he allows the extreme pressure of truth, to evaporate and to escape. These works will for long remain as models of grace and dexterity, but they will not live as models of biography. (Nicolson: 144)

16. For the most recent work see Dellamora and Inman.

17. Henry James and Benson were old friends whose affection for each other seems to have included a passionate friendship in 1896. See James's letters to Benson of 16 January, 5 April, 2 May and 29 June of that year. James's 1906 letter to Benson about Pater's character avails itself of a homoerotic discourse which is much in evidence here. For more about James and Benson, see Masters: 115–16.
18. My italics.

Works Cited

Anon. (1949). 'Worthies of Empire', *Times Literary Supplement* (16 Dec.) 819.
Anon. (1907). 'Walter Pater. Martyrdom by Biography', *Daily Mail Books Supplement* (9 March), II.
Anon. (1904a). 'Literature [review of *Rossetti*]', *Athenaeum* (13 Aug.) 197–8.
Anon. (1904b). 'Books. Dante Gabriel Rossetti', *Spectator* 93 (13 Aug.) 224–5.
Anon. (1901). 'Concerning Biography', *Academy* 60 (23 Feb.) 167–8.
Benson, A.C. (1926) 'The Art of the Biographer', in *Essays by Divers Hands* 6, ed. G.K. Chesterton. London. pp. 139–69.
Benson, A.C. (1906). *Walter Pater.* London.
Benson, A.C. (1905a). Letter from Benson to Macmillan. 25 Aug. Macmillan Archive 55022, Vol. 237. British Library.
Benson, A.C. (1905b). Letter from Benson to Macmillan. 17 June. Macmillan Archive 55022, Vol. 237, British Library.
Benson, A.C. (1904a). Letter from Benson to Macmillan. 12 Oct. Macmillan Archive 55022, Vol. 237. British Library.
Benson, A.C. (1904b). Letter from Benson to Macmillan. 22 Sept. Macmillan Archive 55022, Vol. 237. British Library.
Benson, A.C. (1904c). Letter from Benson to Macmillan. 5 July. Macmillan Archive 55022, Vol. 237. British Library.
Benson, A.C. (1904d). Letter from Benson to Macmillan. 1 July. Macmillan Archive 55022, Vol. 237. British Library.
Cohen, E.H. (1974). 'The Henley-Stevenson Quarrel'. University of Florida Monograph No. 42. Gainesville, Fla.
[Collins, J.C.]. (1886). 'From Shakespeare to Pope', *Quarterly Review* 163, 289–329.
Dellamora, R. (1990). *Masculine Desire. The Sexual Politics of Victorian Aestheticism.* Chapel Hill and London.
Evans, L. ed. (1970). *Letters of Walter Pater.* London.
Froude, J.A. (1882–4). *Thomas Carlyle: a History of his Life in London 1834–1881.* London.
Gosse, E. (1903). 'The Ethics of Biography', *Cosmospolitan* 35 (July) 317–23.
Gosse, E. (1901). 'The Custom of Biography', *Anglo-Saxon Review* 8, 195–208.
Henley, W.E. (1901). 'R.L.S.,' *Pall Mall Magazine*, 25(Dec.) 505–14.
Henley, W.E. (1897). 'Life, Genius, and Achievement [of Robert Burns]' in *The Poetry of Robert Burns*, ed. W.E. Henley and Thomas F. Henderson. 4 vols. 1896, 1897. Edinburgh. IV. pp. 232–341.
Hirst, F.W. (1927). *Early Life and Letters of John Morley,* London.
Howarth, P. (1963). *Squire 'Most Generous of Men'.* London.

Inman, B.A. (1991). 'Estrangement and Connection: Walter Pater, Benjamin Jowett, and William M. Hardinge,' *Pater in the 1990s*, ed. L. Brake and I. Small. Greensboro, NC. pp. 1–20.

James, H. (1897). 'She and He: Recent Documents', *Yellow Book* 12 (Jan.) 15–38.

Kijinski, J.L. (1991). 'John Morley's "English Men of Letters" Series and the Politics of Reading', *Victorian Studies* 34 (Winter), 205–26.

Levey, M. (1978). *The Case of Walter Pater*. London.

Lyttelton, E. (1925). 'Training and Temperament', *Arthur Christopher Benson. As Seen by Some Friends*, [E. H. Ryle, ed.]. London. pp. 141–58.

Macmillan, G. (1904a). MS Letter to A. C. Benson, 10 Oct. Macmillan Archive 55477 (4), f.1545, British Library.

Macmillan, G. (1904b). MS Letter to Aldis Wright, 4 July. Macmillan Archive 55476/4, f.1931, British Library.

Macmillan, G. (1904c). MS Letter to A.C. Benson, [4 July]. Macmillan Archive 54776/4, ff.1934–5. British Library.

[Mallock, W. H.]. (1877). *The New Republic*. London.

Mason, W. (1775). *The Poems of Mr. Gray. To Which are Prefixed Memoirs of his Life and Writings by W. Mason M. A.* London and York.

Masters, Brian (1991). *E. F. Benson*. London.

Morley, J. (1873). 'Mr. Pater's Essays', *Fortnightly Review* 13(April) 469–77.

[Morley, J.] (1866). 'Mr. Swinburne's New Poems', *Saturday Review* (4 August) 145–7.

Newsome, D. (1980). *On the Edge of Paradise. A.C. Benson: The Diarist*. London.

Nicolson, H. (1968; originally 1927). *The Development of English Biography*. London.

Norton, C.E. (1900). 'Gosse's Life of Donne', *Nation* 70 (8 and 15 February), 111–13, 133–5.

Purcell, E. (1896). 'On the Ethics of Suppression in Biography', *Nineteenth Century* 40, 533–42.

Purcell, E. (1895). *Life of Cardinal Manning*. London

Ross, M., ed. (1952). *Robert Ross, Friend of Friends*. London.

Ross, R. (1906). 'Mr. Benson's Pater', *Academy* 71 (21 July) 61–2.

Stephen, L. (1893). 'Biography', *National Review* 22 (Oct.) 171–83.

Strachey, L. (1918). *Eminent Victorians*. London.

Strachey, L. (1921). *Queen Victoria*. London.

Tomalin, C. (1990) *The Invisible Woman. The Story of Nelly Ternan and Charles Dickens*. London.

Van Arsdel, R.T. (1991). 'Macmillan and Company', *British Literary Publishing Houses, 1820–1880*, ed. P.J. Anderson and J. Rose. DLB 106. Detroit and London. pp. 178–95.

[Wilde, O.] (1887). 'The Butterfly's Boswell', *Court and Society Review* 4 (20 April) 378.

Wright, Samuel. (1975). *A Bibliography of the Writings of Walter H. Pater*. New York and London.

Wright, Samuel. (1971). 'Richard Charles Jackson', *Antigonish Review* I (Winter) 81–92.

Wright, Thomas. (1936). *Thomas Wright of Olney*. London.

Wright, Thomas. (1907). *The Life of Walter Pater*. 2 vols. London.

Index